Social Service
Budgets
and Social Policy

by the same author

Willing the Means
Examination of the Cost of Reforming Our Education System

(With Gail Wilson)
Paying for Private Schools

Social Service Budgets and Social Policy

British and American Experience

by

H. GLENNERSTER

*London School of Economics
and London School of Hygiene*

BARNES & NOBLE

BOOKS

10 East 53d St. New York 10022
(a division of Harper & Row Publishers, Inc.)

Published in the USA 1975 by
HARPER & ROW PUBLISHERS, INC.
BARNES & NOBLE IMPORT DIVISION

ISBN 0-06-492435-1

Printed in Great Britain
in 10/11-pt. Times Roman type
by Willmer Brothers Limited, Birkenhead

Preface

This book began as the *second half* of an introductory series of lectures on social administration to students taking an MSc in Social Medicine at the London School of Hygiene. It assumes a basic knowledge of the structure of social service administration in Britain. In particular it is an attempt to show the importance of resource constraints and how the Central Government determines the limits within which those in the field have to work. I have drawn examples mainly from health, education and social security. I hope it will be useful to social administration students who tend to find resource constraints difficult to appreciate, and to economics students who find the world of administration too messy to contemplate.

Above all the book is comparative in emphasis, contrasting throughout United States and British experience. I owe my thanks to the Brookings Institution who offered me a visiting scholarship in 1972 and to the Nuffield Foundation who funded my visit.

I was able to talk both to people who had been concerned with the introduction of the budget reforms during the Johnson administration and to those currently working in the Department of Health, Education and Welfare. This department was one of the very few agencies which the Bureau of the Budget claimed achieved any real measure of success with programme budgeting before 1969. It had subsequently rethought and adapted these activities after 1970 when Elliot Richardson became Secretary of the Department. In addition to interviewing many of those involved and reading examples of work in progress it was illuminating to read the account of past budget hearings on the HEW budget in Congress. They provide fascinating source material and include not only detailed budget 'justifications' submitted by the different agencies but the cross examination of budget officials and others involved by the Congressmen. Against these, the proceedings of our own House of Commons Expenditure Committee appear as pale shadows. It would be foolish to pretend that in such a short time anything more than a general impression could be gained of the budget process in such a vast empire as HEW. To limit the task only two of the agencies in this empire were examined in any detail – that of the Social Security Administration and the Office of Education. Even so the political and organisational differences between the social service departments in Washington and Whitehall are so striking that the observer of both is forced to ask questions that would otherwise probably not occur to him or would seem less important. The advocates of systems analysis and programme budgeting have tended to advocate it as a generally applicable set of principles and to minimise the importance of the varied political, economic and service contexts within which they must be applied. A comparative approach is particularly revealing precisely because it highlights the way in which these different background variables have affected the way the ideas have been implemented.

I should like to thank all those who have been generous in the time they have devoted to discussing their work, and to those who have read earlier drafts especially Professor Abel-Smith, Professor Donnison and Ida Merriam.

Contents

Chapter 1

Social Administration and Resource Allocation

This book seeks to describe and to evaluate some of the important changes that have taken place recently in the way social service resources are allocated. It does so by comparing the fate of similar innovations in Washington and Whitehall. It concentrates on three particular developments – attempts to introduce an element of strategic forward planning, attempts to draw up programme budgets for the social services and attempts to evaluate the 'effectiveness' of social services. All three elements form part of a general approach to public administration that has gained considerable ground in the last decade in North America, Western Europe and many developing countries, at least as a set of ideas. Its practical impact is more debatable. Much of the literature on this subject is abstract and hortatory. We have attempted to describe what happened in practice against different political, economic and service backgrounds.

Why are these changes important to social administrators and why is the emphasis essentially upon a comparison with United States' experience?

Central Dilemma

All of those involved in the social services, whether they provide them, receive them or study them must be continually concerned with the answers to two questions: how much and for whom? The process of public expenditure planning and control in Britain determines precisely that. Each summer, while most teachers and social workers are contemplating their holidays the climax of a complex process is reached and decisions are taken that will determine the size of the classes they will have to teach, the size of their case load and the amount of residential accommodation that they will have at their disposal, in years to come. It is a process very few of them have heard about let alone understand. Yet the nature of their professional lives and the well-being of their clients depend upon the outcome.

The critical conundrum which the social services have to face is how to match supply and demand when the price of the service is zero or near zero?

Some economists suggest that the dilemma is never resolved and that frustrated consumers of the social services are continually demanding more than they as tax payers are prepared to finance. There is, they argue, continual bewilderment and disillusion, tax payers complaining of rising taxes and patients of inadequate care. Since the gap between demand and supply cannot be bridged any other way services are arbitrarily 'rationed' by administrators or bureaucrats. Yet in practice the world does not look like that. Expectations do not persistently and dangerously outrun the levels of service provided. A complex socio-economic market system operates, which we have scarcely begun to understand. In part, of course, the dilemma is not as great as it seems for many social services do carry charges and where direct charges are not levied the consumer has to bear other costs. Earnings which a 16-year-old foregoes to remain at school, are one obvious but important example.

The demand side of this socio-economic market has been explored in a limited fashion by political scientists and social administrators who have analysed the way 'demands' arise within the social service system, and the role which professional organisations and 'cause' groups have played. There is, incidentally, very little work on what consumers or potential consumers actually want, but it is the supply side and the interaction between demand and supply that we know so little about.

All of those concerned with the delivery of social services, whether at the centre or the periphery, are caught up in the rationing process. At the periphery the social worker recognises that there are far more families in need of support than she will ever be able to help. There is an almost infinite amount of further investigation and support which a GP could provide for his patients. How a social worker or a GP deploy their own time, whom they decide to help, how a headmaster or an area team leader deploy their staff, these are the ways in which limited resources are rationed. They determine who benefits and what quality of service which group of users receive.

The distribution of staff within a local authority or area health authority will have been determined, as part of a continuous process of political interplay between the professionals, the administrators and the elected or appointed representatives. In the local authority setting the responsibility for such allocations lies with the appropriate service committee, largely influenced by their chief officers. In the Health Service the Area Health Authorities and the area team of officers will fill a similar role. Both are working within constraints imposed by their respective finance committees or by the Regional Health Authorities. These, in their turn, are constrained by resource priorities laid down by the relevant central government department and this too is constrained by the Treasury and Cabinet decisions on public expenditure. We therefore have a whole hierarchy of rationing decisions which react one upon another since no subordinate level passively accepts the allocations made from above.

Some allocation decisions are open and explicit and planned, others are unrecognised, implicit and unplanned. A social worker or a GP under stress may respond by spending far less time with certain categories of patient or client, or he may merely not object when his receptionist or secretary puts off certain clients or fixes an appointment a long way ahead. The consequences may be unrecognised on the part of the worker; let alone being recognised by some higher authority like the Director of Social Services or his committee.

Conceptually then, it is helpful to think of rationing devices categorised on at least two continua – the degree of centralisation involved and the degree of explicitness. The higher up the bureaucratic or governmental chain allocation decisions are taken the more centralised the rationing process. The more aware the participants are of the consequences of their actions and the more forethought is entailed the more explicit resource allocation can be said to be.

These distinctions are elaborated in the next chapter. It is sufficient, here, to make the point that a central concern for social administrators, both academic and practising, must be to study the way the rationing process works and what are its outcomes. Just as the study of the pricing mechanism is central to the economist's work, so the study of rationing systems must be central to the work of the social administrator.

Parker has argued that the danger is that rationing will be undertaken unconsciously. Instead he claims:

'There is advantage in it being conscious and explicit and in it occurring *before* the service is offered. Otherwise some form of rationing will emerge (by default) through the manner in which the service is provided. Where this happens those who are most easily deterred, least articulate, worst acquainted with the service, least able to wait, or who fall outside the conventional categories of eligibility will tend to be penalised'.[1]

The chapters that follow seek to illuminate the rationing process by examining it at central government level. How far have the rationing decisions at the centre become more explicit, open or rational?

We have tried to ask these questions about education, health and social security and to compare the outcome of changes that have taken place in both Washington and Whitehall. There are clearly disadvantages in trying to paint a picture on such a broad canvas. On the other hand many points emerge from such a comparison that are by no means as clear from a study of the process in one country. Most of the theoretical literature on the subject of public expenditure control is American. It will become clear later that much of this writing is coloured by the particular economic, political and policy contexts which apply in the United States and particularly in Washington. How relevant are the American concepts to British practice? What happened when the United States Department of Health, Education and Welfare (HEW) tried to apply the principles of programme budgeting to different areas of social policy? How does their experience compare with the problems met by those who have tried to introduce some variant of the same procedures within British central government? What lessons can be drawn from such a comparison?

The Argument
The basic argument of the book is first that there were serious weaknesses in the original notion of applying systems analysis and programme budgeting to the social services. Second, the economic, political and policy contexts in which this set of techniques are applied will have a crucial bearing on their success. Moreover, those political conditions which prove favourable to some aspects of the whole process are likely to prove unfavourable to other aspects.

Third, in practice both in Washington and Whitehall, the original ideals have been drastically modified, yet a managerial paradigm still lies behind many of the attempts to carry through changes in resource planning. This is unhelpful and even detrimental to the planning of social services. It can lead to over centralisation and insufficient sensitivity to newly emerging needs, to the conflicts and uncertainties that are inherent in the pursuit of social policies.

Fourth, it is suggested that it would be more appropriate to adopt a pluralist planning model for the social services which explicitly aimed at a more open planning process at central government level and the competitive generation of information from groups with different interests and perspectives.

The argument is pursued in the following way: Chapter 2 reviews the proposals of the original budget reformers in the United States and sets them against the opposing views of those who prefer a political bargaining process. It argues that neither is entirely applicable to social policy.

The second part of the argument involves a brief look at the economic, political and policy contexts within which the reforms had to work in Washington and in HEW in particular. (Chapters 3–5.) These reforms were of three distinct kinds: (i) the attempt to introduce forward planning of public expenditure five or more years ahead; (ii) the proposed changes in the presentation of social service budgets; (iii) the evaluation of programmes' achievements.

Chapters 6 and 7 trace the somewhat frustrated attempts to introduce forward planning in HEW and then, by comparison, in Whitehall. The next chapter compares the development of new budget structures first in HEW and then in the DES and DHSS in Britain. Chapter 9 considers what kinds of programme evaluation have been undertaken in HEW and how the original intentions changed over time. This experience is then compared in Chapter 10 to the varied attempts at evaluation which have been tried in Britain. The book ends by making some proposals about the way in which all three elements – planning, budgeting and evaluation – could be adapted to fit more closely into the model of 'pluralist planning' that is discussed in the next chapter.

REFERENCE

1 Parker, R. A., 'Social Administration and Scarcity: the Problem of Rationing', *Social Work*, April, 1967.

Further Reading

Buchanan, J. M., *The Inconsistencies of the National Health Service*, Institute of Economic Affairs, Occasional Paper, No. 7, London, 1965. (Presents the traditional economist's view of the dilemma posed by free services.)

Crossman, R. H. S., *Paying for the Social Services*, Fabian Society, London, 1969.

Powell, J. E., *A New Look at Medicine and Politics*, Pitmans, London, 1966. (The views of two ex-ministers who were responsible for the Health Service and securing funds for it.)

British Medical Association
  Health Services Financing, London, 1970.
(An account of the financial difficulties faced by the NHS as an advisory
  panel to the BMA saw it. Some useful comparative material.)
Hall, A. S., *The Point of Entry*, George Allen and Unwin, London, 1974.
(One of the few studies of rationing at the periphery.)

Chapter 2

Theories
and Practice

'As the public sector has grown, so have the efforts to improve the basis on which individual policy decisions are taken. Increasing attention has been directed to identifying the nature of the problem or need which calls for action; to specifying as precisely as possible the general aim of the policy and its particular objectives, in terms of standards to be attained or needs to be met; to analysing alternative ways in which these aims or objectives might be achieved; and to verifying after the event that the expected results were achieved, in time, and with the predicted level of expenditure. . . . Cost benefit analysis on a substantial scale is undertaken in relation to both minor and major policy decisions. . . . Studies of output budgeting methods and the introduction of systematic Programme Analysis and Review will help to ensure the regular re-appraisal of policies across the whole field of government.'

(HM Treasury, *Public Expenditure White Papers Handbook on Methodology* (1972) pp. 1–2)

Economy in Government
In order to understand the development of the ideas that are reflected in this quotation it is necessary to go back thirty years or more to the works of Simon and other academic public administrators in America.[1] He had been concerned with decision making in general, and with what constituted rational behaviour by an organisation, but what he had to say was directly related to resource decisions. To operate efficiently, he argued, any organisation must be clear what its goals are and which goals are also means to more distant ends. It must choose from the alternative courses of action available to it the one which will lead to the greatest accomplishment of administrative objectives at the least cost. Later Simon

B

came to stress more explicitly that administrators could only be expected to choose satisfactory alternatives rather than theoretically optimal ones, because of the limitations of time and knowledge at their disposal. He argued that once an organisation's objectives had been determined the structure of the agency should correspond to them. Nevertheless, it is by no means clear in Simon how or on what occasions goals are to be defined or alternative courses of action appraised.

The notable contribution which a group of RAND economists made in the late fifties and early sixties was to suggest that there were techniques that could be used to show which courses of action were cost effective in a wide range of government activities. Moreover, they indicated that there was an appropriate vehicle to which to attach such regular reappraisals in government – namely the budget process.

Far from acting efficiently, they argued, public bodies had no incentives to make them use resources efficiently since there were no market incentives. Instead agencies tended to adopt concepts like 'need', or 'requirements' or 'priorities', which showed little awareness of the resource costs involved nor, in particular, was there any appreciation of the concept of opportunity cost. Budget discussions tended to be couched in terms like 'we need the best facilities available', ignoring the fact that the more resources that were made available to equip, say, a university physics laboratory, the less could be used for other purposes. Finally, they argued, there was no incentive for government agencies to concern themselves with the long term impact or cost of their activities. Politicians were only concerned with short term vote winning advantages. To achieve economy in government, public sector resource allocations should all be subject to 'systematic analysis'.

The essence of this approach emerged most coherently in two publications – *The Economics of Defense in the Nuclear Age* by Hitch and McKean,[2] and *Efficiency in Government and the Use of Systems Analysis* by McKean.[3] The first was the byproduct of cost appraisal work done by RAND for the US Defense Department and the individual services. The second used cost benefit studies of water resource schemes as its starting point but both produced a generalised methodology relevant to all public sector resource decisions and McKean's book in particular argued that systems analysis was applicable to the greater part of the Federal Government's activities.

The essential elements of such systematic analysis were: the clarification of objectives, without this no analysis was feasible; the presentation of alternative means of achieving these objectives; the costing of each alternative approach; the creation of input-output models which would show how much resources had to be expended in order to achieve given outcomes; the choice of some criterion with which to judge between the alternatives.

Both Hitch and McKean were confident from their experience of costing defense contracts and water resource schemes that input-output relationships could be established if agency objectives were clearly specified. It was the last element that posed the most difficult problems, but their solution lay in an apparently common sense procedure they called 'sub-optimisation'. Issues or items for analysis had to be broken down into sufficiently discrete parts to allow acceptable cost comparisons to be made. The usual task of economic or quantitative analysis was to provide information for relatively low level decision making in, for example, the Military hierarchy. At that level it was necessary to take as given the larger questions of military strategy and advise on the cheapest way of achieving a limited goal. 'If the Air Force tries to decide between two gun sights for fighters, taking the general organisation, size and tactics of fighter defense as given, it is sub-optimising'.[4] But the same principle held higher up the decision chain.

The task of breaking down resource decisions into sufficiently discrete issues was an important one. If criteria were adopted at a lower level that were inconsistent with those applied at a higher

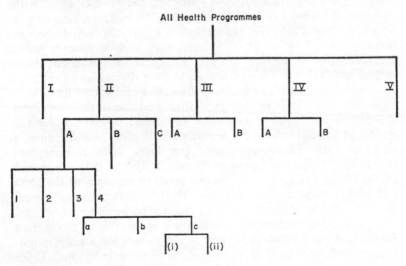

Figure 2.1

level the whole process was vitiated. It was at this point that the programme budget became conceptually important. Hitch and McKean argued that if resources were to be allocated according to specified objectives, the budget must be categorised in the same way. Subsequently the idea was elaborated into the notion of a hierarchical programme structure. The aim was to break down the budget into a logical hierarchy of programmes and sub-programmes[5] (see Figure 2.1). In such a structure activities (i) and (ii) ideally contribute to and only contribute to the goal of activity (c) which along with activities (a) and (b) contribute to and only contribute to the goal of activity 4 and so on right up to programmes I-V which might themselves be subsumed under one general purpose such as 'improved health'. When once this logical categorisation had been undertaken it would ensure that within it sub-optimising analyses between programmes or sub-programmes were consistent right the way through. It would then be possible to make 'trade offs' or adjustments between two sub-programmes that could be said to be fulfilling common objectives.

An example may help to make some of the implications clearer. Let us assume that the objective of activity (c) in Figure 2.1 is to extend the life expectancy of those suffering from kidney failure.[6] The size of the budget that can be devoted to this purpose is already fixed. No questions, at this stage, are being asked about whether such patients ought to be kept alive. There are basically two ways of achieving this end – hemodialysis (purifying the patients' blood with an artificial kidney), activity (i), or kidney transplants, activity (ii). The first of these activities can be further subdivided into dialysis at home or in a hospital. It is not necessary to face difficult issues about the value of life since our aim is to maximise the length of life in both cases. The quality of life could pose difficulties since those who have transplants can lead a more active and varied life. (As it happened transplants in this particular study were deemed to be cheaper so the arbitrary measures introduced to account for the quality of life did not affect the result.) This gives us a situation in which a cost effectiveness study can help. With a transplant operation the high costs come early and in dialysis they are spread over a life time, but they can be compared by discounting the costs and giving each a present value. If the analyst has empirical evidence on the life expectancy of those who are on dialysis and those who have undergone a transplant it is possible to produce an estimate of the cost of each year of life gained for a given population following transplant, or dialysis at home or in hospital. From this it would be possible to shed some light on the appropriate size of (i) and (ii) given the constraints on the availability of kidneys for transplant purposes.

Another example might be that of the maternity service. This could constitute a major programme on its own, say III. The aim might be to reduce perinatal and maternal mortality to a minimum (in practice there would be other considerations). There are two kinds of provision – hospital (A) and domiciliary (B). Let us assume that costs associated with each hospital confinement are twice those associated with each home confinement at present levels of staffing and technology, but hospital confinements are also safer. With a given budget it would be economic to provide the maximum number of hospital confinements consistent with that constraint and ensure that those facing least complicated deliveries had their babies at home. Can the analyst take us further and advise on the size of the maternity care budget? An idealistic society might begin with the idea that it wanted to do the best for its mothers and provide 100 per cent hospital confinements at a cost of £100 million. It may then be established that to have 10 per cent home confinements would not in any way alter the mortality rates. Faced with the knowledge that he could reduce expenditure and still maintain the same 'output' from the programme the minister would be well advised to spend only £95 millions on maternity services – £90m on hospital and £5m on home confinements and spend the £5m he saved on other parts of the health budget. So long as such expenditure had any positive value it must increase the community's welfare. What happens if he reduces the hospital budget a further £5 millions and thus slightly increases the risk of maternal mortality? How are we to set the value of, say, improved geriatric care, that £5 millions would buy against the increased risk of death suffered by the mothers. Some more optimistic exponents of systems analysis would argue a cost benefit analysis could do this. Various methods have been adopted to put monetary values on life expectancy, yet it is doubtful whether any of them satisfy the Pareto criterion that we ought to compensate each person who is to be worse off according to their valuation of the estimated change in risk.[7]

In practice all an economist can do, we would argue, is to show the consequences of spending different sums on maternity care of different kinds and leave the political process to decide. We can, however, say something about the political process. If 'the minister' takes the decision on the basis of his own judgement, or even worse if the medical profession does, with no reference to those affected the decision is less likely to conform to the Pareto criterion than if the decision is decentralised, the alternative consequences made known and discussed and in some way the expectant mothers' valuation assessed. But this is to stray from the original argument which laid considerable stress on what cost benefit and cost effectiveness analysis could achieve.

Next we reach the proposition that the Federal budget itself should be broken down into a hierarchy of expenditure categories each related to one discrete activity. Every activity that was delineated and separately costed ought to be aimed at achieving a measurable goal, for example, raising reading standards, reducing delinquency or speeding traffic flow. This would make cost effectiveness work possible.

When were these systematic analyses to be applied? The only regular assessment of resource priorities takes place within the annual budget cycle both in the preparation of the President's budget within government and in the discussion of it within Congress. Systematic analysis must therefore be applied as part of the budget round. However, the traditional process had major drawbacks. First, the President's budget was only concerned with expenditure covering the next financial year. This was far too short a period within which to seek to undertake strategic planning. New weapons systems had to be chosen far in advance of the period during which they would be operational. Small scale expenditure next year could entail vast sums five years hence. Within a constrained budget this would mean abandoning other projects in five years time or not completing the weapons system you had begun to install. It was necessary to foresee that eventuality. If this were true of military planning it applied equally to the rest of the Federal budget, not least to areas of social policy. Hence budgets should, in future, cover at least a five-year period.

Who was to ensure that this happened? The authors were quite explicit that these changes could only be undertaken if there were greater centralisation within each agency.

Indeed, as we shall see one of the aims of the Bureau of the Budget in extending programme budgeting was to strengthen Departmental heads' control over their agencies – many of which were seen to be virtually autonomous, and to tighten the Bureau's, and hence the President's control over Departments. The budget was the only instrument capable of doing this.

At the end of the day, then, what emerged was a proposal for a budget reform. It was by no means the first or the last of its kind.

The first stage of budget reform in the US had come with the Budget and Accounting Act of 1921. The aim was to create a reliable system of expenditure accounts, and to give the President control of the budget and of agencies' applications to Congress. The Bureau of the Budget was created and situated within the Treasury. The General Accounting Office was also set up. It was, in British terms, a Gladstonian reform, concerned to ensure that money was not wasted or dishonestly used – the financial control function of a Budget.

In 1939 the Bureau of the Budget moved to the Executive Office of the President and became more concerned with management efficiency. Ten years later the Hoover Commission had recommended that the Federal Budget be presented in terms of functions, activities and projects, supported by information about accomplishments. They called this 'performance budgeting'. It could be seen as an attempt to give the budget a managerial function. The reformers saw these latest proposals as adding a strategic planning function to the budget.

At this stage it is worth examining the foregoing propositions as they stand before we begin discussing what happened to them in practice. What are we to make, first of all, of the assumptions with which the argument began, namely that government is necessarily inefficient?

So Inefficient?

This is not the place to enter into a discussion of whether what are now called social services ought to be provided by the private sector. We shall sub-optimise and assume that they are appropriately provided by some organ of government. Is it the case that they are not subject to any economising incentives? Those working for local authorities who are continually being bombarded by demands to economise both from the politicians, the local press and ratepayers organisations, as well as by central government, may wonder somewhat at this statement. It can indeed be countered by considering the political process by which budget allocations are made. Instead of a 'jungle of competing interests' the process can be seen as a political market place in which there is also an 'unseen hand' at work. While it is undoubtedly true that a wide range of interest groups, professional bodies, trade unions, client groups and cause groups are all at work bidding for extra funds, and while it is also true that spending departments and agencies have a vested interest in their own growth, there are also politicians with a vested interest in keeping taxation to an absolute minimum. There is, moreover, the Treasurer's department, the Treasury or the Office of Management and Budget whose role is to be the advocate of economy. Within a constrained budget, if one agency or department 'gets away with it' to an excessive degree other participants in the struggle get less. There is therefore an incentive for all spending ministers or agency heads to ensure that the rules of the game are kept. The more economy minded a department appears to be the better its relations may be with the finance ministry or Treasury. The more constrained the budget – the less growth there is from year to year – the more powerful such competition will be. Clearly the extent to which the Treasury or its equivalent win out will depend not only on the political climate but upon the economic situation and the buoyancy of tax revenue.

The same political market model provides us with another insight into the accusation that agencies or interest groups only talk in terms of absolute levels of need and requirements unaffected by the relative cost of their proposals. If any one such statement or calculation is viewed as the final word on the matter then the criticism is valid.[8] If, however, such a statement as 'we need half a million teachers to reduce class sizes to a maximum of 30' is taken as the opening bid in a competition for resources with other claimants, then it assumes different proportions.

So long as cost consequences are attached different measures and conceptions of need made by different groups of participants are essential if the political resource market is to work properly. Individuals and groups may want to make different 'trade offs' between one view of need and its relative importance compared to the 'need' for another policy. Bradshaw[9] has argued that although need is a normative concept and there are different approaches to measuring it, where these overlap or agree we can be sure there is something for administrators to fasten upon. This may be so, in the sense that if there is widespread agreement that view may carry political weight. But it could well be that agreement amongst numerous experts is not a good guide to political weight. Take 'family poverty' as an example. Numerous experts may agree about subsistence measures – an appropriate dietary and calorific intake that can be obtained from a given income, its historical antecedents, and its appropriateness in comparison with other countries. But another 'expert' may argue that all of these views are wrong and that the only morally justifiable measure to take is one related to average earnings. It will produce a quite different result but its political weight may be greater. So the absolute needs or requirements approach can be seen to be less naïve than it seems if it is viewed as part of a political bargaining process.

Politics also help us to view differently the third criticism we mentioned – the view that governments rarely look or plan ahead. It would be more accurate to say that there are both political incentives and disincentives for government departments and local authorities to undertake long term planning. In pursuing the politics of planning a little further it may help to distinguish four different types of planning that will be useful as descriptive categories in later chapters.

Kinds of planning
As a starting point we shall take *planning* to mean 'an attempt to determine policies that relate to some future time period'.

It is certainly true that planning is time consuming and expensive. It has political costs too. It usually means that difficult choices have to be made earlier than otherwise would be necessary. It is natural for politicians to put off choices in the hope that they will resolve themselves in time. Moreover, plans and forecasts are frequently proved wrong. If the plans are published they may provide ammunition for an opposition party or rival agency. It is clear then that if planning is to take place there must be some political incentives in its favour. It would seem that there are in theory several that can be distinguished. The first two come about through a combination of technical necessity and political advantage – capital planning and manpower planning.

Capital planning first and foremost requires a whole train of decisions to be made well in advance of the time when buildings will actually be needed. If an urban authority like the Inner London Education Authority is to build any schools at all it must begin collecting together the plots of land which it will require to make up a site, seven to ten years in advance. Merely to buy plots and obtain planning permission on the off chance that they might be needed would not only be extremely costly, it would also be highly unpopular with other users – private and public. Land use and building plans in their turn require strategic planning. The authority has to have a fairly clear idea of the likely demand for school places area by area ten years hence, and if the authority also has a clear political intention to which it has publicly pledged itself, going comprehensive in this case, then that policy must be made to bite at the initial planning stage or it will never be attained at all. In exactly the same way if the central government has a clear political pledge to redeem – replacing Victorian primary schools – that too must be made effective at this point. Here we see political commitments and technical considerations combining to force fairly long term planning. Exactly the same kind of factors apply with hospital building, or the provision of old people's homes.

Closely linked to capital planning is *manpower planning*. It takes three years or more to train a teacher, seven or more to train a doctor and two or more to train a social worker. The period of training must be added to the time needed to increase the available building capacity before any impact at all is felt from a decision to expand the supply. Conversely a decision taken now to expand, say teacher supply, based on the existing position in schools could be wholly inappropriate in ten years time when new recruits are entering the schools. Population changes, up or down, prompt attempts at manpower planning. Professional organisations are particularly concerned to see that there will not be an 'over supply' in the future, by which they mean a tendency for their relative salary levels to fall. On the other hand professional and other staff form the major resource input to the social services, so any policy a government may have for extending a service or changing its emphasis will affect demands for manpower.

The technical need to undertake capital planning or manpower planning may come to dominate other attempts by a social service agency to plan ahead but a third important incentive is the political pressure to contain the level of taxation. Just because policy decisions in the social services have such long term consequences on public expenditure, that part of government and those politicians who are anxious to contain or reduce tax levels will also be anxious to get spending departments to produce a statement of the long-term effect that any new proposal will have on expenditure and therefore on taxation. We can call the resultant activities *tax control planning* which is closely associated with *economic planning*.

Fourthly, impetus to planning can arise from outside government altogether. The external stimulus may be a crisis or an issue which assumes major political importance. For a government department *not* to be seen to be planning or producing a long-term policy carries political costs. The perceived shortage of places in higher education in the early sixties is an example. This might be called *responsive planning*. Kahn lists some of the factors which may initiate an attempt to plan.

'Planning begins with a problem, a widely felt need, major dissatisfaction, or crisis. Or it begins with a transfer of power and the decisions of new leadership to systematise their activities. Or it begins with urgent need to allocate scarce resources or personnel. Or it begins with a demand from a source of funds or of power that planning be done to qualify for continued subsidy. Or it begins with the access to considerable new resources (from unprecedented growth or the assignment of revenues from new sources, for example). Or, finally, it is undertaken because "everyone is doing it".[10]

Each of these different kinds of planning are undertaken as part of an organisation's formal activities. It would be wrong to suppose that formal planning activities are the only ones in which government agencies indulge. Those working for an agency will often develop a consensus on which aspect of its activities needs attention next and where the service in question could be expanded or developed. We shall call this activity *promotional planning*. It is the least discussed but probably the most important. Organisations usually seek to expand their activities and powers. The phrase promotional planning is used here to mean the process by which agencies look ahead and make contingency plans for growth, plans which will enable them to take advantage of the political climate when it becomes favourable to that agency or department and the interests it serves. By no means all departments are as skilled at this as others.

We can see, therefore, that the political market offers, first of all, a competitive bargaining situation which does provide incentives for economy and some of the same conditions as a free market. Such a market also provides a forum in which different perceptions of need by different participants can be forced to stand the test of political debate, interdepartmental rivalry and Treasury scrutiny. Finally, there are political and technical incentives which force agencies to take long term perspectives despite pressures not to do so.

Objectives or Increments?
The proposals that had been made to increase efficiency in government, both by Simon, advocates of systematic analysis and later exponents of managerial methods, all begin, it will be recalled, with the proposition that government agencies must determine explicitly what their objectives are and distinguish these *ends* from the *means* of achieving them. Economists tend to say that inputs must be distinguished from outputs. This approach has had numerous critics but it has nowhere been more rigorously attacked than by the American author Lindblom, in his, by now, well-known advocacy of the 'science of muddling through'.[11]

The first characteristic injunction to the policy analyst or strategic planner is to clarify the values and objectives implicit in different policies or programmes before seeking to analyse them. Nonsense, says Lindblom, any programme, and it could be added any social service programme in particular, will be viewed differently by the various groups involved.

A housing redevelopment scheme will be seen differently by those on the council's waiting list, by those owner occupiers in the area, by tenants in the area, by tenants and owners in adjacent areas affected by the scheme, by amenity groups concerned with aesthetics, by the authority's architects who have their professional reputations to make and by local councillors who have their seats to save. Whose interests, whose objectives and which values is the administrator or analyst to take to be the most important? How are they to be measured one against another? If this proves difficult in the case of a simple housing development what price housing policy as a whole?[12] This is of fundamental importance because it means that even if some abstract ranking of objectives or 'needs' by some committee of 'experts' is invented, it has no general validity unless it commands widespread agreement amongst all these competing interests.[13]

Lindblom then turns the original proposition on its head and claims that you can only tell what a government's objectives are by examining in retrospect the policy choices it has actually made. 'I can only know what I believe by examining what I do' – to use the philosophical analogy.

'Except roughly and vaguely I know of no way to describe – or even to understand – what my relative evaluations are for, say freedom and security, speed and accuracy in governmental decisions or low taxes and better schools than to describe my preferences among specific policy choices that might be made between the alternatives in each of the pairs'.[14]

In order to ensure that all these contrasting values and objectives are taken into account and weighed, he argues, we can only rely on the normal pluralist political process. Every value stance neglected by one policy-making agency will be the concern of at least one other agency. Every important interest or value has its watch-dog or if it has not it should rapidly seek to train one.

'In the United States, for example, no part of government attempts a comprehensive overview of policy on income distribution. A policy nevertheless evolves, and one responding to a wide variety of interests. A process of mutual adjustment among farm groups, labor unions, municipalities and school boards, tax authorities, and government agencies with responsibilities in the fields of housing, health, highways, national parks, fire, and police accomplishes a distribution of income, in which particular income problems neglected at one point in the decision processes become central at another point.'[15]

In the same way Lindblom rejects the notion that analysts should seek to distinguish means from ends. Precisely because the ends of a particular policy may be in dispute, groups pressing for change do not seek to agree about ultimate objectives, which would destroy the political consensus on that issue, but to concentrate on the agreed *means* to different ends. This is frequently the situation where social policy is concerned. The recent campaign to extend nursery education is a good example. There were clearly a great many different motives behind that movement. There was the desire of a great many mothers for a bit of peace and quiet or the opportunity to go to work, the belief that education during this period was crucial to their children's intellectual and social development, the desire to give children from deprived homes a 'fairer start' in life, the pressure to employ more teachers in a slackening labour market for teachers and so on. In meetings concerned with pressing for an expansion of nursery provision there was no better way of bringing the whole activity to a halt than to ask what the objective was. The suggestion that pre-school provision should be designed to permit mothers to go out to work was enough to bring angry responses from the most ardent campaigners. Yet on the immediate aim a considerable degree of consensus was possible. *The 'means' was the only 'end' on which agreement was possible.*

Lindblom's conclusion is that the *only* test of a good policy is agreement – not that it is consistent with some abstract objective.

The second characteristic injunction which he challenges is 'be comprehensive', consider all the alternatives. He elaborates his objection to this in the book he wrote with Braybrooke *A Strategy for Decision*.[16] No one can comply with this injunction unless he postulates a single welfare function. What policy makers actually use, he claimed, was the practice he called 'disjointed incrementalism'. That is to say they make small changes about which they have considerable understanding, ignoring most alternatives as impracticable. Even so they recognise there will be unanticipated consequences they would have avoided if they could have foreseen them and which if they monitor they can correct. As an example he cites the gradual liberalisation of the United States social security programme.

The idea is further developed in his later book where he argues that it is wrong to suppose that coordination is best achieved by some central body overseeing the actions of different agencies or ministries.[17] 'People can coordinate with each other without anyone's coordinating them, without a dominant common purpose, and without rules that fully prescribe their relations to each other,'[18] – a process he calls 'partisan mutual adjustment'.

When someone is crossing the road they do not have a clear plan of how they will avoid all the pedestrians coming the opposite way. What they do is to continually change course if they find someone is coming towards them. In the same way one agency may have different aims and values from another but it will still take account of other actions or proposals in making its own. The Appropriations Committee procedure in Congress is an example. One committee responds to what another has done and makes allowances for what another may do. This is equally, if not more, rational than some central agency trying to agree on some overriding strategy which corresponds to an interpretation of 'national interest' on which no one can agree. On the contrary the virtue of the American system lies in the multiplicity of agencies concerned. Where policy making is centralised those responsible for coordinating policy are inevitably found to *over* simplify just to be able to grapple at all with the issues they must decide. If decisions have to be made centrally planners will probably *not* use highly complex methods in order to take account of all the possible important consequences. The central administrator will instead be tempted to use arbitrary or indeed *no* method at all and not publish or give any account of the way he has reached his decisions.

What is more social cohesion is more likely to be promoted through a pluralist system than with central coordination. Where agreement has to be sought and attained before decisions can be made the pressures produce a degree of consensus and the public debate that is involved is a unifying force. If centralised decisions on resource allocation are imposed they merely breed resentment and dissension.

Taken together these arguments present a model for resource allocation very different from the preceding one. Though the model was designed to describe policy making in general it may be argued that it is particularly well suited to social policy where fact and value are so interwoven.

Who Carries Out the Orders?

So far we have been concerned with the difficulties social service organisations might encounter in seeking to formulate agreed goals or objectives. Other considerations may lead us to question whether even when such attempts succeed they can be made operative throughout the service delivery system. In the first place there are general arguments derived from organisation theory which suggest that in any organisation its formal goals are modified by informal procedures which are heavily influenced by the personal goals of officials. While this is a general proposition that may be said to hold for all organisations it is especially true of public bodies where there is no market discipline or easy criteria of success in the organisation's terms which will hold those lower down the bureaucratic hierarchy to the goals formulated at the top. Both Tullock and Downs have extended this argument. Tullock argues that in any hierarchical system 'messages' are cumulatively distorted. The more vaguely defined the functions and the more difficult its outputs are to measure the greater the 'leakage'.[19] Downs emphasises that the particular perspectives and the self interest of bureau officials or civil servants will introduce biases into the transmission of information to their superiors or other parts of the agency – biases towards particular policies or practices or in the budget recommendations they make.[20] This is not to say that all public officials show equal concern for their own survival or advancement. Downs distinguishes five types: the 'climbers' who are primarily motivated by personal goals of advancement, the 'conservers' who are motivated by the desire to stay put and have a quiet life, the 'zealots' with a commitment to the narrow or immediate policies of the agency, the 'advocates' who are loyal to its broad goals and seek power in those terms, while there are, finally, a rare breed of 'statesmen' who concern themselves with societal goals. Nevertheless in public institutions 'a very significant proportion of all the activity being carried out is completely unrelated to the bureau's formal goals, or even to the goals of its topmost officials'.[21] In short, although a particular policy may be chosen because its declared objectives fit in well with a department's overall strategy its implementation may turn out to have quite different effects, which cannot then be altered because entrenched interests have been established and for usual reasons of administrative inertia.

These are general limitations which apply to the pursuit of formal goals within institutions, but in two particular respects the difficulties presented by the social services are even greater. The first lies in the importance of the professional worker who is the major 'factor of production' and whose very professional status provides him or her with a third set of goals or values distinct from both the bureaucratic and the narrow self interested ones. Even more crucial is the general consensus, perhaps more strongly held in the British public service than the American, that the professions, in their day to day dealings with clients, pupils or patients, ought to be the final arbiter of the values, purposes and priorities inherent in their activity. This view lies behind the stress on clinical freedom and the teacher's right to teach how and what he or she considers appropriate. Thus any attempt to set goals or objectives which conflict with professional norms, or an individual's appreciation of what those norms ought to be, will be resisted. Moreover, they can be resisted not merely at the level of the professional organisations, but also by the teacher in her classroom or the general practitioner in his consulting room. Tentative steps by the Ministry of Education in Britain over a decade ago to merely study aspects of school curricula were stamped upon by the teaching profession. An important safeguard to our individual liberty may be seen to rest in the fact that relative valuations of the worth of saving one kind of person's life as opposed to another are not made by politicians or a central authority but by individual doctors. An important safeguard to free personal expression may be seen to rest in the liberty of the teaching profession to teach what it thinks fit. There is certainly no universal agreement on either point but in so far as these views are generally held the pursuit of wider societal interests can be seen to favour maximising the discretion exercised by the individual professional in the field.

The second and related difficulty is that often legal and political responsibility is divided between two or more levels of government, local and central or Federal, state and local. Again the prevailing values inhibit detailed intervention by the centre in the way social service resources are actually distributed at local level. There is therefore little point in central departments making detailed or systematic analyses of the use to which funds are put even assuming they were permitted to do so.

Both factors may be summed up by saying that prevailing values often conflict with the notion that the level of government which provides the funds ought to have any detailed say in the way they are used.

So much, for the moment, for the initial premises on which the systems analysts based their set of proposals. Even if we dismiss the problems that have been raised so far there is still the concept of sub-optimising to be considered.

Sub-optimising?

It will be recalled that the essence of this approach was to break down major resource allocation decisions into a logical series of smaller discrete problems each of which was susceptible to analysis. An extension of the approach was to break down the budget into a logical hierarchy of programmes, between which trade offs could be made. It is crucial to the logic that such programmes represent identifiable activities each of which contribute to and only contri-

bute to one other superior objective. The further real life departs
from that model the more complicated and unworkable it becomes.
Let us assume that sub-programmes (i) and (ii) in Figure 2.1 not
only contribute to (c) but also have different impacts on various
programmes coming under the general headings of I, III and IV as
well as ultimately affecting II. This would involve not only seeking to
measure the impact (i) and (ii) had on these other programmes but
assessing the relative importance of such increments to the output
of I, III and IV. Yet the argument began with the assumption that
such comparisons were essentially political. Therefore, a lot turns
on how far social service activities can in fact be broken down into
discrete activities with single outputs and without large and un-
measurable 'spillovers' into the other programmes. This in turn
depends upon what Simon called their 'technology'. Chapter Eight
is devoted to examining the practical difficulties involved. Let us for
the moment assume that they can be overcome. The second
question is how do we know when the process of sub-optimising has
been well or badly done? To this there is, apparently, no theoretical
answer. It depends upon analysts' 'experience', 'intuition', 'inspiration', 'judgement', 'common sense'. A set of qualities which sound
remarkably like those possessed by the gifted 'greats' scholar of old,
what Vickers called 'appreciation' of a problem.[22]

Finally, and quite apart from the technical problems to be encountered in any actual analysis, there is the objection which
political scientists have made that, so far from making political
choices more explicit, highly complicated cost benefit studies tend to
hide within them all kinds of implicit value judgements and give a
spurious objectivity to the course of action that is judged economically preferable.[23] Economists criticise the use of the word 'need' as
an excuse for special pleading which hides value judgements, but
exactly the same can apply to cost benefit analysis. Both have a part
to play in an open political process where implicit value assumptions can be forced into the open.

An Imperfect Political Market
Taken together these propositions present a formidable counter to
the idealised model for allocating resources advanced at the beginning of this chapter. The first seeks to approximate public sector
allocations to an economic market, the second relies on a political
market. Yet, those who would rely exclusively on a pluralist
political process do so very largely because of the virtues they see in
the *process* without judging the outcomes of that process in policy

c

terms. They are primarily concerned with the achievement of consensus.

Just as the free market theorists have argued that competition between the self interest of individuals will produce an efficient distribution of resources, so pluralist theories assume that free competition between group interests will produce an efficient distribution of public services. Yet, just as there are imperfections in the private market, it can be argued, there are parallel imperfections in the political market.

The political market is just as likely to ignore or at least not give full weight to certain social costs. A large mining corporation or property developers are well placed to mirror, in political power, the commercial power they wield in the economic market. Beside them small scattered voluntary amenity societies may not get very far. Or where they do amenity groups may themselves reflect only one group of interests in the community. Hence the importance of agencies whose role it is to work for other community interests, to analyse and quantify the impact of mining operations or redevelopment on all sections of the community. The potential supply of oil, the profitability of the scheme and much other information will be available to the oil company. At least as competent analytical resources are needed to identify the social costs.

Politically unacceptable degrees of income inequality that are seen to endanger the long term security of the society present difficulties for free market economists. So they do for the parallel political theorist. Poor people cannot work the interest group system as well as the better organised and wealthier sections of the population. The rationale behind, or at least the rhetoric that accompanies, the extension of social service provision is very often in terms of distributional justice. In practice extensions have often benefited the articulate and the rich – those who might be expected to benefit under the private market in any case. It may be that the rhetoric has, indeed, been no more than that. But it is also possible that politicians have often been misled by inadequate information about who was benefiting most from certain social programmes and tax arrangements. There is at least some indication that this has been the case in both Britain and America. If a government wishes to see redistribution of income take place in any direction, it must monitor the impact of its policies to this end.

In brief then, there is no reason to suppose that competition between existing interest groups will of itself produce an outcome that takes account of the full range of community interests.

Specifically this means:

(i) That there must be a substantial input of information and analysis into public debate and decision making which is not tied to particular interest groups. The analytical staffs in government can therefore act as efficiency advocates or 'public interest partisans' who can tackle what Self has called 'higher level problems'.[24]

(ii) That information brings power and should be seen as a way of strengthening weak interests and supporting those individuals, like heads of Departments, who have to make choices between the competing demands.

These might be said to constitute the beginnings of a pluralist planning model. It accepts that the planner cannot have a dominant or decisive a role, that the options he considers and the information system he seeks to create will reflect a variety of political values but unless the politician understands what is actually happening to the resources deployed in his name he cannot translate his values into a consistent set of decisions.

'Participants in the decision process must have some knowledge of the social production functions that translate program specifications (inputs) into program consequences (outputs). Otherwise the advocacy and bargaining process cannot produce a meaningful translation of political values into specific decisions.'[25]

Incremental change is as dependent on understanding the consequences of the previous increments of change unlike a more Utopian planning model. The objective is thus to sharpen and improve political debate not to stifle it in some managerial consensus.

'The most frustrating part of public life is not the ability to convince others of the merits of a cherished project or policy. Rather, it is the endless hours spent on policy discussions in which the irrelevant issues have not been separated from the relevant, in which ascertainable facts and relationships have not been investigated but are the subject of heated debate, in which the consideration of alternatives is impossible because only one proposal has been developed, and, above all, discussions in which nobility of aim is presumed to determine effectiveness of program. There are enough real value conflicts, institutional rigidities, and scarcities of information in the way of effective government action. Let us not add a massive additional obstacle by assuming that complex values can be effectively translated into necessarily complex programmes by nothing more than spirited debate.'[26]

Schultze is here arguing for greater knowledge and greater explicitness but *within* an essentially pluralist system. He also argued later in his book for *decentralisation* in decision making. He was not optimistic about the capacity of centrally controlled management systems to produce results decreed by political heads of agencies. There were too many opportunities for slippage down the chain of command, especially in a country as large and diverse as the States. Instead he argued that relevant positive financial inducements were more effective. It was at least as important to avoid 'negative' financial inducements. (Grant structures or salary structures which may be detrimental to particular policies.) In this way detailed administrative controls from the centre could be relaxed, local officials or professionals could be left to make their own individual or local assessments of particular cases, in the knowledge that the overall outcome would tend to produce the kind of results the central government desired.

One example of the positive inducement principle in America is the health maintenance organisation. This is an organisation which agrees to provide a member with a comprehensive range of medical care in return for a fixed premium. It is argued that this is more efficient than a fee for services basis or the separate public funding of hospitals or family doctor services, which encourage excessive doctoring, rising fees and encourage patients to opt for more expensive forms of care. The HMOs are meant to reduce costs of medical care first because a patient goes on paying – or the State does – through Medicare or Medicaid, whether he is ill or not. Hence the HMO has an incentive to utilise preventive medicine, and to attempt early diagnosis.

If this provides an example of positive financial inducements as a way of rationing resources, an example of a counterproductive inducement can be found in the finance of medical care in Great Britain. The division between central finance of institutional care and the local finance of community care discourages local authorities from expanding what is often supposed to be the cheapest as well as the more humane form of care for many mental patients and geriatric cases.

This, then, is the compromise position occupied by this particular prescriptive model. It accepts, from a realistic assessment of the American situation, that the political process has many centres of power and influence. It can, however, be improved by the injection of information and analysis at every point. The central decision makers in the allocation process should be particularly well equipped with information and analytical staffs. They are, however, only advocates along with all the other participants. Central management is likely to be ineffective unless supported by a system of financial inducements to local government which is consistent with the central department's view of resource priorities.

Once again this model gives little attention to the importance of the professional in the delivery of many public services especially those we normally call social services.

Rationing Processes
The concept which seems most helpful in seeking to understand the way social services are allocated is that which we briefly introduced in the last chapter – rationing. The word carries rather pejorative overtones. For some it raises memories of the second world war and austerity. Some economists see it as an authoritarian alternative to the perfections of a free market and some social administrators view it as a description of the way in which clients are denied their rights. Rationing is usually seen as a negative procedure. Yet it is more appropriately envisaged as a two-way process. Professional workers and other participants seek to regulate the demands made upon their limited resources in various ways, but they also seek to obtain more resources for the task in hand. For example, in 1960 the Ministry of Education imposed a ban on further provision of nursery school places. The ban was only partially raised in the mid-1960s for special categories of children. Thus local authorities were forced to adopt traditional rationing procedures. Waiting lists grew for nursery places, but for the most part headmistresses were given a free hand in operating these and quite frequently the criterion of first come first served was applied. The consequence was that competition for places often resulted in the most informed, active and educated mothers gaining places for their children while those children in greatest social and educational need failed to gain places. Social attitudes to the family and women's role began to change, economic and social pressures on married women and the increased professional attention devoted to the pre-school years combined to make both teachers' organisations and local authorities increasingly perturbed by the rationing process which they were called upon to administer. The pressures on the Department of Education and its pressure on the Treasury and the Cabinet finally broke this very explicit restriction. The fact that success was achieved largely because of the fortuitous decline in the birth rate after 1964 does not alter the basic point that one layer in the political or administrative hierarchy may be enforcing restraint on

those layers below it while at the same time seeking to press its demands for resources on those above.

The participants are reacting upon one another in a continuous chain of events, but it is useful to categorise the locus and nature of resource allocation decisions using four distinguishing dimensions.

Central-peripheral. Resource decisions which affect the social services extend from those taken in full Cabinet about the overall level of public expenditure all the way through interdepartmental bargaining in Whitehall and inter-committee bargaining in County Halls to decisions taken by a receptionist in an area office of a social service department. At each stage constraints are imposed on the level below.

Explicit-unrecognised. It is important to seek to find out how far priorities are determined in an explicit way and how far they have emerged entirely unrecognised. An explicit resource allocation decision may be said to be one which is premeditated or planned, one in which an attempt is made to distinguish who is or has been receiving what resources, and one in which the outcome of the plans or policies are examined or evaluated in some way.

Open-closed. The fact that resources are allocated in an explicit way does not necessarily mean that the knowledge on which decisions are taken are published or open to public debate. The more information on which decisions are based is published and the earlier in the decision process this happens the more open the allocation.

Technical-political. It is also helpful to ask how far resource choices are made on technical or professional grounds and how far they are left to the interplay of political pressures. This is a notably difficult thing to do but it is often possible to trace shifts along this dimension over a period of time. Take as an example the allocation of pupils between secondary schools in Inner London. At one time this was done on the basis of tests and head teachers' individual professional judgements. Later when the responsibility for choice was transferred to area offices criteria were drawn up in order of importance and were discussed by a subcommittee of councillors, eventually becoming the subject of considerable public debate. They were altered in response to public pressure. This represents a shift towards the political end of the dimension.

While none of these dimensions are easy to measure or be precise about they do help to distinguish how the nature of allocation decisions may change over time or differ between countries.

Parker[27] has described some of the ways in which administrators and professionals at the periphery cope with demands on their time or resources. He categorised the following: deterrence, eligibility rules, deflection from one agency to another, delay, client ignorance, and dilution of professional 'standards'.

The practice of deterrence through 'less eligibility' is of course a classic example of a rationing device. As administered under the 1834 Poor Law Amendment Act it was a centrally promoted and explicit device for reducing the burden on ratepayers. It was interpreted with varying degrees of rigour at local level. The same device is still used in the administration of 'Part III' accommodation for the homeless. Until 'King Hill' and the publicity which surrounded it, central government showed no interest in the means by which welfare departments sought to keep demands on such accommodation within bounds.[28] The use of old workhouse accommodation, the separation of husband and wife and the harsh regulations within the hostels were all deterrent rationing devices operated at a local level, though probably not explicitly seen this way by elected representatives and only dimly perceived as such by many of those concerned.

As a rationing device it took place at the periphery, was unrecognised, closed and technical. It became somewhat more a matter of central concern, that was more clearly recognised, slightly more open in that a little more information has emerged about it, and more political.

The stigma which attaches to some services, notably in health and social work, is a common deterrent to their use. Attempts deliberately to stigmatise services may be rare in an explicit way today. Much more often professionals or administrators may tacitly avoid taking active steps to remove the stigma that surrounds that service in the knowledge that to do so would put an unmanageable strain upon it. The same considerations apply when it comes to advertising. 'The idea of a campaign to "sell" a particular service is not always welcome: understandably so, for it might prove impossible to cope with any sudden increase in demand without a simultaneous increase in resources. Such reluctance to advertise a service fully is often justified by the comfortable assumption that those *really* in need will find out about the service soon enough.'[29] This is a very apt description of the attitude adopted by the National Assistance Board in the 1950s and early sixties.

In the same way eligibility or entitlement to a service or benefit can be determined entirely at a professional level. A consultant may decide that priority use of a kidney machine will be given to young men with a family rather than elderly spinsters. Such resource allocation decisions may be largely unrecognised outside the profession and unchallenged politically because of conventions about clinical freedom.

At the other extreme eligibility rules may be determined entirely by central regulations laid down by Parliament as with National Insurance. Supplementary benefits are an example of combination of statutory regulations, a central code of practice which is unpublished and scope for officers' discretion in individual cases.

Again explicit rules of varying secrecy may be locally administered but subject to some central government pressure. The Cullingworth report on council house allocation procedures represents an excellent example of the delicate balance of responsibility in this field.[30] It also shows how one of the most common rationing devices – delay – has in the case of council housing excluded some of the groups in greatest housing need.

So it is possible to see most of the devices operating at any point between the professionals' contact with the client, right the way through to the central department.

It has been the task of academic social administrators to make explicit the unrecognised consequences of many of these practices but it is only relatively recently that government began to recognise the need for greater explicitness.

The apex of the system – the central government's control of public expenditure decisions – is a logical and natural place to begin to understand that rationing process. It is this point in the process which this study seeks to illuminate.

Often advocates of systematic analysis and managerial methods at least sound as if they are advocating more 'technical' and less 'political' choices, hence the hostile reaction of many political scientists. They also seem to favour more centralised decision-taking and indeed not to appreciate the importance of the periphery in the allocation process. They clearly favour explicit rather than unrecognised processes, while the muddling-through school of thought at times seems to make a virtue of the extent to which participants cannot recognise what they are doing. Finally, the managerial method, especially in the hands of the British civil service, appears to make a virtue of secrecy. The pluralist planning model stresses the virtues of open, political and explicit choices, with the periphery responding to appropriate incentives.

In Brief

Social planners need a framework of ideas into which to set their activities. Neither those which derive from management theory or micro economics appear appropriate notably because they give scant attention to the value conflicts inherent in social policy and because they fail to take account of the important part played by the professional provider of the service. Equally a pure pluralist political model has its drawbacks. There are both technical and political factors which make some form of long term planning likely. A pluralist planning model may be of greater relevance combining as it does a stress on open, political but explicit choices. Explicit rationing decisions are ones taken with forethought, over a long time horizon, in the knowledge of how resources are currently allocated, and following an open examination of the outcomes of present policies. It will be argued that it is towards this model that resource decisions have in fact been moving in both Britain and the United States, though in rather varied ways. These reflect the different economic climates, political institutions and social programmes in the two countries.

Both the rational comprehensive and the pluralist models owe a great deal to American authors. It is perhaps inevitable that their theories should rationalise from the American political system. Yet they each owe a good deal to the economic, political and policy context of that country. To these we now turn.

REFERENCES

1 Simon, H. A., *Administrative Behaviour*, (1st Edition 1945, Second Edition 1957) Collier Macmillan, Toronto (see Ch. IX).
2 Hitch, C. J., and McKean, R. M., *The Economics of Defense in the Nuclear Age*, Harvard University Press, Cambridge, Mass., 1961.
3 McKean, R. M., *Efficiency in Government and the Use of Systems Analysis*, John Wiley, New York, 1958.
4 Hitch and McKean, op. cit., p. 129 (1965 edition).
5 See the chapter on programme budgeting for health in Novick, D., *Program Budgeting*, Harvard University Press, Cambridge, Mass., 1965.
6 The example is taken from: Klarman, H. E., *et al.* 'Cost effectiveness analysis applied to the treatment of chronic renal disease', *Medical Care*, Vol. 6, 1968.
7 Mishan, E. J., *Cost Benefit Analysis*, George Allen & Unwin, London, 1972 (see chapters 22–3).
8 See the argument in Culyer, A. J., Lavers, R. J., and Williams, A., 'Health Indicators' in *Social Indicators and Social Policy* (Ed.) Shonfield, A., and Shaw, S., Heinemann, London, 1972.

9 Bradshaw, J., 'A Taxonomy of Need' in G. Maclaghlan, *Problems and Progress in Medical Care*, Oxford University Press, 1972.
10 Kahn, A. J., *Theory and Practice of Social Planning*, Russell Sage Foundation, New York, 1969, p. 12.
11 Lindblom, C. 'The Science of Muddling Through', *Public Administration Review*, Spring, 1959.
12 Ferris, J., *Participation in Urban Planning: the Barnsbury Case*, Occasional Papers on Social Administration, Bell, London, 197.
13 See for example the proposed index of health needs in Culyer, A. J., Lavers, R. J., Williams, A., op. cit.
14 *Public Administration Review*, Spring, 1959, p. 82.
15 Op. cit., p. 85.
16 Braybrooke, D., Lindblom, C., *A Strategy for Decision*, Free Press, New York, 1963.
17 Lindblom, C., *The Intelligence of Democracy*, Free Press, New York, 1963.
18 Op. cit., p. 3.
19 Tullock, G., *The Politics of Bureaucracy*. Public Affairs Press, Washington, D.C. 1965.
20 Downs, A., *Inside Bureaucracy*, Little, Brown and Co., Boston, 1967.
21 Ibid, p. 136.
22 Vickers, G., *The Art of Judgment: Policy making as a Mental Skill*, Chapman and Hall, London, 1965.
23 See for example, Self, P., *Administrative Theories and Politics*, George Allen & Unwin, London, 1972, p. 44.
24 Self, P., 'Is comprehensive Planning Possible and Rational?', *Policy and Politics*, Vol. 2, No. 3, 1974.
25 Schultze, C. L., *The Politics and Economics of Public Spending*, Brookings Institution, Washington, 1968, p. 56.
26 Ibid, pp. 75-6.
27 Parker, R., 'Social Administration and Scarcity: the Problem of Rationing'. *Social Work*, April, 1967.
28 Radford, J. 'From King Hill to the Squatting Association' in *Community Action*, ed. A. Lapping, Fabian Society, London, 1970. Kings Hill was the Kent County Council Hostel that was the subject of a protest movement 1965-6. Ministry of Health Circular 20/66, Home Office Circular 178/66, Ministry of Housing and Local Government Circular 58/66.
29 Parker, op. cit.
30 Ninth Report of the Housing Management subcommittee of the Central Housing Advisory Committee, 'Council Housing, Purposes, Procedures, and Priorities', Ministry of Housing and Local Government, London, 1969.

Further Reading

Simon, H. A., *Administrative Behaviour*, (second edition), op. cit. (Still the classic exposition of the goal oriented approach.)

McKean, R. N., *Public Spending*, McGraw Hill, New York, 1968.
(A student text which gives a balanced but favourable account of the contribution output budgets and cost benefit analysis can play as well as a realistic account of inter-agency bargaining from a US perspective.)

Culyer, A. J., *The Economics of Social Policy*, Martin Robertson, London, 1973.
(A basic textbook which makes a similar case but from a British service perspective.)

Novick, D. (Ed), *Program Budgeting*, op. cit.
(The case for using the Federal budget as a planning tool.)

Etzioni, A. (Ed), *Readings on Modern Organisations*, Prentice Hall, Englewood Cliffs, New Jersey, 1969.
(This contains not only Lindblom's original article on 'muddling through' but Dror's attack on it and Lindblom's reply as well as an article by Drew on HEW and its early attempts at PPB.)

Schultze, C. L., *The Politics and Economics of Public Spending*, op. cit.
(A pragmatic as well as readable view by the ex head of the Bureau of the Budget in Johnson's Presidency.)

Self, P. *Administrative Theories and Politics*, George Allen and Unwin, London, 1972.
(A critical examination of administrative theories, especially Simon, in a comparative context.)

Chapter 3

The
Economic Context

In the past two decades planning procedures have been introduced against a background of sharply increasing social welfare expenditure in both Britain and the United States. To understand the discussion which follows it is important to appreciate the pace of the expansion that occurred and the relative size and scope of the two governments' commitment to social welfare.

We must begin with two key terms: 'the social services' and 'social welfare'.

In the United States the term social services usually means some activity related to social work. It is nearer in meaning to our phrase the 'personal social services'. In the United Kingdom the official statistics have taken the term 'social services' to cover education, the national health service, local welfare services such as the care of old people, child care, school meals, milk, welfare foods, and social security. Social administrators have usually included public housing in their definition. By adding the cost of housing subsidies and new house building by public authorities to the national income definition of social services we have a category broadly comparable to the term 'social welfare' as it is defined in the United States. The Social Security Administration publish figures showing total public expenditure in the United States on social security, health, welfare, education and housing. It would be wrong to suggest that the two categories are identical but they do provide reasonably comparable figures, which show the growth of what will, from now on, be called 'social welfare expenditure' in the two economies.[1]

There is another rather more insoluble problem of measurement. How are we to compare the relative sizes of the social welfare sectors in the two countries? The most obvious approach is to compare total social welfare expenditure with the Gross National Product (GNP). This is the method adopted in the American figures and is often used for this country. However, it does to some degree exaggerate the importance of government activity. To the unwary such figures imply that half the goods and services in our society are actually provided by the government. On closer examination, however, it can be seen that much of the public expenditure total is made up of transfer payments – pensions, other cash benefits and subsidies – which do not appear in the GNP. Hence to express total public expenditure or total social service expenditure, including transfer payments, as a proportion of the GNP is not really legitimate. A more strictly accurate comparison is to express social welfare expenditure on goods and services as a percentage of GNP (currently about 14 per cent in the UK) and express 'current grants to persons' (pensions and other benefits) as a percentage of total personal income (currently about 10 per cent in the UK). However, the sources do not permit us to take this purist approach. We shall therefore express social welfare expenditure in both countries as a percentage of the GNP. The historical pattern is not impaired thereby.

The Growth of Social Welfare in the United States

A popular British misconception about the United States is that it is a basically free enterprise society almost entirely lacking in social services. With the particular and peculiar exception of health care this has never been true. We should not be misled by the rhetoric of American politicians. The American colonies and hence the newly independent states inherited the English Poor Law almost in its entirety. The laws of settlement, the household means test, the workhouse, outdoor relief, poor law hospitals, all these were taken into the fabric of American welfare and remained even longer than in Britain. The Americans introduced public education very early in their history and after the Civil War the Federal Government began its involvement in social security by giving pensions and compensation to veterans and their families on a large scale. By 1890, therefore, the United States was spending more on social welfare relative to its Gross National Product than was the United Kingdom – 2·4 per cent as against 1·9 per cent. It was only by 1900 that social welfare on this side of the Atlantic began to outpace America and not until after 1911 did a big gap really open up following the British Government's introduction of old age pensions, health and unemployment insurance. The United States in contrast was slow to develop social insurance.

In the early part of the century workers' compensation laws were passed by virtually all States compelling employers to insure their employees against industrial accidents. But it was not until the depression of the 1930s that any significant move towards social insurance took place. The key piece of legislation was the Social Security Act of 1935. It established two insurance programmes at a national level, a system of old age pensions for those who were employed in industry or commerce and a combined Federal-state system of unemployment insurance. The same law also provided Federal grants to the states to help meet the cost of public assistance to the elderly, the blind and single parent families. It also enabled the Federal Government to make grants for other welfare services, mainly for children. As more people came to be included within the scope of the legislation and contributors became eligible to draw their retirement benefits its financial importance grew.

During the 1950s social welfare expenditure was held in check while the economy expanded. It was not until the 1960s first under the Kennedy and then the Johnson administrations that Federal involvement in social welfare was extended and local and state spending also rose sharply. Over the decade as a whole social welfare expenditure increased by an average of 8·5 per cent per annum in constant prices. The period falls clearly into two parts: that pre- and post-1965, illustrating the importance of the Federal initiatives. That year marked the legislative fruits of Johnson's re-election and the big Democratic majorities in Congress. Both Medicare and Medicaid as well as Federal aid for secondary education date from legislation passed in that year (see Chapter 4). The rise in the share of the GNP devoted to social welfare had been slow in the first five years – an average of 0·27 a year. In the six years since 1966 the rise was 0·9 per cent a year.

The last ten-year period has indeed been a remarkable one and it is worth examining in more detail. Public expenditure on social welfare has increased from 11·8 per cent of the GNP in 1965 to 18·0 in 1974. If we add private expenditure on the same items, education, health insurance and so on, we find that total social welfare expenditure in the United States now amounts to a figure equivalent to about one-quarter of the Gross National Product, and an increasing part has been publicly financed.

Another way of measuring the growth rate is to express it in constant prices per head of population. In this way we can discount the increases caused by larger numbers and measure the real improvement and cost to the average individual. From 1965–73 this real increase measured 9 per cent per annum, with increases varying from 7 per cent to 12 per cent in any one year. In 1974 inflation and the constraints we shall discuss later began to have their impact. Although in cash terms expenditure rose faster than the year before, the real rate of increase per head fell to 3 per cent.

What services contributed most to this rise? The largest increase was achieved in public aid or assistance programmes, notably Medicaid which assist poor families with their medical bills, the aid to families with dependent children, and the new Federal scheme for supplementary benefits. These increased by nearly 250 per cent in the period 1965–74 in real terms per head. Social insurance, including medical insurance, shows the next highest increase at about half that rate, while education has increased less than the overall average at about 70 per cent.

The Federal Government has been the major initiator. During the early 1960s the share of the total social welfare budget met out of Federal funds remained at about 49 per cent. It was after the legislation we have mentioned that its share began to rise at the rate of about one per cent per annum. By 1974 it met nearly 58 per cent of the total welfare bill. As a consequence social welfare has come to take a rising share of the Federal Government's total budget, well over half of which is now devoted to financing the American 'welfare state'. The United States and the United Kingdom have therefore been moving along converging paths and both have come to face similar economic constraints.

Growth Rates Compared

If we now compare the rate of increase in social welfare expenditure as a whole in the two countries, four separate features emerge. In the first place both countries have devoted a similarly rising share of their resources to social welfare. Since 1950 the ratio of such expenditure (including transfer payments) to the GNP rose by an additional 8·5 per cent in both countries (see Table 3.1). Secondly, social welfare expenditure has taken a larger share of government activity in both countries. Thirdly, the United States' rate of expansion in absolute terms has been much faster than in the United Kingdom. Indeed, expressed in constant prices, the US social welfare sector has expanded at twice the rate of the comparable sector of the United Kingdom economy in the two decades follow-

Table 3.1   *Size of the Social Welfare Budget in Relation to the Economy*

Social welfare expenditure as a percentage of GNP	1928/9	1939/40	1949/50	1959/60	1964/5	1971/2
UK*	9·6	11·3	16·0	17·0	20·3	24·4
US	3·9	9·2	8·9	10·6	11·8	17·5
Government expenditure as a percentage of GNP						
UK	24	30	45	41	44	50
US	18	21	24	30	31	33

* UK figures 1928, 1938, 1950, 1960, 1965, 1972
Source: See notes to this chapter

ing 1950, i.e. at a rate of 7·2 per cent a year compared to a rate of 3·6 per cent a year in this country. Finally, this general picture is only slightly modified by expressing these rates of increase in expenditure per head of population. In the period 1950–70 the United Kingdom's 'real' expenditure on social welfare increased by an average of 3·1 per cent a year for each member of the population. In America the increase was 5·5 per cent a year. It has gradually begun to dawn on some people here that Britain has not kept pace with the extensions in social welfare that have taken place in Western Europe in the last few years. It may come as more of a shock to learn that the same can be said of our position relative to the United States.

The social and political pressures which lie behind both trends deserve closer attention but it is not our purpose to pursue them further at this point. It *is* important to draw attention to the rather different economic and, in particular, fiscal factors at work.

The Fiscal Constraints
General economic prosperity provides the context within which any social welfare system must develop. Americans enjoy a higher average income than we do in this country, but growth rates per head of population in the two economies were rather similar in the period we have been studying. Between 1950 and 1968, excluding inflation, 'real' GNP per head grew at an identical average rate of 2·3 per cent per annum in both countries. The crude growth rate,

Table 3.2 *The Growth of the Social Welfare Budget in absolute terms at constant prices and per head of population*

		Percentages		
Social Welfare Expenditure in constant prices		*1950/60*	*1960/70*	*1950/70*
Rate of Growth per annum	UK	2·6	4·6	3·6
	US	6·4	8·5	7·2
Rate of Growth per head per annum	UK	2·1	4·1	3·1
	US	4·0	7·2	5·5

Note: In the UK the base years are 1951, 1960 and 1970
In the US the base years are 1949/50, 1959/60 and 1969/70
The growth rates are an average compound interest over the periods in question
Source: See notes to this chapter

discounting population growth, has been faster in the US but not dramatically so.[2] It is all too readily assumed that this country's 'low growth rate' explains almost anything. It is true that the United Kingdom has suffered a series of balance of payments crises which the United States has, until recently, avoided. Tighter control of public expenditure has been an almost inevitable reaction to each successive crisis. How far politicians ought to have been so dominated by the 'need' to limit public spending for this reason is quite another matter.

One important explanation for the different trends in expenditure lies in the fiscal situation which confronted the two central governments. Ever since the early nineteenth century the US Federal Government has tended to raise more tax revenue than it knew what to do with. Federal tax revenue tends to increase as the economy grows and to increase at a faster rate. Most economies experience this phenomenon but it has been more important in the United States for a number of reasons. Perhaps the most important in recent years has been the fact that Federal income tax is progressive over the whole of its range. It begins at a bottom rate of 14 per cent and rises as an individual's income increases. The US has not had anything equivalent to our old 'standard rate' – a single rate of tax covering most of the population. During the 1960s the British income tax system became even less progressive. The United Kingdom tax base has therefore been less 'buoyant' than that of the US Federal Government.

Taken in conjunction with this there was the very real political reluctance to see the Federal Government undertake social welfare functions, hence the almost negligible role it played up to the New Deal era. This reluctance was only broken by the economic crisis of the 1930s. Even so it remained in many fields outside income maintenance until the 1960s. The conservatives in Congress, from both parties, successfully resisted attempts to get the Federal government to give financial aid to education which was administered and financed locally. It was possible for Washington to aid universities only indirectly.

In the late 1950s and early 1960s this tendency for Federal expenditure to increase more slowly than Federal revenues was seen as a critical economic problem and to be one of the causes of slow economic growth. The solution was either massive and continued tax cuts or big increases in expenditure and preferably both. Economic pressures in the US therefore pointed in precisely the opposite direction to the conventional wisdom in the UK at the same point in time. At the same time concern grew over social issues, racial inequality and poverty, providing the rationale for more social expenditure.

Hence, the 1960s saw a boom in Federally funded social welfare programmes. Nor is it surprising to find, as we shall see later, that attempts to impose stricter budgetary control on social welfare programmes were far less successful in the US in the 1960s than they were in the UK. By the early 1970s, however, the US position was changing.

Over the period 1963–73 if both Federal programmes and Federal tax rates had remained unchanged there would have been a budget surplus of $68 billion by 1973.[3] Of this 'potential fiscal dividend' $26 billion went in tax reductions. Even so the Federal Government was able to increase expenditure by over 50 billion dollars without raising tax rates. The scale of this increase more than absorbed the potential surplus. The remainder was financed out of sales of government assets, receipts from royalties and in 1973 by a sizeable budget deficit. In October 1972 Nixon proposed a budget ceiling for the 1973 budget proposals coming from Congress and proposed cutting certain social programmes in his own 1974 budget. The 'natural' growth rates of these and other programmes had begun to equal if not surpass the likely tax receipts at full employment levels. Rising expenditure would mean raising tax rates, though something could be found in theory by closing 'tax loopholes'. It was a situation with which the United Kingdom was familiar. During the 1960s and early 1970s all British governments have been faced with the continual tendency of public expenditure to outpace potential tax revenue. The object of the public expenditure control strategy as it emerged in the late fifties and early sixties was to make local authorities and nationalised industries finance more of their own

Table 3.3   *The Division of Social Welfare Expenditure between Central and Local Authorities in US and UK – 1929–70*

	Percentages				
US	1928/29	1939/40	1949/50	1959/60	1969/70
Federal funds as a percentage of Social Welfare Expenditure (including grants to states)	21	39	45	49	55
Direct expenditure by the Federal Government as a percentage of all social welfare expenditure	21	31	41	42	43
UK	1929	1938	1950	1960	1970
Central government expenditure on social services as a percentage of social service expenditure (including grants to LAs)	65	67	78	75	83
Direct central government expenditure as percentage of all social service expenditure	49	49	65	63	63

Source: *Social Security Bulletin*, Statistical Supplement 1971.
Office of Research and Statistics, Social Security Administration (unpublished figures)
Alan T. Peacock and Jack Wiseman: *The Growth of Public Expenditure in the United Kingdom* (1929/1950 UK figures)
National Income and Expenditure 1971 (UK 1960 and 1970 figures)

activities thereby containing the level of central government taxation required. In the event this strategy failed. Central government revenue, including national insurance contributions, rose from 27·4 per cent of the GNP in 1960 to 39 per cent in 1970. Hence, in contrast to the American situation, it is not surprising to find that centralisation and detailed control over public expenditure developed much faster in the United Kingdom. This is, indeed, the single most important difference between the economic situations of the two countries as far as this study is concerned.

The Role of the Central Governments
It will already be clear that the role of the Federal Government is very different from that which United Kingdom government plays

in social service provision. The constitutional differences and the political resistance to a major Federal activity have been mentioned already. Even so, generalisations are not easy. At one extreme the social security programmes are administered almost entirely at Federal level, they are highly centralised and in most essential respects are very similar to the United Kingdom system of National Insurance. At the other extreme education is largely financed and administered locally.

Just before the Great Depression roughly 20 per cent of all social welfare expenditure was funded Federally (see Table 3.3). It was either undertaken by the Federal Government directly – mainly Veterans benefits – or else it took the form of Federal Government grants to states. The really big jump occurred in the 1930s when major Federal aid was given for public assistance and unemployment benefit schemes run by the states and the Federal social security provisions began. By 1939–40 the Federal share of social welfare expenditure had almost doubled – to nearly 40 per cent. Ever since it has consistently grown as these programmes developed and major new ones have been added, until today the Federal Government funds well over half the social welfare expenditure in the United States.

In the United Kingdom the major switch from local to central finance and administration came between 1945 and 1950 when the post war Labour Government passed a whole series of measures which either:

established completely new provisions financed by the exchequer and administered centrally (family allowances are the obvious example);
established national services which replaced and extended services previously provided by local authorities (National Assistance and the National Health Service are examples here);
extended or universalised services already financed nationally on a restricted basis (National Insurance is one example).

As a consequence, the proportion of social service expenditure met directly by central government rose from 49 per cent pre-war to 65 per cent in 1950 and the overall share of financial support grew similarly.

However, since 1950 no major new programmes have been added, nor has the financial or administrative structure changed dramatically. The growth in the share of central government funding has been slower and has primarily resulted from the fact that the services like social insurance and higher education, for which central government has most responsibility, have grown fastest. Over the last twenty years no British government has had to cope with the massive and rapid accumulation of new programmes such as the Federal Government in Washington faced in the 1960s. This, as we shall see later, had important consequences for Washington's inability to control the use to which Federal funds were put.

Nevertheless, the degree of UK central government involvement in the social services, simply measured in financial terms, is overwhelming. More than four-fifths of all social service expenditure is either directly met or funded by central government. We shall describe these differences in more detail in the next chapter.

In brief

We can now answer the two questions posed at the beginning of the chapter. How important is social service expenditure to the economies of the two countries and how much of it lies within the financial control of the central governments?

It is clear that in the aggregate such spending does still form a significantly larger part of the nation's economic activity in the UK – equivalent to over 24 per cent of the GNP as against nearly 18 per cent. Moreover central government's direct financial stake is much higher in the UK and hence its power to intervene. Finally, the political and economic pressures to constrain growth have been greater for much longer in Britain and hence controls have been further developed. This need to impose restraints and to make difficult choices has added to the powers of the centre. It has changed the power structure and created new political or constitutional conventions. For most of that period we are studying, the economic climate and the financial facts of life favoured stronger budget controls in Britain than in the US. Another factor likely to prove unfavourable to tight budgetary control in the US was the rapid introduction of new programmes and the expansion of Federal activity into new fields. In some ways US experience in the 1960s parallels that in the UK in the 1940s.

REFERENCES

1 The US figures are taken from the following sources: *Social Welfare Expenditures under Public Programs in the United States 1929–1966*, Research Report No. 26, Office of Research and Statistics, Social Security Administration, Department of Health, Education and Welfare; *Social Security Bulletin*, Annual Statistical Supplements and

January 1975; and US Bureau of Census, *Census of Governments, 1967, Historical Statistics,* and *Economic Report of the President, 1972.* UK figures: Peacock, A., and Wiseman, J., *The Growth of Public Expenditure in the United Kingdom,* George Allen and Unwin, London, 1961 (1928, 1938 figures). *National Income and Expenditure,* HMSO, 1973 and previous issues.

2 The actual figures in detail are as follows:

	US		UK	
Years	Overall	Per Capita	Overall	Per Capita
1950–68	3·9	2·3	2·8	2·3
1950–60	3·2	1·5	2·7	2·3
1960–68	4·8	3·4	3·0	2·3

Source: *US Statistical Abstract* 1971 (Table 486)

3 Shultze, C., *et al., Setting National Priorities: The 1973 Budget,* Brookings Institution, Washington, 1972, p. 407.

Further Reading

Abel-Smith, B., 'Public Expenditure on the Social Services', *Social Trends 1970,* HMSO, 1970.

Musgrove, R. A., *Fiscal Systems,* Yale University Press, 1969.

(This book contains a comparative analysis of the growth of public expenditure in Britain, the USA and Germany, but requires a basic knowledge of economics.)

Schultze, C. L., *et al. Setting National Priorities The 1971 (1972, 1973 and 1974) Budget,* Brookings Institution, Washington.

(This series of books contain the best accounts of Federal expenditure on social programmes in recent years.)

Chapter 4

The
Programme Context

The word programme, or program in its American spelling, comes from the Greek word programma – to write publicly – which adds a touch of irony to the secrecy in which the programme budgeting activities of Her Majesty's Government are conducted. Until recently most people associated the word with radio and television or a concert but not much else. Its Oxford English Dictionary definition is 'a definite plan of intended proceedings' and that comes very close to the meaning it now has in budgeting terminology. Yet it is no accident that the word has little general political application in Britain. We have tended to talk of a 'social service' or a social or economic 'policy' not a government 'programme'. The stated intentions of Acts of Parliament in the social welfare field are extremely general. Instructions to the Minister are couched in terms like the following:

It shall be the duty of the Secretary of State for Education and Science to promote the education of the people of England and Wales and the progressive development of institutions devoted to that purpose. (Section 1 of the Education Act 1944.)

There follows an Act entirely concerned with specifying the structure of the system – the ages and stages of the education process. The National Health Service Act 1946 was scarcely more helpful. In contrast social legislation enacted by Congress has empowered the Federal Government to act on behalf of specific defined groups of people for particular purposes. Precisely because Americans have been so suspicious of collective action, especially by the Federal Government, Congress has been careful not to give wide ranging general powers that are the characteristics of social legislation in Britain. When an American talks about a 'Federal program' it tends to be a specific and clear cut activity directed at a particular client group – the blind, or the disabled or the coal miner with 'Black Lung Disease' or it is a grant of money provided for the purchase of library books or school equipment. That legislation which most resembles the British is the social security law. Yet it is the one part of British social legislation that is most specific about the client groups it is to serve, retirement pensioners, the short term sick, the long term sick, those who have suffered industrial injuries, the unemployed and so on. This is an extremely important if little recognised difference. When the Americans came to transfer the concepts and techniques of programme budgeting to social programmes it was nothing like as difficult as it turned out to be in the British case. The kind of difficulties are elaborated later. First it is necessary to grasp the scope and nature of the legislation which is administered by the Department of Health, Education and Welfare.

It would be quite wrong to think of the 'Department' as some equivalent to the Department of Education and Science in London, or to the Department of Health and Social Security. It is more like the United States Government itself, a federation of very largely autonomous agencies. The Social Security Administration is just one of these agencies, though the largest by far. It employs 25,000 staff in a huge complex of office blocks 20 odd miles away from Washington, in Baltimore. Then there are the National Institutes of Health, themselves a loose federation of separate research institutes each responsible for different fields of medical research. They occupy a vast site also outside Washington. Scattered in and around the city are other parts of the empire, which was formed in 1953 from what were then separate social agencies. At the centre is the Secretary.

With the help of the Office of the Secretary he seeks to control this immense agglomeration. By 1973 the department had become the largest spender in the Federal Government, outpacing even the Defence Department. What was the scope of its activities in that year?

The HEW Programmes
The largest and most directly comparable to their British counterparts are the Social Security programmes.

Social Security[1]
The American system of social insurance has always been wage

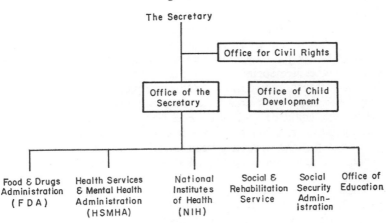

Figure 4.1

related. There is no general contribution from ordinary tax revenue, i.e. no 'exchequer contribution'. Pensions, widows' benefits (survivors benefit in US terms) and disablement benefit are financed by a social security tax which is a flat percentage of earnings up to a 'wage ceiling'. The tax is paid half by the employer and half by the employee. In 1972 the rate of tax relevant to these benefits was 4·6 per cent for employer and employee – i.e. a total of 9·2 per cent (self-employed workers paying 1½ times the employee's rate). In order to qualify to draw benefit the worker must have contributed for so many years. This varies depending on his age. The size of the benefit is related to previous earnings – not total previous earnings but only earnings up to the wage ceiling. Moreover the formula which relates these previous earnings to the total benefit rate is so geared that low earners receive a higher ratio of benefit to earnings than high earners. As in the UK a retirement test is applied and the regular retirement age is 65. Pensioners can take a reduced pension at the age of 62. A reduced widow's benefit is payable at 60. An old age pension, regardless of the retirement condition, is paid at 72. The ages are the same for both men and women, i.e. there is no earlier retirement age for women as there is in the United Kingdom.

Disability benefits are paid to those unable to work because of physical or mental illness which can be expected either to lead to death or to prolonged absence from work of twelve months or longer. But there is a waiting period of six months before benefits are paid.

Medicare

Since 1965 another important insurance programme has been added – hospital insurance. Under it an additional 0·6 per cent social security tax is paid by employee and employer. In return those eligible to receive social security benefit are automatically eligible for hospital insurance coverage. Other people over 65 can qualify if they have some work credit, i.e. they have paid social security at some time, again depending on age. Nearly all people over 65 do qualify. More recently Medicare has been extended to cover disabled beneficiaries who have been receiving benefit for two years or more, and those suffering from kidney disease who are on social security.

These benefits cover the major part of important hospital expenses up to 90 days in any one 'benefit period'.[2] The scheme also covers 'extended care' after you leave hospital – nursing home care, or continuing drugs. The patient must pay the first $68 of expenses if he is in hospital for up to 60 days. After that he must also pay $17 a day up to the 90th day (1972 rates). Then he pays the full cost unless he wants to use up his 'life time reserve' of 60 hospital days. The expenses thus covered, in part, include the cost of a bed in a semi-private room, operating room charges, nursing, lab tests, X-ray and radiology and appliances but it does not pay for doctors' services. These can be covered under a different programme – medical insurance.

Medical insurance for the over 65s together with hospital insurance for this age group constitute what is generally referred to as 'medicare'. The medical insurance element is voluntary. An old person had to pay a basic premium of $5,80 a month in 1973. This is matched by equivalent Federal funds. For it, an old person can have 80 per cent of his doctor's charges paid after the first $50 in any one year. This means that all bills must be sent to the appropriate insurance company who handle Medicare in that State. They must be adjudged reasonable expenses on approved types of treatment before they can count towards the $50 'deductible'. In 1972 nearly 50 million doctors' bills were reimbursed. It is a vast administrative undertaking. Information is collated centrally but the day-to-day procedures in handling claims are dealt with by the 'carriers', usually one insurance company in each State.

These are the two major health programmes administered and financed at Federal level by the Social Security Administration. There is no local government involvement. They are comprehensive in coverage and highly centralised in operation. For the most part few of these characteristics apply to the remainder of the HEW's activities. One form of income maintenance considered inseparable from the rest in the UK, unemployment insurance, does not form part of HEW's responsibilities. Unemployment compensation was part of the original 1935 social security legislation but apart from a period during World War II it has never been directly administered by the Federal Government. Employers pay a Federal tax – 3·2 per cent of their employees' wages up to a given ceiling of $4,200 in 1973. Little more than 10 per cent is actually collected by the Federal Government which is used to cover administrative expenses. The rest is refunded to the states to finance their unemployment compensation schemes. They must in their turn conform to various minimum standards laid down by Washington – in fact the Department of Labour. There are special provisions to aid states with persistent high unemployment and the Federal Government also finances special unemployment benefit programmes for veterans, Federal civilian employees and unemployed persons who have exhausted regular benefits. Since states are under no obligation to standardise benefits there are wide divergencies.

The other main area of income maintenance which is administered by HEW is public assistance (including Medicaid). It is the responsibility of the Social Rehabilitation Service, an agency within HEW, like the SSA but far smaller and mainly responsible for administering grants to the states.

Public Assistance

The current debates and developments in American public assistance are, in some ways, reminiscent of the British history in the 1930s. The US took over Britain's Victorian model of the Poor Law. It has been administered by state and local authorities. In the 1930s the Federal Government gave grants to encourage the development of assistance programmes for specified categories of people – the aged, the blind and families with dependent children. The permanently and totally disabled were added in 1950. States fix eligibility rules and the levels of benefit which vary not merely between states but between categories of assistance. They can give benefits to families with unemployed male heads of households but some still do not. This is not the point at which to go into the complexities of what Americans call 'the welfare mess'.[3] It is enough to point out that in the late sixties it became a national issue and that after prolonged Congressional debate about the various reform proposals produced both by the Administration and individual Congressmen, the adult groups, the old, the blind and the disabled were removed from the locally administered system. They now receive means-tested assistance payments from the Social Security Administration. Even so these Federal payments only represent a national minimum. Well over half the states were paying benefits above the level the Federal Government used for its basic income guarantee. Under the legislation the states had to supplement the Federal payment up to the amounts they were paying before January 1974. States can make a contract with the Federal Government so that the recipient can actually receive one cheque from Washington. The least 'deserving' group of all have been left with the states – the single parent families, the mainly negro 'welfare mums' who come under the Aid to Families with Dependent Children (AFDC) programme. The numbers receiving these benefits have increased nearly fivefold since 1955 and constitute a major political issue. Various attempts to be tough or to get these mothers into work have been tried. One of these is the Work Incentive programme (WIN) which aims to train the mothers for work and make their receipt of an allowance dependent upon such training. The whole AFDC programme appears highly unpopular with both the general tax payer and those who receive its 'benefits'. A great deal of Federal money is spent, yet Washington can only exert limited control on the way it is spent. This is even more true of the related system of social services (what we should call personal social services) also provided through the same public assistance agencies. Social work in the agencies is still an adjunct of financial assistance as it was in Britain earlier this century. The 1967 Social Security Amendments authorised 75 per cent grants towards the cost of state and local social services for 'needy' children, to keep families together, to reduce illegitimacy and to provide support services for the aged, blind and handicapped adults. Very soon states found they could classify activities they were already undertaking under the heading 'Social Services' and obtain 75 per cent Federal support. Vast increases in the budget were required. One state would find a loophole that others would then exploit. Congressmen were in two minds about clearing up these abuses because it meant more Federal funds for the home state. It is an episode which illustrates very well the limited control in a Federal system where Congress has the final say on what controls are exercised.

The other major programme, funded Federally but administered locally, is 'Medicaid'. Under it HEW gives grants to states whose plans for medical assistance it approves. The grants vary from 50 per cent to over 80 per cent depending on the average income levels in the state. All those on public assistance must be included in the scheme and it can be extended to other groups. The state can either meet the whole cost of doctors' or hospital charges or ask the patient to pay something towards the cost. The overall administration of this programme is in the hands of the Medical Services Administration, which is part of the Social and Rehabilitation Service.

Medical Research and Training

One important agency in the medical field is the National Institutes of Health, itself a federation of separate institutes covering different areas of medical research. Between 1960 and 1965 its budget more than doubled. In British terms NIH combines the functions of the Medical Research Council, the DHSS's responsibility for medical manpower and the UGC's responsibility for the medical schools. In addition to supporting research it gives capitation grants to institutions training physicians and other health professionals, nurses and dentists. It also covers the work of the National Library of Medicine. Its total budget amounts to over $2,000 million. It is not far short of the total budget of the other agency concerned with health services: the Health Services and Mental Health Administration (1974).

Health Services

The Health Services and Mental Health Administration (HSMHA) gives grants to a wide variety of private and voluntary organisations and to state and local governments, to assist in and promote a whole range of activities that have at various times caught the attention of Congressmen or Presidents as special cases. HSMHA has rationalised these under four broad headings: mental health, health planning, health service delivery and preventive services.[4] The mental health heading alone covers research grants on the use and misuse of narcotics, grants to agencies providing care, treatment and rehabilitation of drug addicts, grants for the construction and staffing of community mental health centres, grants and contracts for the prevention and treatment of alcoholism, the construction and staffing of child mental health treatment facilities, establishment of a National Institute on Alcohol Abuse and Alcoholism, and the mental health of minority groups.

Under the second broad heading grants are given to state agencies who may undertake comprehensive health planning, i.e. attempts to assess health needs in local areas and involve local organisations in this planning. One of the largest items is the Hill-Burton programme funding new hospital construction or modernisation. This has provided nearly half a million beds and has more than eliminated what was once viewed as a national shortage of beds – one in five beds were *unoccupied* in 1973. More recently grants have been made to support neighbourhood health centres originally set up under the poverty programme to support about 60 maternity and infant care centres, and so the list might be extended. It is a bewildering variety of highly specific projects stemming from different pieces of legislation. As someone who was trying to get a local health centre under way pointed out, you could raise grants for this purpose under something like 20 different headings administered by several different agencies.

Health care is the responsibility of four separate agencies within HEW without counting the Food and Drug Administration that has had such an important role to play in trying to prevent the marketing of drugs which have dubious or dangerous medical results. In addition other departments of the government are involved in a much more tangential way – the Department of Defense, the Atomic Energy Commission and so on. The Office of the Secretary has recently been making determined attempts to coordinate all these disparate programmes but it is a daunting task. If we turn to education a similar and, if anything, more confusing situation is to be found.

Education

The Federal Government is not a major participant in education.

In 1973 it financed no more than 11 or 12 per cent of education expenditure compared to the central government's 60 per cent in the United Kingdom. There are many other agencies involved apart from HEW but that is the largest by far and the Office of Education is responsible for most of the programmes which give direct support to educational institutions. Federal programmes of aid to the land grant colleges and for vocational education have a long history but were very tiny. Washington then became more involved when it made grants to areas affected by large concentrations of troops in the period of the Korean war. It is a programme that has continued ever since. But Federal involvement in education began in a significant way only after the first Sputnik went into orbit. In 1958 the National Defense Education Act was passed – 'a hodgepodge of categorical aids for instructional equipment in science and other subjects, language instruction, guidance and testing, student loans, and graduate fellowships'.[5] Then in 1963 came the Higher Education Facilities Act providing funds for university and other higher education buildings. If the pressure for these changes had to do with perceived danger to national security, the Elementary and Secondary Education Act 1965 came about as a result of very different and rather confused pressures. Under 'Title I', i.e. the relevant opening section of the act, it authorised the Federal Government to make grants to school districts which had high concentrations of low income families 'to expand and improve their educational pro-grammes by various means (including pre-school programmes) which contribute particularly to meeting the special educational needs of educationally deprived children'. The legislation was to last from July 1965 to June 1973. It enshrined the concept of 'compensatory education'. It was very much under discussion when members of the Plowden Committee visited America and it undoubtedly influenced their thinking about the similar concept they called 'positive discrimination'. It will be discussed in more detail in later chapters. For the moment it is sufficient to see it in its context as part of the total Federal education budget. Other sections or 'titles' in that Act gave grants to states to promote experiments and dis-seminate new developments. Yet the 1965 Act was only one of many much smaller provisions that have accumulated. Although the Federal Government only finances 7 per cent of all elementary and secondary education the budget covers over 30 separate pro-grammes directed to this sector alone. For the third time in the 1974 Budget the administration sought to replace this 'hotch potch' by a measure it calls 'educational revenue sharing' in other words five block grants to cover the following purposes: compensatory pro-grammes at elementary and secondary level, assistance to 'im-pacted' areas i.e. those with large military or other installations, education for the handicapped, vocational and adult education and the school meals programme. For the previous two years Congress had refused to pass the President's legislation. Even if it did there would remain three other programmes in the field of elementary and secondary education. One is 'Head Start', which originated under the old poverty programme in the Office of Economic Opportunity and is now run by the Office of Child Development in HEW. There are funds to help school districts which are being desegregated (Emergency School Assistance). Finally, the bilingual programme gives special aid to districts which have large numbers of children needing to be taught English as a second language.

The other major area of Federal expenditure has been that on higher education. It constitutes roughly half the Federal Govern-ment's outlays on education and finances about 20 per cent of the expenditure of institutions of higher education. Again in British terms this is a very small contribution. Here, the central government directly finances about 90 per cent of the expenditure of Univer-

Table 4.1   *US Federal finance of social welfare programmes compared to central finance in the UK – 1971*

	Percentages			
	Federally or centrally administered		*Centrally financed*	
Social Services	*US*	*UK*	*US*	*UK*
Social Insurance				
Old Age	100	100	100	100
Sickness and Disability	100	100	100	100
Widows or Survivors	100	100	100	100
Unemployment[3]	—	100	27[3]	100
Health[1]	16	92	16	96
Education[2]	nil	nil	12	60
Social work/personal social services[4]	nil	nil	73	57
Public Assistance[5]	nil	100	53	100

NOTES

[1] US: Office of Research and Statistics (ORS), Social Security Administration (based on information published in *Social Security Bulletin*, January 1973). UK: Expenditure by central government as a percentage of total NHS expenditure (*Social Trends*) 1972 Table 150. Since 1974 the whole of the NHS is both financed and administered directly by the central government with regional and local delegation of responsibilities.

[2] US: Federal funds as a percentage of spending by all educational institutions – i.e. excluding student support. ORS figures (*US Budget 1973 Special Analyses* gives a figure of 12 per cent). UK: Central funds allocated directly or indirectly to educational institutions as a percentage of expenditure of all educational institutions (Peacock *et al. Educational Finance*).

[3] Federal unemployment taxes as a proportion of total state and federal contributions to unemployment insurance funds (*Social security Bulletin* Table M4).

[4] US: ORS figures. These include housing, food stamps and poverty program items. Federal Matching grants for personal social services are 75 per cent. UK: financed in part from Rate Support Grant.

[5] US: ORS figures. UK: Supplementary benefits wholly financed and administered centrally.

sities, and indirectly through the fees which local authorities pay on behalf of students, it meets most of the rest. Of the US Federal contribution only about half actually flows from HEW, and only about a third of that comes via the Office of Education. This, too, is utterly different from the situation in Britain where although the research councils provide funds for the Universities they finance a tiny fraction of the institutions' activities.

Federal support for higher education, therefore, comes from: (i) grants and loans for college students organised and funded by the Office of Education; (ii) Grants and loans for college building paid not only by the Office of Education but by the National Institutes of Health and the Housing and Urban Development Department; (iii) Fellowships and grants made by a whole range of other agencies.

The basic piece of legislation is the Higher Education Act also passed in 1965. Under this students from poor homes could get grants or loans, or guarantees for loans. The 1974 Budget proposals asked Congress to approve a much larger grants programme. The aim was to spend $590 million on $1\frac{1}{2}$ million 'needy' students, compared to $210 million on 300,000 students the previous year.

Other parts of the 1965 Act authorised grants to mainly negro colleges who trained teachers.

The HEW Budget

Perhaps the best way of illustrating the relative importance of this wide range of programmes is to show the contribution they make to the total HEW budget, and to group them under the administrative agencies responsible, within broad functional categories. Table 4.2 shows the total budget obligations of the Department at five yearly intervals from 1955. In the early days the overwhelming emphasis was on income maintenance – social insurance and public assistance. Health and education expenditure at a Federal level was minimal. Funds under the health heading were largely confined to support for medical research and grants for new hospital building.

Twenty-one years afterwards the budget had been transformed. It increased by more than fourteen times. The Old-Age, Survivors and Disability Insurance scheme was the oldest and the largest programme, and it had grown almost as fast as the total budget. Several factors contributed to this rise: more occupational groups were included (today 90 per cent of the population is covered). The number of old people has increased, and the level of benefits has risen. In 1956 benefits to disabled workers were added to the original scheme. As a consequence the total number of people receiving pensions, widows or disablement benefits increased from 3 million in 1950 to nearly 30 million today. The average value of pensions received in constant prices more than doubled between 1950 and 1973. The largest single increase occurred in 1972 – an all round 20 per cent rise in benefits.

The peculiarity of the Social Security Administration's budget, apart from its size, is that the greater part operates through separate Trust Funds. Some contributions are made from general taxation, but for the most part the funds are financed out of the Social Security Tax. Until recently these Trust Funds did not even appear as part of the total Federal Budget. They are now consolidated in

E

Table 4.2   *The Budget obligation of the Department of Health, Education and Welfare*

Programmes and Agency	1955	1960	1965	1970	1974 (estimated outlays)
		Millions of Dollars			
Social Security Administration					
Old Age Survivors and Disability Insurance	4,414	10,981	16,944	31,911	56,345
Medicare	—	—	—	9,426	15,056
Adult Assistance	—	—	—	—	2,208
Total	4,414	10,984	16,950	41,366	73,609
Health (exc: Medicare and Medicaid)					
Research	87	372	947	1,072	1,688
Training	11	90	357	938	705
Construction	62	161	264	309	187
Total National Institutes of Health and Health Services and Mental Health Administration	288	933	2,280	3,594	4,240
Social and Rehabilitation Services					
Public Assistance	1,402	2,904	2,966	4,697	5,528
Medicaid	—	—	290	2,827	5,247
Work Incentive (WIN)	—	—	—	130	597
Other Social Services	26	75	165	670	2,835
Total	1,428	2,979	3,421	8,324	14,207
Education					
Elementary and Secondary	286	381	748	1,994	3,011
Impacted areas	256	254	408	201	—
Disadvantaged children	—	—	—	1,226	—
Other	30	128	340	566	—
Revenue Sharing	—	—	—	—	1,693
Other Elementary and Secondary	—	—	—	—	1,318
Higher Education	5	58	585	837	1,636
Other	—	6	112	408	328
Total Office of Education	302	470	1,498	3,370	4,975
TOTAL HEW	6,458	14,588	24,209	56,888	93,822

Source: C. Shultze, *et al.*, *Setting National Priorities; The* 1971 *Budget* Table 3–1. *The Budget of the United States Government Fiscal Year 1974* Office of Management and Budget, 1973. (Totals net)

the overall budget figures, yet the degree of independence they give from detailed Congressional and executive control is important. There are four such funds, the Old Age and Survivors Insurance Trust Fund, by far the largest, with an estimated outlay for 1974 of about $50,000 million; the Disability Insurance Fund, the Hospital Insurance Fund and the Supplementary Medical Insurance Fund. Until recently these were run on a partially funded basis, that is running a surplus to meet future claims for benefit. They have moved to an explicit 'pay as you go' basis since 1972, annual income is merely meant to cover the expected cost of benefits that year. In total these trust funds accounted for an expected outlay of $67,000 million, or about 70 per cent of the total HEW budget in 1974. The new adult assistance programme is financed from general revenue and is outside the scope of the Trust Funds.

The impact of the new programmes of the 1960s – Medicare, Medicaid, and support for elementary and secondary education and higher education – are clearly to be seen in Table 4.2. They had added a further $24,000 million to the budget by 1970. The rapid rise in public assistance and social service spending is also evident.

In Brief

With the exception of social security the work of the Department of Health, Education and Welfare presents a very different prospect from its British counterparts. The programmes it administers are narrow or specific, very heterogeneous, controlled by a wide range of agencies with overlapping fields of responsibility and in many important areas, notably health and education, they actually only affect a small part of the nation's provision. Even the social security programmes are more clearly categorised than in Britain.

The head of the Bureau of the Budget in Johnson's period summarised the situation in 1971 in this way:

'By the close of the 1960s, HEW was administering dozens of specific categorical programs each of which had developed a supporting clientele on Capitol Hill and in the field. Vocational educators lobbied hard for aid to libraries, manufacturers of instructional equipment extolled the benefits of equipment programs, hospital associations fought for hospital construction money and so forth.'

In contrast British social legislation tends to be all embracing, very general, to place considerable responsibility on a single department, a department which after its tussles with the Treasury will determine virtually the total resource allocation in that field. The basic legislation setting the framework for the service will in some cases have remained little altered in a generation. Despite the new *structure* the basis for health *provision* is still the 1946 National Health Service Act, the basis for the education system is still the 1944 Education Act. The point has frequently been made that to extend 'programme budgeting' from the Defense Department to social agencies was to extend it to a very different kind of activity. That was true in both Britain and the US. What has been less readily appreciated is that the nature of a 'social programme' is really very different in the two countries.

The very term 'programme' is an American importation which fits somewhat uneasily into the context of broad legislative intent characteristic of social legislation in Britain.

REFERENCES

1 The US Federal Social Security legislation is described in numerous publications of the Social Security Administration. The Office of Research and Statistics regularly revise a useful summary entitled: *Social Security Programs in the United States.* Technical details are summarised in the *Annual Statistical Supplement* to the *Social Security Bulletin* published by the same office. Perhaps the best critical assessment of the whole scheme is to be found in *Social Security: Perspectives for Reform* by J. A. Pechman, H. J. Aaron and M. K. Taussig, Brookings Institution, Washington, 1968.

2 The complexities of Medicare were summarised for the beneficiary in a document called: *Your Medicare Handbook*, Social Security Administration, July, 1972.

3 The difficulties of tackling this 'mess' are well discussed in *Why is Welfare so hard to Reform?*, H. J. Aaron, Brookings Institution, Washington, 1973.

4 *Departments of Labour and HEW Appropriations for 1973, House of Representatives Committee on Appropriations Hearings, HEW Sub-Committee, Part 3*, also the source for other figures in this section.

5 Shultze, C. *et al.*, *Setting National Priorities: The 1971 Budget*, Brookings Institution, Washington, 1970, p. 58.

Further Reading

Apart from the references above the following is still a useful account of the development of Social Welfare in the United States:

Wilensky, H. L., and Lebeaux, C. N., *Industrial Society and Social Welfare*, Free Press, New York, 1965 edition.

Mencher, S., *Poor Law to Poverty Program*, University of Pittsburg Press, 1967.

(Includes a comparison of English and American developments.)

Chapter 5

The
Political Context

Budget reformers on both sides of the Atlantic have often been criticised for ignoring or underestimating the 'political' element in expenditure decisions. This was the main burden of the early attacks made by political scientists in the United States[1] and similar warnings have been given in Great Britain[2]. Our purpose is to be more specific. What kind of political factors have forced what practical modifications to the idealised models that were originally proposed? By comparing the fate of these reforms in two countries with very different political contexts some pointers emerge. At this point it is necessary to emphasise what political differences there are. They may be summarised under three broad headings: constitutional, institutional and sociological differences. For all the importance we attach to them, it remains true that there are probably even more similarities in the way social service departments bargain with their respective 'Ministry of Finance' than there are differences. In the second part of the chapter these similarities are elaborated under two headings: the strategies and the tactics of the bargaining process.

Constitutional Differences, Federal and Unitary
The United States is a federation, the United Kingdom is not. This constitutional difference has profound implications for the control of public expenditure. In the United States the Federal Government can only influence the spending plans of the states indirectly by changing the levels of grants or by general measures such as interest rate policy which affect the economy as a whole. The President can only control *his* budget, in other words the spending plans which his departments and agencies present to Congress. When the Treasury

seeks to control public expenditure in Britain this means *all* expenditure in the public sector, local authorities' spending as well as that of central government, and the capital investment plans of nationalised industry. It is possible for central government to seek to maintain this control in the first place because its constitutional powers are so much greater. As we saw in an earlier chapter local councils deliver most of the education services and nearly all the public housing and personal social services. But every local authority in Great Britain is a creation of Parliament. Indeed a completely new set of local authorities has only recently been established by an Act of Parliament.[3] Moreover no local authority may undertake any functions, however minor, which are not laid down in an Act of Parliament. District auditors – employees of the Central Government – ensure that no money is spent on activities which are *ultra vires* i.e. unauthorised by statute. More than that, it is their job to ensure that a local council does not spend 'unreasonable' sums even on items that have been permitted by Parliament. In practice the district auditor's powers under this last heading only rarely bring him in conflict with the locally elected authorities but this can happen and when it does the outcome is instructive. In the 1920s a number of poor law authorities with Labour majorities deliberately provided higher benefits to those on poor relief than the central department approved. They also paid their employees above the nationally agreed wage rates. This led to a series of famous confrontations. The Poplar Guardians (the elected members) were sent to jail in the most famous case and in the end the central government took additional legislative powers to control such spending.[4] Again in the 1950s and 1960s there were a number of court battles between the district auditors and local councils over the very low rents charged by some Labour authorities for their public housing. In the end a Conservative Government passed the Housing Finance Act 1972 which essentially fixed a national system of assessment for council houses, and a national system of rent rebates based on a common means test scale. These cases illustrate both the extent to which local authorities are bound by the legal framework and the power that central government has to amend the rules if they are not tight enough for its purposes.[5]

In the last resort if a local authority refuses to comply with an Act of Parliament or fulfil adequately the duties laid upon it the central government can step in and run that service itself funding it from the local rates. This has quite recently happened in the case of one council which refused to implement the Housing Act that has already been mentioned. In short the central government has quite draconian powers to circumscribe the activities of local authorities in Britain if it wishes to use them. The normally polite relationships which exist between civil servants and local government officials in Britain are merely the velvet glove that hides the mailed fist. The important consequence is that the central government has at its disposal an impressive array of economic levers or rationing devices with which it can control resource allocation by locally elected councils. It can control the capital building programmes of each local authority in considerable detail determining not merely the size of each authority's school building, house building and social service building programme, but its composition: which schools, where and of what size and character, built with what building materials, all of this has ultimately to be appraised in Whitehall.[6] The central departments have considerable say in the overall manpower situation. University places are funded almost entirely by the central exchequer and polytechnics and local authority colleges of education are subject to large elements of central government control. The upshot is that through a complex apparatus of national advisory committees, training councils, formal and informal pressures, the central departments, the Department of Education and Science and the Department of Health and Social Security between them, determine how many school teachers, social workers, doctors and nurses are trained each year. The flow of new recruits into the social service professions is thus closely controlled and largely through that mechanism the size of the total stock can be determined. In addition both departments have powers to control the geographical distribution of certain staff. Local authorities may not employ more than a given number of full time teachers for example. This 'quota' system, as it is called, was introduced in a period of extreme teacher shortage in the mid 1950s and was an attempt to prevent the more prosperous and attractive areas taking more than their fair share of the total available teacher supply. More recently financial incentives have been introduced, to persuade teachers to come to, and to stay longer in, schools serving poor neighbourhoods. Similar inducements exist for doctors. Salary scales not only for teachers but for other groups of local authority employees are negotiated nationally and the departments have an important say in the outcome. This is all but inevitable since indirectly central government meets the larger part of the salary cost even though it does not employ the staff directly. Finally, the total grant which the central government provides is such an important source of income that changes in it have a direct impact on the total level of spending which local authorities feel able to embark upon.

Central government meets about 60 per cent of local expenditure on the social services. Even relatively small changes in the rate of increase in this grant compared to previous years can produce repercussions throughout all the social services. Local authorities have not in the past been willing to finance a higher proportion of their services from rates if the government grants are cut. Thus although it is a general grant not tied to a particular service or to a particular authority's spending central government has been able to exert considerable leverage on the total level of local authority current spending.[7] Finally, central departments have more informal methods of control, notably the circular or letter written to all relevant authorities giving advice or information. At times circulars can be used to request particular action and call for authorities to submit plans by a given date to achieve such and such a goal. The circular asking local education authorities to submit plans for the reorganisation of secondary education in their areas was such an example and it had far-reaching consequences.

Each of the methods that have been mentioned have been used by central departments for a long time, but in the last twenty years they have been developed into far more sophisticated tools of resource allocation. This is especially true of the loan sanction procedure which is the basis of Whitehall's control over local building programmes. In the nineteenth century it was thought necessary for the central government to retain control of local authorities' borrowing powers to ensure that they did not incur massive debts. More recently this power has become the foundation of an elaborate process controlling local capital expenditure almost as if it were central government's direct responsibility. But if Whitehall has considerable say in the resource allocation decisions of locally elected bodies its say in the National Health Service and the National Insurance Scheme is greater still. The Insurance system is in this respect no different from the American, except for Unemployment Insurance. The British Health Service is utterly different. Federal health programmes in the US still leave a great deal of room for local initiative and discretion. In contrast the newly reorganised Health Service has removed even that element of local discretion that used to exist. The domiciliary services used to be administered by locally elected councils. Now the whole service is Exchequer financed and the Secretary of State for Health and Social Security is directly responsible for the whole enterprise. Moreover the new centralised structure lays heavy emphasis on resource allocation.[8]

In short if the Treasury can control the social service departments it has charge of an extremely powerful economic regulator of a kind that no American President could ever wield.

The Separation of Powers
The second major constitutional difference between the US and the UK is, of course, the separation of powers between the executive and the legislature. This is nowhere more important than in the field of financial legislation, and the economic consequences are considerable. In Britain no private member of Parliament can propose legislation which has financial consequences. Under a long-standing rule no proposal 'causing a charge on the public revenue' can proceed unless recommended by the Crown. This derives from a standing order that dates back to 1713. Equally strong conventions and party discipline ensure that government estimates are not cut. In consequence, once a particular spending proposal or the total package of annual estimates have been settled within government their approval is all but automatic, assuming the government has an overall majority. This is *not* to say that governments are never forced to bring in supplementary estimates, far from it, or that they never change their expenditure plans for one reason or another. They frequently have to do so in response to political or economic pressures. However, whenever such changes are made, it is the government which proposes the changes, not individual members of the House of Commons. Indeed the House is weaker in its impact on expenditure decisions than on almost any others.

In contrast the United States Congress does not suffer such limits to its financial power and the extent of party discipline is traditionally weak. Not infrequently the President will have to get his budget through Congress in the face of a hostile majority just as President Nixon had to do in each of his terms. Congress may not only cut a President's spending programme, this has been its traditional role, but it may also increase it. Some committees and their chairmen have made names for themselves as 'budget boosters'. This has second order reactions. An agency and the Office of Management and Budget will not want to be seen to be continually underestimating or continuously 'being mean' if the programmes are politically popular. The result is that the agency and the President will raise their proposals next year. There is evidence of this process from various sources: discussion with those who make up the budgets, simple observations of the successive adjustments over time and more rigorous statistical analysis.[9]

Each part of the President's budget is considered first by one of the specialist sub-committees of the House of Representatives'

Appropriations Committee. The HEW budget is the responsibility of the Labour-HEW subcommittee. At the hearings the Budget officer and then the Secretary give an overview of the whole HEW budget and its rationale. They are questioned by members of the committee. Then each agency's section of the budget is considered separately and the head of that agency, his budget officers and heads of division accompany him. Each programme or set of programmes is accompanied by a 'budget justification' giving the legislative and factual background. The record of the 1972 public sessions of this committee alone amounted to five volumes and nearly 5,000 pages of text.[10] At the next stage the committee goes into closed executive session. A draft appropriations bill for that part of the budget is thus hammered out and reported to the full Appropriations Committee. Usually the full committee will not question the detailed recommendations. Next the bill as a whole is reported to the House. There again it may be changed. Thence it goes to the Senate's Appropriations Committee and the process is repeated. In some sense the Senate acts as an appeals court for interests who have lost out in the first round. As with other legislation, if the Senate version differs from the House version, the two have to go to a joint Conference Committee of the two Houses. This meets in executive, or closed, session to work out an agreed version. It is not uncommon for wild but popular moves to be included on the floor whereas in secret session, when no individual congressman can be blamed, it will be safely cut out again.

If the outcome of this whole process is not to the President's liking he can veto the bill but this is not likely to be popular politically. Nixon did veto the HEW budget Congress had voted in 1972. The whole process is particularly complicated in the case of HEW because the largest chunk of HEW's budget does not come from the Appropriations Committee at all. The Trust Funds are the responsibility of the Ways and Means Committee of the House and the Finance Committee in the Senate who are both responsible for taxation. They approve the level of benefits and the social security tax rate whenever new legislation is needed which is not, of course, every year.

The final shot the President has in his locker is to 'impound' the funds voted by Congress i.e. to refuse to spend them, but even here he has recently run into difficulties in the courts. Where the money is voted under a grant formula it is beyond the President's reach.

It is very difficult for a British observer to understand how the process works at all. At first sight the President, and those particularly responsible for his Budget – The Director of the Office of

Management and Budget and those in that office – seem all but powerless. In practice, the appropriations legislation that eventually emerges is rarely very different from the President's budget at least as far as established programmes are concerned. There are many reasons for this. The most important is the situation familiar to budget compilers in any system – the burden of past obligations. Existing legislation pre-empts the greater part of each year's budget. Social security legislation is the most obvious example. It guarantees specified levels of benefit for certain contributions. Many other programmes guarantee states or institutions a certain level of grant on the basis of some set formula. These programmes have been grouped together and referred to both by Congress and the President as 'uncontrollables'. Of course the original piece of legislation can be amended in the long term and indeed even in the short term it can in theory be repealed but in everyday practice this is most unlikely. Altogether in the 1974 budget 75 per cent of the President's budget was classified as 'relatively uncontrollable'.[11] To a lesser extent the same political constraints make radical changes in other existing programmes unlikely. Even at the margin where the real debate centres, the informal contacts which exist between Congressional committee members, their staffs and those who work in the agencies ensure that there is enough common understanding of the issues and the constraints to reduce the number of serious battles to manageable proportions. A number of studies have analysed this 'mutual adjustment' process in some detail and we shall return to some recent examples of it later. The simple and crucial point to grasp here is that Congress's constitutional position makes the task of controlling the Federal Government's own expenditure far more complicated in the United States than is the comparable task for the central government in Britain, and the precise outcome of the process is always uncertain.

Institutional Differences

As the executive's power to control the budget is fundamentally different in the two countries so too is the relative power of the Treasury and the OMB within the government machine. Their formal roles are similar. They are both responsible for advising the Cabinet in one case or the President in the other about the size of the total budget in view of the overall economic prospects. They must also advise on the relative claims of different Departments. They are the 'economy advocates' or the 'safeguarders of the public purse'. They oversee the activities of the spending departments and try to ensure public money is not wasted. In practice their political power and significance are very different. In part this is a matter of history.

The British Treasury emerged as long ago as 1688 as a separate department and as Parliament gained control over financial matters this power was largely vested in the Treasury. The reforms of the mid-nineteenth century finally established it at the very centre of the government machine. Indeed the system of expenditure control that operated until 1961 was essentially that which had been developed in the Gladstone era. The Treasury's power derives from a series of rules or conventions: first, there is the Standing Order of the House of Commons which denies individual MPs the power to move a Financial Resolution. This is backed up by the convention that no Financial Resolution can actually be tabled in the House of Commons unless it bears the initials of a Treasury Minister. No piece of legislation involving public expenditure can therefore even be discussed by the House of Commons without Treasury approval. A government department must seek authority from the Treasury for any new project or significant departure from past practice. In the same way it has been a long-standing rule laid down by Prime Ministers even before the 1960s that no memorandum proposing extra expenditure could be circulated to Cabinet or Cabinet sub-committees without the Treasury having seen it and commented on it.[12] As we shall see these basic constitutional conventions have been elaborated in important ways in the 1960s but even before this the control of public expenditure was highly centralised in the hands of this one department.

There is an interesting account by R. M. MacLeod[13] of the early history of the Local Government Board which was created in 1871 and took over very wide responsibilities overseeing the activities of local Poor Law Guardians and public health as well as local government. After a honeymoon period the Board gained a reputation for restrictive meanness and historians' judgements on it have been harsh. MacLeod argues on the basis of department files for the period that to a large extent this image was primarily the fault of the Treasury.

However justified this particular view of history, it does illustrate the power which the Treasury had already acquired in this period. The basis of its influence lay not merely in its control over expenditure. It was the department responsible for the recruitment and promotion of civil servants as well as for taxation policies and the general control of the economy. In 1968 following the Fulton Commission's Report[14] recruitment and promotion, i.e. the management of the Civil Service itself, passed to the Civil Service Department. During the 1964–70 Labour Government a separate department took over long-term economic planning, but the Treasury again took charge of this at the end of 1969. In short, it remains the premier department of state with a long history and an important range of inter-connected responsibilities over and above expenditure control.

Neither situation applies to the present Office of Management and Budget. Its present title only dates back to 1970. Its predecessor, the Bureau of the Budget, was only created in 1921.[15] Before that date each separate agency could submit its own expenditure proposals to Congress. Since then only the President has been able to do so. The Bureau of the Budget was originally a part of the Treasury and only in 1939 did it become part of the Executive Office. Its task has been to put together a complete set of requests to Congress from all the agencies and departments of state and to impose the President's own set of priorities and limits. Together, these bids to Congress constitute the President's Budget.

The Office of Management and Budget therefore has a shorter history than the Treasury and carries less prestige. In talking to the participants in the American bargaining process one gains nothing like the same feeling of respectful awe which the Treasury commands throughout the Civil Service and amongst Ministers. This is not primarily a matter of tradition, it is quite simply a matter of power. The OMB has no responsibility for the raising of taxes; that is the task of the US Treasury, a separate Department of State not part of the White House at all. It does not have the responsibility of giving the President advice on economic management; that is the task of the Council of Economic Advisers. Nor has it ever controlled the recruitment and promotion of staff.

The Sociology of Spending Control

No account of formal differences in the constitutional or legal powers of the Treasury and the OMB can indicate the complexity and the subtlety of the bargaining process. Nor does it bring out the informal ways in which the President or the Treasury can seek to exercise their influence over departments' spending plans. In a recent highly entertaining book Heclo and Wildavsky[16] have described the informal and personal contacts that make the process work as well as it does in Whitehall. The number of people involved at the top is much smaller in Britain than in America. The majority of those who enter the Civil Service still come from Oxford or Cambridge and a disproportionate number from a few private schools.[17] The pre-conditions for mutual confidence and shared values exist. The higher up the hierarchy the more the atmosphere of a select club prevails. In this intimate atmosphere the individuals concerned must keep on reasonably good terms with each other and learn to co-operate as well as bargain. The vital part played by such co-operation and intimacy is well illustrated in Heclo's and Wildavsky's detailed account of the bargaining processes. But although such co-operative values are clearly important other tougher factors are at work and ones which smack more of conflict and the strategic use of power. Essentially what is at stake in this whole process is the size and scope of government – the most basic of all ideological differences. The Treasury has stood, traditionally, for the minimum feasible scale of government intervention. It forms the implicit basis for the more elaborate Treasury norms into which each new recruit is socialised. Against these values are those of some at least of the spending departments. It is natural that any civil servant who has spent a period in a department like Education or Health should acquire a considerable sympathy for the service he helps to administer and for the professionals and administrators in local or regional authorities with whom he is in regular contact. There is a clear community of interest especially between those in the policy branches of a spending department and their 'constituencies'. The 'Schools Branch' or the 'Further Education Branch' or 'Teachers Branch' readily identify with those in that part of the education service and act as its advocates. This feature was evident in the American context and was especially noticeable in an agency like the Social Security Administration where some of the senior people had served together since they joined the organisation in the New Deal era and held firmly to what could be called 'social welfare' values.

In Britain there is, or was, no such clear pattern. One of the few studies of a piece of social legislation in the 1950s, the 1957 Rent Act, shows how passionately the appropriate civil servants in the Ministry of Housing were committed against government intervention in the housing market.[18] Griffith has shown that different ministries have very different traditions in their relations with local authorities.[19] But it is surely reasonable to suggest that there is a tendency for longer service in one department to encourage more enthusiastic advocacy of its activities. It is also difficult to believe that this fear has not been an important reason why civil servants have been moved so rapidly from post to post. In the period between 1961 and 1971 the average period for which a Permanent Secretary held office was 49 months compared to 66 months in the inter-war period, and the rapidity of transfer seems to have increased in the late sixties.[20] The department responsible was of course the Treasury. The Fulton Commission criticised this tendency and went on to recommend that recruitment and promotion within the Home Civil Service should be specialised, recruits should be grouped for promotions within two sets of departments – social administration and the economic departments.[21] Most civil servants would spend most of their careers in one or the other group. Much scorn has been poured on this proposal. It has been rejected, and perhaps not surprisingly, for part of the Treasury's influence has come from the fact that its own men have gone on to 'colonise' the major social service departments.

Kogan, an ex-civil servant himself, pointed to this phenomenon in a paper he wrote in 1969.[22] He grouped departments under four broad headings: the central departments – Treasury, Cabinet Office, Civil Service Department; the Economic departments – Trade, Employment, Economic Affairs, Agriculture, etc; Defence and Overseas: and finally Social Services – Education, Health and Social Security, Home Office and Housing. Those who reached the top, either as Permanent Secretaries or Deputy Secretaries, had spent more of their careers in either central or economic departments than would be expected given the number of lower level posts available in the various groups of departments. Permanent Secretaries had spent 39 per cent of their careers in the central group of departments – notably the Treasury, although only 12·6 per cent of the total posts in the administrative class in 1967 were in those departments. Permanent Secretaries had spent only 15·2 per cent of their careers in the social service departments but 27 per cent of all administrative class posts in 1967 were in these departments and as Kogan argued 1967 figures probably understated the career opportunities available in those departments in the 1930s and 40s. Permanent Secretaries in social service departments had spent 44 per cent of their careers within that group of departments, a lower percentage than that for any other group, especially in the central departments. In 1969 the Department of Education and Science, the Ministry of Housing and the Department of Social Security all had Permanent Secretaries who had spent most of their careers in the Treasury, the Board of Trade or the Admiralty. Heclo and Wildavsky add a historical perspective. They show that between 1928 and 1938 16 per cent of all new Permanent Secretaries had had Treasury experience. The proportion grew to 38 per cent in the period 1961–71 and was even higher at the end of the period – 44 per cent from 1968–71. This reflects a deliberate policy of recruitment to the Treasury of young Principals with several years

experience in other departments. It is interesting that of those who
have been employed on the task of controlling public expenditure in
the Treasury those who have climbed highest afterwards have spent
longer on average in public expenditure control than those who
have not climbed so far.[23]

In short the means of control that have been open to the Treasury
are subtle and extensive. They have in part depended on career
management, responsibility for which has now passed to the Civil
Service Department – though even that was headed by an ex-
Treasury man. The Treasury's key position in this respect has also
depended on the fact that the Treasury has had the pick of the new
recruits. This may also be changing somewhat as we shall see later.

These more subtle mechanisms are not really translatable into
American terms. The OMB is merely one part of the Executive
Office of the President. Nor has it been at the centre of the career
structure. A large number of senior posts in the agencies come up
for Presidential appointment after each presidential election and a
President who is keen to economise can ensure that men of the right
persuasion and temperament for such an activity are appointed to
key posts while others are removed. In 1972 after Nixon's re-
election the former head of the Office of Management and Budget,
Casper Weinberger, was moved to be Secretary of HEW – a move
that was generally interpreted as a means of giving greater emphasis
to an 'economising' strategy in that department. Other changes
seemed to bear this out.

So far it is the differences between the bargaining process in
Whitehall and Washington that have been emphasised. Despite this
the similarities are considerable.

Similar Tactics and Strategies

In his classic account of the American budgetary process
Wildavsky[24] not only emphasised the pluralism of the system as we
have done but he also maintained that the process of budgeting
within agencies, within Congress and within the BOB was non
comprehensive, non rational and conformed closely to Lindblom's
model of 'muddling through'.

The participants in all parts of the process used tactics or 'aids to
calculation' to help them *simplify* the process and avoid conflict.
Budget officials and congressmen on appropriations committees
concerned themselves with a small number of minutiae, not grand
objectives, they experimented cautiously, they 'satisficed' or in other
words they aimed for budget totals which would 'go' or 'get by'
rather than maximise returns or optimise. Above all budgeting was

'incremental'. 'The largest determining factor of the size and content of this year's budget is last year's budget.' By this Wildavsky clearly meant not only that the nature of the budget changed little but that the total budget increased slowly. He pointed out that most bureaux' budgets increased most years by less than 5 per cent. Decisions were not comprehensive. It was 'the beginning of wisdom' for an agency *not* to consider all the possible alternatives before it. It was not 'rational'. In making judgements about cuts the Bureau of the Budget worked to rough rules of thumb. This account of the BOB official deciding how to limit the budget of the National Institutes of Health is quoted as a classic case by Wildavsky.

'How did the BOB decide where and how much to cut the NIH request?'

'This is a very good question. I wonder how we will decide. I would say as a generalisation that it was some kind of mechanical factor like "let's hold it to last year's budget" or "last year's budget plus 10 per cent. ..."'

'How did you arrive at this figure?'

'We do it on an *ad hoc* basis. 10 per cent sounds right ... We were playing around with graphs and figures ... projecting growth to 1965 and say the figure was 1·3 billion. The people in the BOB will say, let's reach 1·3 billion not by 1965 but by 1975. ... Comments might go like this. "We have to put a stop to this NIH." "Congress will up it anyway whatever we do. ..." Then someone will say "Let's hold it to last year's level". But somebody else would reply: "No, that is no good. That is not realistic at all. There has to be some increase." Then another would say, "can we raise them 10 per cent and get a rationalisation for this?" and we try to figure one out ...'[25]

Discussions did not centre on whole programmes, merely on minor items that created controversy. There were enough of these not to want to raise issues about the virtues or vices of a whole programme. Once a problem had been 'solved' one year it was not returned to the next. The outcome was a slow but steady expansion to the budget. Wildavsky explained this by outlining numerous 'strategies' employed by government agencies to maintain or increase the resources available to them. He gave these strategies titles like 'serve your clientele', 'expand your clientele', and 'secure feedback', in other words, make sure your clients or related pressure groups let congressmen know what a fine job you are doing for them. Advisory committees are a very good way of drawing congressional and specialist attention to new areas of activity or to 'gaps' in the programmes an agency is administering. 'Get a group

F

of people together who are professionally interested in a subject no matter how conservative or frugal they might otherwise be, and they are certain to find additional ways in which money could be spent.'

It is of crucial importance for agency officials to keep on good terms with and secure the confidence of the relevant congressional committee. This goes not only for the members of the committee but for its staff. Contact between the staffs of a committee and an agency will be frequent during the passage of a bill or when hearings are in progress. How much will such and such a proposal cost? What are the implications of such an amendment on the complex entitlements under the Social Security laws? Prompt, accurate and well-informed answers to that kind of question can increase 'confidence' in the agency. The ability to handle a committee during congressional hearings is another important facility. Although agencies are not supposed to seek to promote their part of the budget in conflict with Presidential priorities, Congress can get a pretty good idea what the agency wants, and indeed will ask 'what did you put in for?'

In Britain strategies of a directly comparable kind are not appropriate. Parliament does not play the highly significant role that Congress does. The bargaining process is conducted, with rare exceptions, in secret. Yet the strategies spending Departments use in their battle against the Treasury are just as varied as those in the US. They apply in part to the tactics used against the Treasury in direct negotiation and in part to the strategies used to create a climate of opinion which will, in the longer term, have its impact on cabinet priorities. What might seem the most obvious tactic, which is simply to add on a percentage to your estimates over and above what you need to meet any commitment, is too obvious. Yet in any forecast of future expenditure numerous assumptions have to be made and any spending department will adopt generous ones and these will be questioned and cut down as the interplay continues.

The Treasury cannot keep large numbers of staff combing every programme and has tended to pool its resources and make concerted attacks on particular areas. Heclo and Wildavsky discuss these tactics and strategies in general terms but they can be usefully elaborated, especially as far as social service spending departments are concerned.

Tactics include the 'thin end of the wedge'. This means getting a relatively unimpressive proposal or piece of legislation through when the costs appear small knowing that the growth potential is great. The Crowther committee proposed raising the school leaving age for a point in time when the school leaving population was to be at its lowest in 1966–9. Afterwards numbers would rise steeply. Tactics also include the 'new building lever'. Any building programme which will replace old buildings will be certain to gain public support. Replacing Victorian hospitals or primary schools over 100 years old is not only a first-class campaign slogan, it can also have the appearance of being economic. Old buildings are inefficient, expensive to heat and maintain. Undoubtedly so, but new buildings also make it possible to install hospital equipment that could not previously be used, higher standards of care and better facilities for staff. If there simply was not room for a staff-room in a small Victorian primary school, or room for children to eat their lunch except at their desks, if there was no room for a playground except on the roof and no room at all for playing fields – so be it. Everyone will accept the situation. But the DES cannot *plan* to *build* schools with no staff room or dining room, no playground and no playing field. If the hospitals contain facilities for modern surgery then plainly it is a *waste* not to use them – hence more staff, more maintenance, more drugs. If more laboratories are provided in schools more laboratory assistants are needed.

Then again there is 'the more machines less men' argument which turns out to be 'more machines therefore more men'. Schools have much more equipment in them now than ten years ago. But, teachers claim, it is underused because it is always going wrong or takes too much time to install in a classroom before the lesson begins. A technical assistant will ensure that the equipment is fully and effectively used.

Or there is the 'training facilities time bomb'. A programme to expand training facilities for staff to meet a perceived staff shortage does not in the short run cost a great deal of money, especially if it can be combined with a proposal to make more effective use of the buildings. The 1966 expansion of places in Colleges of Education with no extra capital expenditure is a case in point. Yet, the long term expenditure consequences of such a move are considerable. An increase of 50 per cent in the annual output of Colleges of Education or medical schools or social work courses may not cost much now but it will eventually produce a 50 per cent rise in staffing costs and to the extent that other costs are linked to staffing costs it may increase the total cost of the service by nearly 50 per cent.

Finally, if a department can maintain that there are long term economic gains involved in a proposal this is always felt to be helpful in convincing the Treasury. Short-term wage related social security benefits for the unemployed, and therefore, in justice, for the sick, would help increase the pace of technical change, it was argued. A surplus of council housing would increase labour mobility and the raising of the school leaving age would make labour more adaptable. If a department has to accept cuts it tries to ensure that these are 'paper cuts'. It will cut building 'starts' knowing that local authorities had already got more starts approved than they could hope to turn into bricks and mortar that year. Or the department will attempt to get cuts made to programmes that can only be delayed and will have to come in a later year's programme. The postponement of the raising of the school leaving age is a case in point. The DES probably made money out of that skirmish. Or again a department may seek to cut public expenditure as defined but to avoid cutting the actual service commensurately, e.g. by raising charges. This may be especially attractive when it is combined with complex arrangements to ensure that most of those who might be deterred do not in fact have to pay the charges. The reimposition of prescription charges in 1968 is the classic example of this tactic. Fees for overseas students is another and so are increases in school meals charges. Nevertheless the ultimate defence is a powerful minister in Cabinet.

These are the tactics. The strategies for expanding the budget are in the end more important. Three stand out. They all have parallels in the US.

One of the most important is the use of the advisory committee. It was used successfully by the old Ministry of Education. The succession of reports by the Central Advisory Council for Education in England, and other *ad hoc* committees, the most influential of them being the Robbins Committee on Higher Education, spotlighted deficiencies in the system systematically and helped to create a political climate in which a head of steam built up behind a succession of expensive developments.

The Housing Advisory Committee proposed a significant improvement in the standard of council house building.[26] As a result 'Parker Morris' minimum standards were introduced with some modification after tussles with the Treasury. It is particularly useful if, through a committee of this kind, the minister can be prevailed upon to commit the government publicly to a target – eliminating oversized classes by 1980 or removing all Victorian primary schools by 1975. It is also helpful for interest groups to get a political party to commit itself as specifically as possible to certain targets in a manifesto. Opposition parties are usually fairer game in this respect just because they do not have the Minister concerned straight from his monthly battles with the Treasury bringing a sense of realism into the discussion on a Party committee.

The skilful use of crises is another strategy that a good spending minister can adopt. A succession of damaging revelations about the conditions in mental subnormality hospitals were used by Crossman as the justification for a major reappraisal of expenditure in this field. The initiative was kept up despite the change of government and the result was a white paper outlining a programme involving more resources for the mentally handicapped.

Third, a spending department and its minister can 'orchestrate' and encourage pressure groups who are being highly critical of them and their niggardliness. This undoubtedly happened in the case of the Child Poverty Action Group's various attempts to get family allowances raised during the Labour Government's period in office.

All these strategies are more difficult to bring to successful completion in Britain than they are in America because the immediate audience is less certain and the channels of influence more diffuse. Back bench opinion cannot easily be aroused by an individual minister for his own purposes unless it is done very subtly. This would arouse the anger of other ministers and be self-defeating. There are specialist back bench committees that a minister would do well to keep briefed on what is happening in general but the expenditure control process is sufficiently secret to prevent them from playing any effective role. The new House of Commons Committee on Expenditure, though it has specialist subcommittees, is being kept very much on the periphery and has not sought to comment on the general expenditure proposals, pursuing instead special topics that interest them. There is no audience akin to the US Appropriations Committees who actually hold the purse strings. The audience is the press, specialist public opinion and via them other cabinet ministers.

In Brief

The Treasury has more power than the US Office of Management and Budget and was in a much stronger position to launch a new expenditure control system.

Constitutionally the central government in Britain can regulate resource allocation decisions of local authorities and directly control social security and health care. Parliament, unlike Congress, has little real power over expenditure. The Treasury is in a far more powerful position not only because of numerous constitutional conventions on expenditure control but because of its other linked responsibilities for economic policy and previously civil service management.

Yet despite these differences the bargaining process until the early 1960s was probably rather similar. Expenditure had been edged forward by a combination of tactics and strategies countered as best they could by the Treasury and the Bureau of the Budget.

REFERENCES

1 See, for example, *Public Administration Review*, Vol. 26, No. 4, December 1966, especially Wildavsky's article.
2 Self, P., ' "Nonsense on Stilts": Cost Benefit Analysis and the Roskill Commission', *The Political Quarterly*, Vol. 41, No. 3, 1970.
Klein, R., 'The Politics of PPB', *The Political Quarterly*, Vol. 43, No. 3, 1972.
3 Local Government Act, 1972.
4 Keith Lucas, B., 'Poplarism', *Public Law*, Spring, 1962.
5 For a full account of central departments' powers and relationships with local authorities see: Griffith, J. A. G., *Central Departments and Local Authorities*, George Allen & Unwin, London, 1966.
6 Ibid. Chapter 2.
7 See the written evidence of the County Councils Association to the Education Sub-Committee of the House of Commons Expenditure Committee Session 1970-1 HC 545, p. 138. The differences between the forecast of total expenditure relevant to the Rate Support Grant and the eventual out-turn in the late sixties was:

	Forecast £m	Out-turn £m	Difference %
1967–8	2,619	2,663	+1·7
1968–9	2,793	2,842	+1·8
1969–70	3,144	3,126	−0·6

8 See later discussion, p. 153.
9 Fenno, R. F., *The Power of the Purse*, Little Brown, Boston, 1966.
Fenno shows Congressional appropriations as a percentage of budget bids 1947–62 for different agencies. Here are the HEW examples:

Food and Drug Administration	99·1
Office of Education	97·5
Social Security Administration	97·2

See also Davis, O. A., Dempster, M. A. H., and Wildavsky, A., 'On the Process of Budgeting: an empirical study of Congressional Appropriations', *Papers on Non-Market Decision Making*, Vol. 1, 1966, pp. 63–132.
Equations were fitted to time series data on appropriations of 56 non-defence agencies for the period 1947–63. One of the equations used was designed to test this theory and generally supports it. Simple linear growth patterns that shift when a new administration takes office, seem the best interpretation.

10 Hearings before a subcommittee of the House of Representatives Committee on Appropriations, 92nd Congress.

11 *The Budget of the US Government, 1974*, US Government Printing Office, Washington, 1973, p. 44.

12 See Lord Bridges, *The Treasury*, George Allen & Unwin, London, 1966, pp. 34–7.

13 MacLeod, R. M., *Treasury Control and Social Administration*, Occasional Papers in Social Administration, No. 23, Bell, London, 1968.

14 *The Civil Service*, Cmnd 3638, 1968.

15 For an account of the history of budget control in the US (and elsewhere) see J. Burkhead, *Government Budgeting*, Wiley, New York, 1956. For an account of the Bureau just before its change of title and functions see P. F. Brundage, *The Bureau of the Budget*, Praeger, New York, 1970.

16 Heclo, H. and Wildavsky, A., *The Private Government of Public Money*, Macmillan, London, 1974.

17 Boyd, D., *Elites and their Education*, NFER, 1973, also *The Civil Service*, op. cit., Vol. 3.

18 Barnett, M. Joel, *The Politics of Legislation: The Rent Act, 1957*, Weidenfeld and Nicolson, London, 1969.

19 Griffith, op. cit., pp. 515–28.

20 Heclo and Wildavsky, p. 81.

21 Cmnd 3638, paras. 41–58.

22 Kogan, M., '*Social Services: their Whitehall Status*', New Society, 21 August, 1969.

23 Heclo and Wildavsky, pp. 82–3.

24 Wildavsky, A., *The Politics of the Budgetary Process*, Little, Brown, Boston, 1964.

25 Op. cit., p. 45.

26 Central Housing Advisory Committee: *Homes for Today and Tomorrow*, HMSO, London, 1961.

Further Reading

Wildavsky, A., *The Politics of the Budgetary Process*, op. cit. (A highly readable account of the budget process in Washington as seen by participants.)

Heclo, H., and Wildavsky, A., *The Private Government of Public Money*, op. cit. (Chapters 1–4). (An equally readable account of the process in Whitehall.)

Griffith, J. A. G., *Central Departments and Local Authorities*, op. cit. (Important for an understanding of how the central government in Britain can seek to control the whole field of public expenditure including that undertaken by local authorities.)

Chapter 6

Forward Planning — US Style

High Hopes

It was in President Kennedy's term that the first attempts were made to introduce a longer term perspective into the normal budget sequence. Presidents normally present their spending proposals to Congress in January, and this has been traditionally preceded by hard bargaining in the autumn. In 1961 Departments were asked to submit tentative estimates for *five* years ahead assuming current policies held. These estimates were to be with the Bureau of the Budget in the summer. At that point in time tax yield forecasts were also projected ahead by the US Treasury on the basis of an economic assessment. This set the stage for the Budget negotiations and was consequently called the 'summer preview'. It was similar in outline to the procedure recommended by the Plowden Committee in the same year. What the first US exercises showed was that on reasonable assumptions tax revenue would rise faster than projected expenditure – the opposite of the British situation. The whole exercise was evidently rather half-hearted and crude.[1]

Much more significant in the end was the appointment of Robert MacNamara as Secretary of the Department of Defense and the changes he made there. For more than a decade various attempts had been made to gain some kind of coordinated control over the separate armed forces. The Office of the Secretary for Defense had been created in 1947 and strengthened in 1958, to no great effect. Each service largely went its own way, each seeking to introduce weapons systems that had profound long-term expenditure consequences and could duplicate the efforts of another service. MacNamara made a determined attempt to centralise and co-ordinate planning activities within the Office of the Secretary. He appointed Charles Hitch from RAND to be Comptroller of the Department, a post which carried responsibility for drawing up the Department's budget. Numerous participants and observers have written about this experience.[3] The reforms that were introduced were, at the time, considered to be an outstanding success. MacNamara evidently gained a hold on the Department and co-ordinated the activities of the separate services in a way that no other Secretary had done. The first step in the new planning process was the determination by the Secretary of State of overall defence priorities. This meant providing broad guidance on constraints within which the services had to work – Tentative Force Guidance as it was called. Then came the creation of the detailed programme budget structure of the kind we have discussed earlier and at the end of it all came a Five-Year-Defence-Plan, with costs covering a five-year period and manpower forecasts an eight-year period. The expenditure forecast for the first year of the plan was then trans-lated into the necessary appropriations categories required by the BOB and Congress. Those involved argued that the whole process enabled the Secretary to gain a much clearer idea of future cost consequences, to form judgements on the respective value of com-peting proposals and above all it gave him the means to impose some set of priorities on defence expenditure.[4]

It was probably these features that appealed to President Johnson most and led him in 1965 to instruct all agencies to introduce a similar system. The traditional pattern of incremental budgeting left the head of a department little scope for imposing his own pattern upon the final package. This new system seemed to offer a chance of doing just that and with it the chance that the President could exert his influences too. It was a period of legislative activity. The 'Great Society' programmes were being launched and it was a time of optimism about man's capacity to solve the great social issues of the time – poverty, racial discrimination, delinquency – through selective government intervention guided by the contributions of social scien-tists. Moreover, Schick argued, 'the President viewed PPB as an opening prong in a major overhaul of federal organisation, an expectation that was aborted by the Vietnam situation.'[5]

Once again RAND made the case for the change. The findings of its 1965 study (discussed in Chapter 2) were evaluated within government prior to publication. A powerful case was made for using the whole Federal budget as a basis for strategic planning. As we shall see in the next chapter the earlier British reforms had been prompted by a concern to find some means of containing excessive and 'uncontrollable' increases in public expenditure. In contrast, the

Johnson reforms formed part of a more interventionist philosophy. This is well illustrated in the tenor of the President's press conference on August 25, 1965, announcing the institution of this new planning system. He said:[6]

'This morning I have just concluded a breakfast meeting with the Cabinet and with the heads of Federal agencies and I am asking each of them to immediately begin to introduce a very new and very revolutionary system of planning and programming the budgeting throughout the vast Federal Government, so that through the tools of modern management the full promise of a finer life can be brought to every American at the lowest possible cost.

'Under this new system each Cabinet and agency head will set up a very special staff of experts who, using the most modern methods of program analysis, will define the goals of their department for the coming year. And once these goals are established this system will permit us to find the most effective and the least costly alternative to achieving American goals.

'This program is designed to achieve three major objectives: It will help us find new ways to do jobs faster, to do jobs better, and to do jobs less expensively. It will insure a much sounder judgement through more accurate information, pinpointing those things that we ought to do more, spotlighting those things that we ought to do less. It will make our decisionmaking process as up to date, I think, as our space-exploring programs.'

These changes were to be sudden, sweeping and all-embracing. Two things followed fairly soon, first the employment of specialised staffs to operate the new system, and second the formal set of procedures that were laid down by the BOB under which the agencies had to submit their proposals to the Bureau.

Between 1966 and 1968 virtually 1,000 additional staff were recruited or transferred to work in the new PPB system in 21 non-defence agencies. In 1968–9 a further 150 were added. Of this total of 1,150 new posts nearly 300 were filled by analysts or support staff working for the heads of departments or agencies. A further 160 were concerned with programme monitoring, i.e. producing statistics on the progress of the various programmes for the heads of agencies, while a further 700 were employed mainly by subordinate agencies.[7] Inevitably few of these staff had any experience of the kind of work that was required. Indeed notions on anyone's part of what was required were hazy. Nevertheless by 1969 26 agencies had central units producing programme budget analyses of some kind for the heads of their department.[8] They were employed for much of their time in responding to the complex demands of the BOB. These requirements firmly tied both planning and analysis to the annual budget cycle (see Table 6.1). The first task was to group together agency activities which had similar objectives – in short the creation of a programme structure on which the RAND study had placed such emphasis. This could well mean grouping together money voted by Congress under differ-

Table 6.1   *The PPBS Process in a Typical Budget Year*

November 1968– February 1969	Identification of major policy issues affecting the fiscal year 1971 budget and/or subsequent budgets, or having major social impact.
	Issue letters sent by the Director of the Bureau of the Budget to each agency head.
1969 May–June	Results of issue analysis reported to agency heads and then to the Budget Director. Commitments or uncontrollable budget expenditures based on past decisions are identified and projected five years ahead along with the identification of proposed additional or new expenditures and the identification of low priority expenditures for the fiscal year 1971 budget.
June–July	Bureau of the Budget holds spring preview of major policy issues and plans for the reorientation of existing programs and/or identification of new low priority programs. The implications of changes in policy and spending levels are projected ahead for five years.
August	The Budget Bureau releases tentative guidance by agency and selected programs for each agency to develop final budget requests.
September– October	Final budget and program and financial plans are submitted by each agency to the Bureau of the Budget.
October– November	B.O.B. holds final agency hearings and budget review.
November– December	President decides on the major budget issues.
1970 January	Presidential budget message transmitted to the Congress.
February–June	Hearings on the budget by various committees of the Congress.
March–July	Congressional approval of the major items in the fiscal year 1971 budget.
July	Fiscal year 1971 begins.

ent acts or administered by different parts of the agency or by different agencies. A translation or 'cross-walk' from this set of categories to Congressional appropriation categories was needed. Once agreed within departments and between the department and the Bureau it provided a framework for future budget discussions. It meant that all the disparate programmes that supported health delivery or helped support students in college could be discussed as one block of expenditure. Basic ground rules were laid down by the BOB. We shall discuss the particular difficulties encountered in connection with social services programmes in a later chapter.

The second element in the system devised after 1965 was the choice by the Bureau in consultation with the agency, of 'Major Programme Issues'. These were issues that needed decisions in the current budget round, and would have major implications in terms of future cost or the future direction the programme should take. The Bureau sent out 'Issue Letters' in theory, although not always in practice early in the calendar year. In response each agency would produce a 'special analytic study' by May or June to be available as part of the Bureau's 'spring review'.

Then in the autumn the agencies were to submit their complete budget proposals to the Bureau accompanied by 'programme memoranda'. These should set out the objectives of the agency and describe all the various ways that they might be pursued, ending with the reasons why a particular set of choices had been made. This part of the exercise most of all gave the procedure a bad name. It fell into the trap Lindblom had foreseen. No one, not even a group of young analytical whizz-kids, could undertake such a superhuman task for all parts of all programmes. The result was variously described by participants as 'a considerable degree of high level generalisation' or 'mountains of garbage'. The Bureau soon adapted its instructions to emphasise that it only wanted the major issues and alternatives argued in detail. Nevertheless the instructions (to agencies received) were daunting enough. For example:

'In addition to identifying the strategy upon which agency plans are built, the PM should show how the resolution of major program issues fits into or modifies the program strategy. . .

The PM also shows why particular choices have been made, by identifying agency objectives in a measurable way, and comparing alternatives programs in terms of their costs and who pays them, and their benefits and the group benefited.'[9]

The third element in the whole procedure was for the agency to submit its 'Programme and Financial Plans' (PFPs). These were meant to cover the whole of the agency's activities. They were to include costs, data on finance, and output figures for each of seven years – last year, the current year, the immediate year ahead (i.e. the figure they hoped would eventually enter the President's Budget) and forecasts for four subsequent years. These figures were to be included separately for not only the whole of the programme, but for each sub-programme and programme element (i.e. a sub-subprogramme). To take one example, this would mean providing cost estimates for 'vocational education aimed at the economically and socially disadvantaged', and the outputs expected. Elaborating in its guidance on the 'concept of outputs' the Bureau said:

The PFP is intended to reflect, for decisions reached, the outputs in relatively unambiguous terms. Outputs in these terms might include the number of B52 squadrons, number of workers trained, etc.

This would not be good enough for the special analyses, however, where the concept would have to be extended to such measures as the impact of training on workers' earnings.[10]

Low achievements
This was, in outline, the system that was adopted in the 26 agencies mentioned previously. In practice nothing like the rigour implied in the instructions was achieved. There was growing criticism of the results which fell so far short of the high claims that had been made. The Bureau and the General Accounting Office (GAO) undertook a survey to assess practical results and in Congress the influential joint Economic Committee undertook what is still the most comprehensive official survey of the whole process that has been published.[11] The evidence to this committee both from officials and outsiders ranged from the mildly critical to the highly critical. There was some agreement that more information was now available about non-defence programmes, that the procedures had stimulated more research into public programmes and that there was wider recognition of the relevance of analysis in making resource decisions. Yet even these achievements were recognised to be extremely patchy. Marvin and Rouse, one from the General Accounting Office and the other from the BOB, listed thirteen separate reasons for the patchy response.[12] There was, they claimed, continuing confusion as to whom PPB was intended to serve, the managers of the separate programmes, the head of an agency or the Bureau. Support for the whole exercise within even the Bureau of

the Budget had been ambivalent. But it was the attitudes of the various agency heads that made the difference. Where they were keen to use analysis the system developed, where they were not, it tended to become merely a time-wasting duplication of the existing budgeting process. Other less important factors had to do with the varied training and experience the 'analytical' staff had had. In all these comments about comparative success HEW was almost always mentioned in a favourable context. It was one of the few domestic agencies which had really 'made a success' of the new system.

On one point many supporters and out and out critics agreed. The attempt to tie policy analysis too closely to the hectic and complex budget process was a mistake. It simply lead to inadequate and superficial work. The dilemma remained. The outcome of the budget process effectively determined agency priorities. Yet the budget cycle had proved a difficult vehicle to couple to systematic planning and analysis. Schick, from Brookings, in a paper that was highly critical of traditional incremental budgeting, argued that PPB had fallen foul of precisely the deficiencies it was supposed to remedy. Formulating a budget is inevitably largely a matter of routine:

'The forms and routines force one's attention to the work sheets and the ledgers, away from the ghettos, hospitals or school rooms.'[13]

Yet the PPB system with its numerous forms, and even more numerous empty boxes to be filled, routines and timetables to be met, had done precisely the same thing. 'Routine drives out analysis' he concluded. Yet some routine use of analysis had to be employed, systems could not be dispensed with altogether. He described four ways of trying to link analysis and budget discussions. Even if they suggest a railway system rather than a budget, they highlight some of the procedures later adopted in HEW.

1 A *cross walk* system in which budgeting and analysis are closely linked as in the procedure initiated in 1965.

2 A *two-track* system in which analysis is conducted largely independently of the budget process but is aimed indirectly at affecting future budget decisions.

3 *Analytic budgeting* which means sweeping away the normal budgeting process altogether, essentially putting the analysts in charge and relying entirely on a programme budget structure.

4 A *policy planning system* which largely lets budgeting go its

own way and concentrates policy analysis on new legislative proposals or major developments in existing programmes.

It was the last model Schick himself favoured. In evidence to the same committee Wildavsky came to similar conclusions on the drawbacks of linking policy analysis to the budget process. He claimed that for policy analysis to be done well, it could only be undertaken on a few key issues that were then dealt with in depth. It was up to agency heads to decide what these areas should be, but the BOB should insist that any major increases in agency funds or new programmes would have to be justified by such an in-depth study. He outlined the following sequence of steps, which closely resemble the Programme Analysis and Review procedure the British Conservative Government adopted a year or more later.

1 Secretary of agency and top policy analysts review major issues and legislation and set up a study 'menu' for several years. Additions and deletions are made periodically.

2 Policy analysts set up studies which take anywhere from 6–24 months.

3 As a study is completed for each major area, it is submitted to the Secretary of the agency for review and approval.

4 If approved, the implications of the study's recommendations are translated into budgetary terms for submission as a program memorandum in support of the agency's fiscal year budget.[14]

The last link in the chain, the *use* of the analysis, depended on the agency head. It depended on whether he was seriously interested – a chancy procedure perhaps, but that was real life.

The committee evidence therefore showed a strong undercurrent of criticism of the way the reform had gone. It had been oversold and introduced in too much of a hurry. It was open to some basic criticisms on which there was a wide measure of agreement. By this time – mid-1969 – there was also a new President, Richard Nixon and his appointees were at the Budget Office and in the agencies. PPB was strongly associated with the Johnson administration. Yet its more managerialist assumptions fitted the values and rhetoric of the new administration. In 1970 the BOB became the Office of *Management* and Budget.

What then happened to PPB? Most noticeably after 1970 public discussion simply petered out. Those Johnson appointees who had been involved in the practice wrote about their experiences, explained why it had failed, published their books and then stopped talking about it. The new administration ceased to use the elaborate PPB language. The programme structure – or programme budget –

so important to the original reformers was 'de-emphasised'. Individual agencies were left freer to devise their own planning, but more emphasis was laid on the special analyses within a revised budget timetable. In short a good many of the lessons pressed by the critics were taken to heart. By 1972 those in the OMB seemed unsure whether to say that PPB continued to exist or not. Agencies no longer had to return programme memoranda or PFPs or maintain separate programme structures. Yet many of the principles remained, particularly the emphasis on analysis and evaluation. Perhaps most significant of all, the bureaucracy that it had created remained. Each agency had acquired its team of analysts, its planning and evaluation or programme planning officers. The system had required expertise and the universities had begun to provide training courses. These 'experts' did not decline in number and the offices did not disappear. This is illustrated well in the experience of HEW.

HEW Experience
Planning of a less 'systematic' kind was not a new activity, at least for the Social Security Administration. The original Social Security Act of 1935 had given it the power to undertake research, unlike most other agencies. Since then its research activity had grown despite cuts imposed in 1947 and the Eisenhower period.[15] By 1965 the agency had a long-established reputation for research and its studies were summarised monthly in a journal called the *Social Security Bulletin*.[16] The agency had evolved its own informal planning strategy, mainly centred on the regular Advisory Councils on Social Security. At regular intervals since 1935 distinguished outsiders had been appointed to review the scope of social security legislation, identify gaps and propose changes and extensions. Their role was very similar to that of the Education Advisory Councils in England during the late 1950s and 1960s. The Office of Research and Statistics and its predecessors had spent a considerable part of their time preparing reports and basic material that could be used by these bodies.

The first Advisory Council had reported in 1938 and it resulted in the complete overhaul of the 1935 Act which Congress undertook in 1939. Research staff then were employed costing the numerous alternative benefit structures that were considered. The 1948 Advisory Council prepared four reports. One proposed changes in the old age and survivors insurance scheme, the second recommended the establishment of a permanent and total disability insurance programme, a third made recommendations on public assistance and maternal and child health, the fourth dealt with unemployment insurance and disability. By no means all their proposals were legislated but they did have a major impact on the 1949–50 Social Security amendments. Robert Ball who became the Commissioner for Social Security in 1961 and remained through to the beginning of 1973 was Staff Director for that Council, and knew the on-going research very well and used it to the full. The 1953 and the 1959 Councils had a more limited impact. Perhaps the most notable recent council was that of 1965 whose report was entitled *The Status of the Social Security Program and Recommendations for its Improvement.*[17] This included proposals for Medicare that were close to those eventually legislated. Yet it was but one part of a much longer saga which it is relevant to indicate very briefly.

Organised pressure for health insurance in the States dates back to 1910 at least. In the 1930s President Roosevelt's Committee on Economic Security worked on a plan for health insurance. The American Medical Association managed to prevent any proposals reaching Congress, but one sentence was included in the draft social security legislation stating that the Social Security Board should study the subject and report to Congress. That aroused so much opposition that any reference to health insurance was dropped. Instead a section was retained which called on the Social Security Board to study and make recommendations regarding the 'improvement and completion' of the social security system. It was used by the Board to justify later research and policy analysis work. Clearly health insurance has remained on the mental agenda of many of those who worked for the Board and its successor ever since. In the 1940s, in Truman's Presidency, bills were introduced which aimed at providing health insurance cover for the whole population. The AMA successfully opposed this, defeating, as it put it, 'The Federal Security Administration, the President and every leftwing organisation in America including the Communist Party'.[18] Indeed the head of the research section who had actually prepared an outline plan for a National Health Service for the United States was dismissed by the incoming Eisenhower administration so unpopular was he with the AMA. The political climate became more favourable around 1959 and 1960. A special Senate Sub-Committee on the problems of the aged had before it a lot of evidence from the Social Security Administration about the financial burden of health costs on old people, as did the House Ways and Means Committee two years later. The AMA claimed that the elderly were neither poorer nor more sick than the rest of the population – a proposition that the SSA statistics were able to conclusively disprove. As far back as

G

1950 it had been undertaking studies on health expenditure that were published in the *Social Security Bulletin*. Later surveys showed the cost of health care to the aged as well as their general financial circumstances.[19] It was no accident that so much information was available from the on-going research activity of the organisation. It sustained the case for medicare – which in the end the Social Security Administration came to administer.

Another example of the use of research strategy as part of an informal planning process was the publication of regular surveys of the aged. They were used over and over again in Congress and by the Advisory Councils. Indeed their timing was geared to successive Advisory Councils and likely Congressional consideration of the need to increase benefits. Research on the extent of disability and wage loss from disability began in the mid 1940s or even earlier. They played a part in educating opinion though it took time. It was not until 1956 that benefits were provided for disabled workers aged 50–64. The age limit was removed in 1960 and the programme has been an important one ever since. This strategy does not always produce results of course. It seemed obvious to many in the organisation in the early sixties that there were still gaps in the disability programme and that within five or six years there would be more legislative pressure to extend the programme.

Given the resources that were available at the time a decision had to be taken whether to go for a survey of the disabled or for a survey on 'survivors', widows mainly, and other single parent families; the decision favoured the disabled. The design of the survey took a long time mainly because of the need to get agreement with other agencies. It was not launched until 1966 and in the event 'disability' went off the boil politically, whereas 'single parent families' boiled over. The 1971 Advisory Council returned to the theme of disability and made some concrete proposals on which it was hoped legislation would follow.

All of these examples indicate that long before 1965 the Social Security Administration had evolved a planning strategy which in Chapter 2 we categorised as 'an informal promotional planning process'. It was no less effective by virtue of not being centred on some complicated set of documents which fed into some kind of 'system'. Indeed much of its effectiveness sprang from the fact that it was not formalised – hence the suspicion which many of its participants shared of the attempts to promote systematic formal planning. Its Commissioner and his staff already knew more or less where they wanted the agency to be heading in the next five years even though there had never been a formal five-year plan.

The Systems Approach

In comparison with this experience many of the other agencies were either small or new or both and none had a significant policy research base. The major innovation following the Johnson PPB 'dictat' was therefore the creation of an analytical team in the Office of the Secretary under an Assistant Secretary for Program Coordination, William Gorham. This office initiated three new developments. The first was the attempt to create a program structure, or output budget of the now familiar kind, which sought to specify objectives and produce output indicators over the whole of HEW's range of responsibilities. What this meant in practice is discussed in a later chapter. The second major activity and one which gained the most notice outside the department was the mounting of a relatively small number of detailed studies, designed to illuminate budget priorities.[20] These were, in the first instance, attempts to apply cost/benefit analysis to particular health and education programmes. They were therefore relatively novel in approach though the subject matter seems to have been chosen more with an eye to illustrating the possibilities of the analytic method than the strategic importance of the programmes that were considered. For example, the programme analyses undertaken in 1966 covered four programme areas – disease control, human investment (i.e. education and training), maternal and child health, and various strategies for income maintenance.[21] The disease control studies concentrated on five topics: motor vehicles passenger injury prevention, cancer, arthritis, syphilis and tuberculosis. The resulting documents pulled together what was known about prevention and treatment and the possible success rates of different strategies. They ended up with estimates of 'cost per death averted'. Some of the documents were substantial pieces of work. They were undertaken with the technical advice of outsiders – e.g. doctors as well as economists. The first, on prevention of motor accidents, came to over 180 pages and explored the costs and benefits of eight different ways of reducing injuries.[22] A final document compared the relative benefits that might be gained from each of the disease control programmes.[23] The maximum return, it was concluded, lay in getting people to use seat belts!

One of the most interesting documents was the paper on child health which compared the costs of seeking to find and treat handicapped children in poor areas.[24] Yet as Alice Rivlin later commented:

'It uncovered more questions than answers. I remember being

astonished when we first started that study that doctors could produce no evidence that children who saw their doctors regularly were healthier than children who did not.'[25]

The attempts to obtain rate of return figures for the education programmes did not get very far. Six years later the same office was still grappling with the problems of measuring the impact of the compensatory programmes. However, the office had begun by seeking to follow the injunctions of the BOB guidelines and the hopes of the original reformers by seeking to compare at least a few of the potential and existing programmes in cost/benefit terms. Yet they were operating on only a small fraction of the Budget. A similar set of studies were undertaken the following year.

In 1967 this section of the Secretary's Office was given a new title, it was now to be responsible for 'Planning and Evaluation' which implied a rather more positive conception of its role than mere 'coordination'. The Assistant Secretary in charge until March 1969 was Alice Rivlin, an economist, who came from and returned to the Brookings Institution. In her evidence to the congressional committee she outlined the main achievements of these years as she saw them. First, instead of a single programme budget related to one set of 'objectives' the office developed several analyses of the budget by population group served, by the source of finance, by type of activity and so on. They were able to illustrate in fairly simple terms where the money was going from as many perspectives as possible. This brought to the Secretary's notice trends he might have otherwise missed. She illustrated the point in the following way:

'In my opinion, the greatest impact of the program information system has been in facilitating some simple calculations at high levels of aggregation. My favourite example is Secretary Cohen's astonishment at a table showing that most of the Department's recent budget increases had been devoted to older people and relatively little to children. Why the father of Medicare should have been surprised at this, I do not know, but he was; and he immediately began talking about a new emphasis on programs for children.'[26]

The office began, and indeed continued, to obtain some measures of 'output' for the various programmes, but for reasons we shall discuss later it moved on to lay stress on deeper 'evaluations' of programme activities. It was from this office, at that time, that the proposal came to get Congress to authorise a proportion (0·5–1 per cent) of education and health programme expenditure – to undertake 'program evaluation' studies.[27] This was a significant achievement on its own and even though the actual permission to spend only came through slowly, these authorisations laid the foundation for the substantial evaluation activity of the early 1970s.

The office also began, as a rather separate exercise, the first attempt to produce a set of social indicators. The result, *Toward a Social Report*,[28] was a kind of state of the nation report on social conditions and helped to stimulate the work in Britain that produced the first issue of *Social Trends* over a year later.[29]

Finally, there was the attempt to establish a planning cycle, in which the information and analysis that had been generated could be brought to bear at the right moment. Despite the fact that the BOB withdrew its insistence on each agency presenting longer term expenditure estimates, HEW sought to present full five-year costed plans beginning with fiscal years 1968 and 1969. The planning office instituted a procedure in which the Secretary met with his advisers and heads of different sub-agencies to consider how the resources of the Department might be deployed over the next five years. Decisions were made in the spring or early summer which were to be translated into budgetary and legislative decisions in the autumn. At least, this is what was supposed to happen. But a number of factors tended to throw the timetable out. The original strategic choices were delayed. Detailed proposals and plans had to come in the first place from the separate agencies within HEW before a discussion on cash priorities could take place. These proposals were often late and discussion about the current budget in the autumn then swamped the longer term considerations. Then White House 'task forces' tended to produce their suggestions for legislation in the period just before Christmas upsetting any forward planning HEW itself had been able to do based on its own legislative plans.

The next phase in the HEW planning system was virtually a 'stand at ease' period, but it teaches an important lesson. The new Secretary for Health and Welfare, Robert Finch, gave up in 1970 without making much impact. The planning process largely lapsed in this period. Its importance depends much on the personality of the Secretary and the extent to which he wants it to be a positive force. This point is reinforced in the next two years. Finch was replaced by Elliot Richardson. He was very much the 'managerial man'. He thrived on memoranda and 'issue papers'. It was he who revived the planning apparatus. He invited a former Department of Defense analyst, Laurence Lynn, to head the planning and evaluation activity in his office. Management consultants were brought in and partly as a result of them and partly as a result of the advice of staff who had experienced some of the previous frustrations an elaborate new information and planning system was introduced. It is discussed in more detail later. Here it is sufficient to note that it was a determined effort to get the subordinate agencies more under the Secretary's control. One of the very few tools the Secretary possessed was control over budget submissions to the Office of Management and Budget. Hence the system turned essentially on that fact. It abandoned the PPB emphasis on programme structures and indicators. It was designed instead to ensure that the Secretary had determined his priorities and had considerable analytical work already completed before the point in time at which the OMB sent down its 'guidelines' in July and before the round of intense budget bargaining which takes place in the Autumn. The process was entitled *The Master Calendar* to emphasise the importance of timing. The planning process began nearly a year before the guidelines arrived when meetings were to be held in the agencies and then between the agencies and the central planning staff to determine what key issues would require to be discussed the following summer. In other words the planning process for the budget which took effect in July 1974* began in July 1972, two years previously (see Table 6.2). Much earlier it should be noted than in the original

Table 6.2 *The HEW Master Calendar*

Identification of issues for analysis (1 August–20 September)
    Agencies, and the various assistant secretaries for planning and evaluation and the Regional Offices identify major issues facing their agency and the department in the next three years.
    The Assistant Secretary for Planning and Evaluation consolidates these issues, produces briefs and passes them on to the Secretary.

Analysis Agenda (20 September)
    Specific areas for detailed analysis are agreed by the Secretary of the agencies.
    The Planning and Evaluation staff in the Secretary's office agree who is to undertake the analyses and within what time tables.

Regional Memoranda (1 November)
    Regional Office submit memoranda which explain major problems facing each region.

Strategy Discussion (Through November)
    Major strategic issues facing the Department discussed on the basis of agency and regional memoranda.

* The Americans confusingly call this the Budget for 1975.

Planning Guidance Memoranda (15 February)

The Planning Office gives guidelines on budget targets over the next four years and summarises the priorities which emerged from autumn meetings. On this basis the agencies draw up a Forward Plan for the next fiscal year plus four succeeding years. This includes plans for legislation and its cost implications as well as expenditure associated with current legislation.

Evaluation and Research Plans (15 April)

Agencies submit their evaluation plans for the next financial year – which research projects they will commission on what aspects of their programmes. The appropriate section of the Planning and Evaluation Office comments on the priorities and adds proposals and adds its own. (Final Evaluation Plans prepared for 1 July.)

Agency Policy and Programme Alternatives (15 May)

The Agencies' Forward Plans are received and modified in the light of any new developments.

Over-view and Programme Memoranda Discussed (June)

The agency proposals are put together in groups related to the programme structure. For example, all the health related agency programmes are considered in one programme document prepared by the planning staff. Major alternatives assessed.

There then follows discussions between the Secretary, agency heads and their planning staffs on the Forward Plans and the planning staffs document.

Budget Ceiling arrives from OMB (July).

Detailed discussions with agencies and the OMB on the budget for the next financial year (October–December).

President's Budget presented in Congress (January).

Congressional discussions (February–August or longer).

cycle designed in 1967–8. The work on these 'issue papers' continued from September through to May if necessary. Some were undertaken in the agencies, some largely in the Secretary's planning office, many jointly, but someone in the Secretary's office was responsible for keeping an oversight on each.

In November the Secretary had 'strategy' discussions with the heads of the agencies determining his priorities, legislative priorities that would bear upon the budget – still over a year away.

In the following February planning guidance was sent out by the

Secretary's planning office to each of the agencies. In 1972 the guidance indicated expenditure targets for each agency not merely for Fiscal Year 1974, but for the four subsequent years. 'Guidelines' are crucial to any planning process. How were they arrived at? The Department's budget planners analysed trends in previous budgets both in terms of the rising percentage they represented of the Federal budget and of the Gross National Product. Both shares had increased sharply since 1965. They took the rising share of GNP as the crucial predictor and extrapolated the 1965–73 trend. In the first year of that series, 1965, the Department's budget had formed 3·5 per cent of GNP. By 1973 it had risen to 6·5 per cent.[30] The planners therefore assumed that it was reasonable to expect their budget would amount to about 7 per cent of national output in 1974 and rise to about 7·9 per cent in Fiscal Year 1978. By combining the projected share of the GNP with forecasts of economic growth they gained a figure for the total resources available to the Department. This was then divided between the separate agencies. Special account had to be taken of the important bills pending in Congress at the time – the social security changes and the Family Assistance Plan – but apart from that it was assumed that each agency could plan to keep its share of the rising budget. A high and a low target was set to permit each agency to show items it could cut or add to the basic plan.

This procedure is interesting from a British point of view for three reasons. It is significant that the budget planners had to go through this kind of exercise at all. As we shall see in the next chapter, the limits within which a British department has to plan are pretty well understood. The basic economic parameters are clear from regular experience of the Treasury's PESC negotiations, and the figuring derives from the Treasury. The rules of the game are now well known. The second interesting feature is the optimistic outcome of the assumptions that were used. The expenditure control procedure in Britain has been aimed at stablising the share of the GNP taken by public expenditure overall and even social service departments have recently had to accept that they cannot be exceptions to that rule without making an exceptionally strong-case. HEW was assuming that it was possible to plan on the basis of gaining a rapidly rising share of the GNP. It is a specific illustration of the different economic constraints we described in Chapter 3. The third feature that strikes a British observer is the relatively unsophisticated, even crude procedures, that were adopted in arriving at the various planning totals, not only in the targets but the eventual submissions. Nowhere to be found were the complex assumptions about the factors likely to affect unit costs or relative prices. Indeed for the most part it was difficult to discern what price assumptions were being made. This is not a reflection on the professional expertise of the participants. It does reflect the tougher constraints on the bargaining process on this side of the Atlantic. In Britain even small differences in the statistical forecasting assumptions used can make all the difference between having a new programme accepted or having an old one cut. So they will be argued at length and in detail.

These, then, were the expenditure guidelines to which the Forward Plans of each agency were supposed to be geared. The Plan itself should begin by describing programme trends, population trends, need and political pressures, assessing gaps and estimating what expenditure would be required to meet existing legislation. Plans then had to list possible additions or developments beyond the target set and possible priority cuts. Where any major new developments were planned a separate detailed justification was required. These Plans together with the specialised studies mentioned earlier were to arrive in the Secretary's office in their final version in May. It is at this point that the planning staff in the Secretary's office undertake their major role in the process. Their task is to identify alternatives on the basis of which 'trade offs' can be made when the OMB ceilings arrive. These are normally less than the agencies have asked for and it is this margin that gives the Secretary's office its power. A paper is prepared for each major group of programmes: one on health programmes, one on income maintenance, one on education. A section of the planning and evaluation office is responsible for each broad area. The income maintenance section alone contained 17 people at the end of 1972. The total size of the planning staff in Lynn's office had reached about 100.

Each of these overview papers which were prepared by the Secretary's own planning staff and the Forward Plans of the agencies were considered at a series of meetings attended by the heads of the agencies and their planning staffs, Richardson, his planning staff and the Comptroller, who was directly responsible for the budget. The meetings themselves were not of central importance, the key fact was that the Secretary had obtained a body of information, proposals and alternatives that would be helpful in making decisions about how to conduct the autumn budget round.

Clearly if all this had worked as intended there would have emerged a very centralised planning and management system. Needless to say it did not work like this, or only to a very limited degree so far as an outsider could see.

In the first place the priority issues had to be decided a long way ahead which required considerable skill as a political crystal gazer. Secondly, the agencies retained their political independence, their own constituencies and their links with Congress which have already been described. No systematic planning exercise could alter that. This basic political independence was reinforced by each agency building up its own analytical teams or planning and evaluation sections. The Social Security Administration already had the basic research capacity and a considerable accumulation of knowledge and expertise on its programmes which was a powerful force in its own right. In response to the new planning procedures it developed a method channelling the work of its research and statistics group into the Secretary's Forward Planning mechanism. Discussing their contribution to the 1973 budget round Lynn is reported to have said:

'SSA has easily the most competent research and analysis staff of HEW's agencies. It is fair to say that because of the quality of the operation the Secretary's office has not been able to lay a hand on SSA'.[31]

In the same way during 1970–72 the Office of Education built up a larger and more effective Planning and Evaluation Section.

In the third place the greater part of HEW's budget funds were pre-empted by previous legislation. They were 'uncontrollable' as the jargon put it. There are the social security programmes based on accumulated 'rights' to benefit and the open-ended commitments to those qualifying for Welfare. HEW is particularly unfortunate, looked at from the planner's point of view, in having so many matching grants and grant formulas, which tie it down to paying so much per dollar spent by the state or some other local agency. The central government in Britain, even in the days of the percentage grant, always had the power to approve first the total expenditure on which it was giving grants. It thus had the final say on the total grant.

The response from the various agencies to this new process was mixed. Some appeared not to have taken it seriously at all in the first two years leading up to the 1973 and 1974 budgets but were beginning to do so in the next round of discussions. The National Institutes of Health had stoutly maintained the irrelevance of the whole procedure and had kept out of the planning system as much as possible. They appeared to rely on Congress to put back any cuts made by the rest of the administration. The planning staff denied that analysis could throw any light on priorities between research projects or justify the total scale of funding. This depended firstly on how many good research workers or promising research areas there were and this could only be judged by fellow academics. Secondly, it depended on what Congress was prepared to pay. In contrast, the Office of Education had used the new planning time-table to give its senior staff the chance to discuss the Office's priorities and long term strategy.

The original idea of asking all agencies to produce plans that met two overall objectives for the Department fell flat. The two object-ives chosen, 'reducing dependency' and 'institutional reform' had been so general that almost anything could go under either and when it came to the point there was no hard evidence on the extent to which programmes did actually reduce dependency. The National Institutes of Health, for example, could argue that all medical research may ultimately be directed at reducing disease and therefore dependency.

All in all the shift towards centralised decision-making within HEW was probably not great, but by 1972 the *nature* of the inter-agency bargaining had changed. The battles were more explicitly about programmes and what they had achieved or could be ex-pected to achieve. Perhaps one of the most valuable parts of the process was the selection of topics for special analysis rather like the programme analysis and review procedure in Whitehall (see chapter 7). For example, studies undertaken from autumn 1972 to summer 1973 on income security included work on the impact of different benefit formulas, and the kind of criteria that could be used for determining 'replacement rates', i.e. the relationship of benefits to previous earnings. The content of these studies indicated the extensiveness of the basic survey material available and the pre-vious work done by the Social Security staff.

How successful was the Secretary's Office in its attempt to impose its priorities on the whole departmental budget? As it turned out the planners had made a pretty good guess at HEW's share of the President's budget. They had produced a basic target for Fiscal Year 1974 of $93,000 million, with a high estimate of $94,500. In fact, the figure turned out to be nearly $94,000 million. The share taken by HEW was 35 per cent of the President's budget compared to 33 per cent the year before, again more or less on trend.[32] Yet the composition was not what had been expected a year before. The Food and Drugs Administration, the Health Service and Mental

Health Administration, the National Institutes of Health and the Office of Education were all well below forecast, the Social and Rehabilitation Service responsible for welfare and the social service programmes, and the Social Security Administration were well up, especially the latter. The reason for both lay in the outcome of legislation during 1972.

It is to the legislative process that we must now turn, for the President's budget is only the first part of the story. It is the very uncertainty about the outcome of legislation that makes long-term planning *within* the Department so difficult. Congress' role is still crucial especially where new legislation is being considered; the White House too can play a maverick role. The 1973 and 1974 budgets of HEW were cases in point. Both were affected by the outcome of the 1972 Congressional process.

The Impact of Congress on Planning

In 1972 problems arose in the four major areas for which HEW was responsible. A major piece of legislation was being considered by the Senate Finance Committee. The bill, already passed by the House of Representatives in 1971 (HRI as it was called), incorporated both a major package designed to 'reform the welfare system', to increase social security benefits by 5 per cent, and tie future benefits to the cost of living as well as a host of important detailed changes in social security law.

The administration's welfare reform plans provided for a guaranteed minimum income met out of Federal funds whether the head of household was working or not. The proposal had first been made by President Nixon in 1969 and had already been thrown out once before by the Senate Finance Committee in 1970. The Chairman of the Committee was bitterly opposed to a measure he felt would reduce work effort. Once again in 1972 the Committee, having sat on the bill for 14 months, dropped that part of the package which aimed at guaranteeing the incomes of the working poor and of single parent families with dependent children, while the more 'deserving' poor, the aged, the blind and the disabled, were more favoured. The 'adult assistance' programme under which they would receive the equivalent of supplementary benefits from the Social Security Administration survived. Even so, the question of who would administer the benefit remained in doubt until the last moment.

By June 1972 it was clear that welfare reform would be rejected by the Finance Committee and that the only way to save it was to create a coalition of left of centre Senators. Those in HEW who had been planning the reform package entered into negotiations with Senator Ribicoff – a Democrat – to prepare a more generous version of that part of HRI which incorporated the family assistance provisions. Richardson, Secretary of HEW, then tried to persuade the President that the only way to keep welfare reform alive was for him to support the compromise his department had worked out with Ribicoff. A few days before the meeting with the President, Richardson evidently asked a liberal republican Senator to get some of his colleagues to urge the President to adopt this plan.[33] When it came to the point, however, the President refused to back the compromise. His advisers in the White House on domestic policy were opposed to it. It could upset the conservative Republicans on the Finance Committee whose votes the President needed on other matters. Moreover the whole issue of welfare reform seemed now to be a political liability, especially since McGovern's similar plan had been attacked. Indeed, by the time the Bill was discussed on the Senate floor the President intimated to the Press that he would not be sorry to see it killed.[34] This episode illustrates the difficulty any administration has in planning ahead beyond one year and it illustrates the extraordinary complex power situation. It is further illustrated by what happened to the proposed social security benefit increases. The budget, as it was presented to Congress, and the relevant sections of HRI, proposed a 5 per cent flat rate increase. Since HRI had passed through the House of Representatives the Advisory Council on Social Security had strongly recommended that the Trust Funds formally abandon any notion of 'funding' (building up large balances to finance future pensions), and instead merely operate on a 'pay as you go' basis,[35] so that the social security tax together with other income would just meet current outgoings. In practice this is what had tended to happen already, but its explicit recognition would make unnecessary tax increases proposed in the bill and could have justified a reduction. Alternatively they could be used to give a much larger benefit increase. In fact the Secretary of HEW took the view that the 5 per cent limit should be retained. Priority should go to welfare reform. Nevertheless, the Chairman of the House Ways and Means Committee proposed using the potential surplus to raise benefits by 20 per cent. This proposal was removed from the main legislation and enacted early so that the benefits could be distributed prior to the election.

Knowing the close historical ties between the Social Security Administration, especially its Commissioner Robert Ball, and the Chairman of the Ways and Means Committee, it was generally taken that Ball was happy with this outcome. Indeed some people went so far as to say that the Social Security Administration had 'busted' the Department's budget. This irritation was only increased by the knowledge that in the previous year something similar had happened. Prior to the White House Conference on Ageing,[36] some Democrats, in particular Senator Edward Kennedy, had used the general public interest that had been aroused as background support for a bill authorising the creation of a nutrition programme for the elderly, which the Administration had opposed. President Nixon, in order to wrest the political credit from Kennedy, proposed to increase the budget of the Administration on Ageing fivefold, but in addition other initiatives from the Social Security Administration which were presented at the Conference were legislated though they had not originally featured in the HEW budget.

Social service provision was another part of the budget to present major difficulties. The services are provided by state public assistance departments – and include social work help, family planning clinics, services to secure financial maintenance for deserted mothers or to establish paternity, foster care, day care and anything which could be said to 'strengthen family life' (see Chapter 4).

The scope of these services was expanded and eligibility was extended to former and potential, as well as to existing, welfare recipients in legislation between 1956 and 1967. In the latter year state welfare agencies were given power to purchase services from other private or public agencies. The Federal Government met 75 per cent of the costs of these services. States, led by California and Illinois, managed to put more and more services under this heading thus attracting more Federal money. In 1969 HEW grants amounted to $350 million. By 1971 the total was $750 million. Then in 1972 the figure rose to $1,300 million. The budget contained an estimate of $1,241 million but as the year passed more and more requests from states pushed the estimate up to well over $2,000 million. In 1970 and 1971 HEW sought to get an upper limit imposed by Congress on the total funds that could be dispensed, but Congress under pressure from state Governors and Mayors as well as local constituents refused. It was not until 1972 that Congress finally fixed a limit at $2,500 million. Thus a very small programme had become a large one almost overnight. It was clear that Congress frustrated the administration's attempts to control the programme.

As Richardson was reported as saying:

'It's frustrating, indeed exasperating, to sweat over the budget and see this open ended matching program absorb funds in a manner unrelated to our attempts to establish priorities.'[37]

In the education and health fields too, changes proposed by the administration failed to get past Congress. The aim was to consolidate 30 or so separate education grants into one 'revenue sharing' bill with five elements, aid for the disadvantaged, the handicapped, schools affected by Federal activities, vocational education, and help in purchasing material of certain kinds. Congress would have none of it. The chairman of the Appropriations Sub-Committee seized on the fact that 'the only increase you are representing in this entire appropriation is $10 million for strengthening State departments of education'. Under questioning the Office of Education witnesses admitted that this was to make the State departments capable of handling the administration of these more general grants. That proved they were not ready this year, the chairman maintained.

'You can't do it this year. If they are not ready this year, then you can't have a revenue sharing bill. You have just proved it, and I warned you – you both went on the attack, now you have got your pants down around your ankles, and you can't give revenue sharing to the States this year'.[38]

Even more speculative were the administration's health proposals. Basically these would have meant compulsory private health insurance for those at work and special coverage for low income families. A number of other health insurance bills were before Congress at the same time promoted by Congressmen – notably the far-reaching Kennedy-Griffith plan for universal national health insurance. None of these were enacted. Thus the eventual appropriations legislation failed to include many items in the original Budget presented to Congress and did include items the President's Budget did not. This one year's experience merely illustrates Congress's continued power in resource allocation, particularly where new legislation is concerned. It also illustrates the existence of many centres of power within the administration as well as outside it. Even with on going programmes Congress shows its independence. Congress has consistently been more generous to the National Institutes of Health, the Social Security Administration and the Office of Education than the Bureau of the Budget or its successor have proposed. Within these broad areas too priorities of congressmen have been different from the agency concerned.

The inability of the administration to be sure what Congress will do with its proposed legislation and its budget has an impact on any attempt by the agencies to plan ahead. One member of a planning staff argued, 'We still have a responsibility to present a budget we believe represents the right priorities for the Department whatever Congress does with it.' In practice, such a neat division as is implied by that remark between the 'rational' Department and the 'disjointed Congress' will not do.

Table 6.3 *An Example of Congressional impact on the Budget: Elementary and Secondary Education 1963–72*

Year	Budget Estimate put to Congress $	House Allowance $	Senate Allowance $	Final Appropriation $
1963	16,700,000	16,700,000	16,700,000	16,700,000
1964	19,035,000	18,285,000	18,285,000	18,285,000
1965	25,800,000	25,800,000	25,800,000	25,800,000
1966	1,411,434,000	1,083,250,000	1,083,250,000	1,083,250,000
1967	1,269,660,000	1,269,660,000	1,269,660,000	1,242,660,000
1968	1,444,250,000	1,494,250,000	1,494,250,000	1,433,126,000
1969	1,448,163,000	1,280,753,000	1,402,626,000	1,334,753,000
1970	1,384,143,000	1,608,601,000	1,608,601,000	1,499,643,000
1971	1,489,193,000	1,667,143,000	1,684,143,000	1,673,143,000
1972	1,676,343,000	1,676,393,000	1,838,393,000	1,744,343,000

NOTE
In two early years before the programme became as large as it is now the estimate was let through unchanged. But in only one year – the first after the new act, have the changes been really big, for the rest the eventual outcome has been within 10 per cent of the original estimate. Larger cuts or additions occur in the House or the Senate but are then evened out in conference.

Source: House of Representatives Labour HEW hearings, Part 2, p. 266.

In the first place as we have implied the horizontal lines of power and influence between agency and congressional committee mean that an agency that wishes to maximise its budget has to play a dual game. It can play its cards in the inter-agency game in such a way that it gets Presidential backing for the items least likely to gain Congressional favour, but hope that the Congress will increase other programmes. The end of the game is not the President's budget message but the final act of Congress. Those agencies who have little support in Congress must play the formal planning game for all they are worth – argument and analysis are their only weapons. More powerful agencies need to bother less at that stage. This probably explains in part the different degrees of seriousness with which the various agencies in HEW seemed to take their planning activities and budget justifications for the 1974 budget.

In the second place the uncertainty about Congress's response meant that complex and detailed projections of Forward Plans were difficult for many of the participants to take seriously.

In Brief

We have described the original high-optimism which accompanied the attempts to introduce an element of systematic strategic planning into the Federal budget process.

The large claims may have been necessary for the changes to achieve any impact at all, but they were in consequence followed by a period of pessimism and disillusion. Many argued that it was disastrous to attempt to force policy analysis into a necessarily rushed budget timetable and various proposals were made for separating the two activities – policy analysis and budgeting. HEW had also identified timing as an important issue, but many of the planners in that agency were convinced that the budget had to remain the major planning tool; it was the strongest – or almost the only – one the Secretary possessed. They sought to resolve the problem by extending the time scale of the planning cycle so that it began a whole year before the intense round of budget negotiations between the OMB, the Secretary's office and the constituent organisations within HEW. By the time these began it was hoped that issues and priorities would have been clarified by the preparation of special studies and forward plans. These were finished and discussed with the Secretary in the summer. He would then have an information base on which to decide his budget tactics in the autumn. The aim was to tie future legislative plans and research and evaluation activity to the budget cycle. It was the uncertainty about new legislation and Congress's role in it and the budget process which made it so difficult to produce and stick to a long-term strategy. Nevertheless, the new system was succeeding in introducing more informed discussion about expenditure priorities. This worked most successfully where the specialist groups producing the issue papers could draw upon basic on going research and evaluation studies. In short, HEW went for a 'crosswalk' system of combining analysis with the budget cycle but in an extended cycle. Long before these formal planning systems had been instituted HEW's largest component – the Social Security Administration – had been operating an informal planning procedure that worked through regular Advisory Councils. It continued to work alongside and indeed in competition with the formal planning cycle. It was much more explicitly geared to influencing

H

the Congress and it too had relied for much of its effectiveness on a long-term research strategy. This is one clear lesson to draw from the HEW experience.

In the second place the HEW experience illustrates that it was the use of analysis at the appropriate time that affected decisions rather than the shape of the budget structure. Analysing and presenting the budget documents in different ways was only one form of analysis among many others and probably less important than many.

Thirdly, the HEW case illustrates the limitations of relying on the budget process alone. Precisely because the main emphasis even in 1972 was the current budget, long-term legislative planning still did not fit in very effectively. Most participants firmly claimed that what they were doing was participating in incremental budgeting. Yet, as we have seen, some very big 'increments' came about in the period between 1965 and 1974. They constituted wholly new departures – Medicare, Medicaid, federal support for secondary education, a federal public assistance programme. The flexible legislative time scale and congressional independence made the budget calendar approach, with its hard deadlines for analysis and forward plans, difficult to tie in with the highly uncertain outcome of legislation. Thus the precise problem identified by the Plowden Committee in Britain in 1961 remained largely unsolved.

Finally, HEW experience illustrates both the virtues and drawbacks of a pluralist planning system. Competition between the centre and the sub-agencies, between them and the OMB and Congress became more informed. In order not to lose out in the balance of power an increase in analytical capacity by one competitor tended to be matched by another. If the outcome did not dramatically change the power structure it was beginning to change the nature of debate and increase knowledge about how the programmes operated or failed to operate, what the issues were and what the major areas of ignorance were. Moreover, this knowledge was being diffused. It was in the interests of the competitors to diffuse it. Hence staff working for the appropriate specialist committees and the staff of congressmen who were specialising in these areas could be and were informed about the work that was going on.

On the other hand the very plurality of the process detracted from the likelihood that any forward plan could be kept to. Often projections made at one point in time would be made irrelevant by some other competitor in the process. If there is little pay off from looking ahead, busy staff and capable researchers are not going to waste their time on it even if they are forced to produce pieces of paper purporting to have 'looked ahead'.

The last word may be left with Richardson:

'It is important to have fully and clearly in view the limitations of a purely rational process for allocating resources. What we need to do in substance is to make the decision process – the difficult choices among competing claims – as conscious and articulate as possible while recognising at the same time that in the end feelings, attitudes, values must have ultimate and controlling weight'.[39]

REFERENCES

1 Schick, A., 'The Road to PPB', *Public Administration Review*, Vol. 26, No. 4, December, 1966.
2 Hitch, C. J., *Decision-Making for Defense*, University of California Press, Berkeley, 1965.
3 Novick, D., 'The Department of Defense' in *Program Budgeting*, Ed. D. Novick, op cit. Enthoven, A., 'The PPBS in the Department of Defense: some lessons from experience' in Vol. 3 of *The Analysis and Evaluation of Public Expenditures: The PPB System*, a compendium of papers submitted to a sub-committee of the Joint Economic Committee of Congress, 91st Congress. In the same volume see the paper by A. C. Enthoven and K. Wayne Smith: 'The PPBS in the Department of Defense: Current status and next steps'.
4 See Chapter 2. pp. 18–19.
5 Schick, A., 'Systems Politics and Systems Budgeting', *Public Administration Review*, Vol. 29, No. 2, 1969.
6 *New York Times*, 26 August, 1965 (quoted in Novick).
7 Joint Economic Committee papers, Vol. 2, p. 636.
8 Ibid., p. 637.
9 Bureau of the Budget Bulletin, 68–9.
10 Ibid.
11 A summary of the Committee papers was published as a volume edited by R. Haveman and J. Margolis, *Public Expenditures and Policy Analysis*, Markham, Chicago, 1970.
12 Joint Economic Committee Papers, Vol. 3, pp. 805–814.
13 Ibid, Vol. 3, p. 819.
14 Ibid, p. 847.
15 A Report of an Advisory Group on the Social Security Administration Research Program, a review prepared by B. Bernstein, Fall 1960.
16 This journal was first published in 1938.
17 Social Security Administration, Washington, 1965.
18 Quoted in E. Feingold, *Medicare Policy and Politics*, Chandler Publishing Co., San Francisco, 1966.
19 *Social Security Bulletin*, January-February, 1950, July, 1950, October 1957, August, 1964. Also see Feingold.

20 Gorham, W., Evidence to Joint Economic Committee, Subcommittee on Economy in Government, Hearings, 14 September, 1967.
21 Drew, E., 'HEW grapples with PPBS', *The Public Interest*, Summer, 1967.
22 HEW Office of Program Coordination, Program Analysis 1966–1.
23 HEW Office of Program Coordination, Program Analysis 1966–5.
24 HEW Office of Program Coordination Program Analysis 1966–6. Reproduced as an annex to Gorham's evidence as an example of PPB at work.
25 Joint Economic Committee Papers 1969, op. cit., p. 917.
26 Ibid., Vol. 3, p. 911.
27 See Chapter 9.
28 *Toward a Social Report*, Department of Health, Education and Welfare, Government Printing Office, Washington, 1969.
29 *Social Trends*, no. 1, 1970, Central Statistical Office, HMSO, 1970.
30 Planning Guidance Memorandum, 1972, HEW, February, 1972.
31 *National Journal*, January 29, 1972, p. 180.
32 *The Budget of the United States Government, Fiscal Year 1974.*
33 *National Journal*, 5 August, 1972, pp. 1245–57.
34 *Washington Post*, 6 October, 1972.
35 *Social Security Advisory Council 1971.*
36 *National Journal*, 29 January, 1972, p. 173.
37 *National Journal*, 17 July, 1972, pp. 1007–14.
38 House of Representatives Labour HEW Appropriations Committee Hearings for 1973, Part 2, p. 174.
39 *National Journal*, 29 January, 1972, p. 180.

Further Reading

Haveman, R. H., and Margolis, J., *Public Expenditures and Policy Analysis*, Markham, Chicago, 1970.
(An edited version of the papers submitted to the Joint Economic Committee of Congress in 1969).
Moynihan, D. P., *The Politics of a Guaranteed Income*, Vintage Books, New York, 1973.
(An account by a participant with very decided views, on the fate of the Family Assistance Plan and the subsequent legislation referred to in this chapter.)

Chapter 7

Forward Planning — UK Style

In Britain, as in America, the introduction of a government-wide system of public expenditure control has had profound consequences for the planning of individual social services. Despite some similarities both in conception and timing the new system of expenditure control in Britain differed from the American in several important respects. In the first place the Johnson Administration was pursuing a strongly interventionist strategy and the new planning system was perceived as part of that approach. Secondly, its advocates pressed for the sudden, sweeping introduction of a highly formalised system throughout government. Thirdly, considerable stress was laid on the role which social sciences and economics in particular could play in illuminating choices between different courses of action. Finally, the early optimism soon gave way to a good deal of disillusion and the adoption of a more piecemeal approach. In contrast, in Britain the reforms shared none of these characteristics. They were largely prompted by a desire to constrain the growth of government. They were introduced in a gradual way, with very little publicity or political bally-hoo, and have evolved gradually and continuously ever since. Initially they laid very little emphasis on the role of analysis in determining choices or indeed on the process of *choice* at all. However, as time went on a more American emphasis was introduced and the two traditions drew closer together. Finally, as the system evolved, larger claims were made for it, its inventors and practitioners as well as independent commentators have come to praise and publicise its achievements. It is worth briefly developing these contrasts before asking whether the achievements are indeed as great as has been claimed. The last part of the chapter concentrates on the impact the system has had on social service planning.

Containing Growth

The origins of the new system of public expenditure control lie in the frustrations experienced by the Treasury and its Ministers in the late 1950s. Earlier in that decade the Conservative Government had managed to contain the growth of public expenditure. Indeed, in real terms, it had been allowed to grow at less than one half of a per cent a year between 1952 and 1958. As a proportion of the Gross National Product it had fallen steadily from 47·0 per cent in 1952 to 41·6 per cent in 1958. See Table 7.4. Excluding transfers there had been no increase in the actual resources devoted to the state sector in this period.[1] As a consequence the Conservatives had been able to reduce taxation steadily throughout the period. How had this been achieved? The main contribution had been the run-down in Military expenditure following the end of the Korean War, but the social services had played an important part too. From the beginning of the period the National Health Service was held sharply in check and took a declining share of the GNP until the middle of the

Table 7.1   *Growth Rates in Public Expenditure in the UK – 1952–74. Annual Average rates of Increase – per cent*

	1952–8	1958–60	1960–5	1965–8	1968–70	1970–74
Social Services						
Education	6·0	6·3	8·1	6·9	2·6	5·9
National Health Service	2·3	7·0	4·8	8·4	4·7	
Local Welfare Services	3·5	12·1	10·0	10·4	3·4	6·4
Child Care	2·5	0·0	7·9	10·1	2·9	
School meals, milk and welfare foods	—3·2	2·6	5·2	2·3	—0·3	—
Social Security Benefits	5·1	3·5	6·5	7·1	1·9	4·7
Total Social Services	4·3	5·1	6·6	6·6	2·7	5·5
Housing	—6·4	7·1	10·7	2·2	—2·6	20·7
Total Housing and Environment	—3·6	6·7	9·9	4·3	0·0	15·3
Military Defence	—3·6	2·2	2·3	0·5	—5·2	1·6
Total Public Expenditure	0·4	4·6	5·2	5·2	0·1	6·5

Sources; Sir Samuel Goldman *Public Expenditure, Management and Control* Table Aii and *Public Expenditure to 1978–9* (Cmnd 5879).
    Constant prices with relative price effect attributed. The 1970–74 figures are for Great Britain.

decade,[2] council house subsidies were substantially reduced, and local authorities were confined to the residual and, as it was thought, temporary role of slum clearance just as they had been in the 1930s.[3] A series of restrictions were imposed on local authority spending,[4] and the percentage grants system for local services was replaced in 1958 by a General Grant, the purpose being to instil a more 'responsible' attitude to spending on the part of local councils and so check the rising demands on the national exchequer.[5] Food subsidies had been abolished and family allowances were allowed to decline in purchasing power. The 1959 Graduated Pension Scheme was essentially an attempt to gain larger graduated contributions and reduce the expected contribution from general taxation.[6] So much of the government's social policy was designed to reduce or contain the growth of government expenditure and, at least until 1957, it had some success despite suggestions to the contrary.[7] But after 1957 the strategy did begin to fail. The last three years of the 1950s are an important turning point in the management of public expenditure and for social welfare too. They deserve a detailed study which we cannot give them here, but a number of factors are clear. The armed forces could not be scaled down indefinitely at least without a fundamental reappraisal of Britain's international role especially in view of the deficiencies Suez had shown up. So defence spending begins to rise again in real terms. The pressures within the social welfare sector were growing too. The Guillebaud Committee, set up to help the government economise on health expenditure, showed instead that the service was being neglected.[8] Hospital building was running far below the levels reached in the 1930s. 'No hospital built since the War' became an election propaganda weapon. There was a limit to the extent to which economies could be demanded from a service without unacceptable political costs being incurred. The same held with council house building. Demographic trends were also against the government. The size of the pensioner population was rising. The large post war cohort of school children were passing through secondary school and steadily increasing numbers were staying on at school, the birth rate began to rise for the first time since 1948.[9] Moreover the Labour Party was switching more of its attention to social welfare policies and away from a more traditional emphasis on industrial policy.[10] In 1957 and 1958 the Conservative government was highly unpopular if Gallup polls and bye-elections were any guide. It was against this background that the spending ministers began to win more battles. The strategy of the early 1950s was collapsing. At the end of 1957 the Cabinet rows and the Treasury's unease broke the political surface. The Chancellor Thorneycroft and his two junior ministers – one of whom was Enoch Powell – resigned ostensibly because the cuts they insisted on in Cabinet had not been accepted. In fact the resignations had been prompted by a series of defeats for the Treasury ministers in Cabinet and in its 'sub-committees'.[11] The Treasury might have concluded that there were strong underlying political reasons for this state of affairs and that it should accept the new situation. It did not. It concluded that the system it was operating was at fault. As Heclo and Wildavsky put it:

'In the end Treasury officials such as Richard Clarke, David Serpell, Matthew Stevenson, William Armstrong and others won out because a strong feeling crystallised in the Treasury that it was being defeated far too often. Spending, the victorious faction believed, was not being controlled by anyone'.[12]

The resignations high-lighted the 'problem' and the House of Commons Select Committee on Estimates 'properly briefed and encouraged'[13] by the Treasury, produced a report which voiced many of these fears and proposed a course of action.

'It became clear early in the course of the enquiry that it is really an abuse of language to speak of a "system" of Treasury control if by the word "system" is meant methods and practices that have at one time or another been deliberately planned and instituted. What is called "Treasury control" is better described as a complex of administrative practice that has grown up like a tree over the centuries, natural rather than planned, empiric rather than theoretical.' (para 94, H.C: 294 1958.)

The report recommended that an independent Committee be set up to report on 'the theory and practice of Treasury control of expenditure'. The result was not an independent committee but an internal group chaired by an outsider from industry – Lord Plowden. The group consisted of senior officials from various departments including the Treasury and a number of other 'outsiders'. It was appointed in mid-1959 shortly before the General Election.

The Plowden Committee's report, published two years later in July 1961, became a key document.[14] The contents almost entirely derived from the Treasury. It makes very clear how the Treasury saw the basic issues and it is worth quoting at some length:

'The system of control of public expenditure depends upon the attitude to public spending both of Parliament and of public opinion. In former times, there were strong external pressures on the Government to reduce both expenditure and taxes, and every Minister who wanted to spend had to run the gauntlet of severe criticism from his Cabinet colleagues, from Parliament and from the public. The system was then effective at keeping expenditure down. This was the instrument, indeed, by which an austere discipline was maintained throughout the public service for generation after generation up to World War I in marked distinction to many other countries' experience. In the inter-war period, although public attitudes were changing, there was still a strong body of critical opinion which served as a check on the growth of public expenditure.

'In our judgment, the social, political and economical changes of the last twenty years have created a new situation. First, the scale of public expenditure is far greater ... Second, public expenditure has become more complex including, as it does, the cost of the most advanced technological projects and of scientific research; the financing of commercial risks that the private sector cannot take; aid of many different kinds to a variety of under-developed countries; and social insurance schemes of unprecedented scope. All of these activities involve commitments, contractual or moral, extending several years ahead. Third, there has taken place a great change in economic thought; the Keynesian revolution in the role of public finance and its relationship to the national economy as a whole ...

'These, and above all the fact that the main weight of Parliamentary and public pressure, central and local, is for innovation, or improvements which cannot be brought about without increases in public expenditure, have created a situation in which, in our opinion, the traditional system of decision-making can no longer be expected to be effective *in containing the growth of expenditure within whatever limit the Government have set.* If, as must be expected, these changes are permanent, the system needs to be reconstructed accordingly.' (paras 9–11. Cmnd. 1432 our italics.)

The report then proceeded to outline what was called 'a reconstruction' based on four particular objectives.

The first was that regular surveys be made of public expenditure as a whole over a period of years – five were recommended. All decisions involving substantial future expenditure should be taken in the light of these surveys. Expenditure should be 'properly aligned with prospective resources'. This was in fact the crux of the whole report. It could be seen to constitute a 'counter strategy' to those employed by the spending departments which we have described earlier. If the long-term implications of policy proposals were fully examined they would often be seen to have large consequences on the future levels of public expenditure. Sudden impulsive decisions to expand or adopt an expensive policy might then be put off, or made to wait until 'room could be found' for them. If all ministers could be persuaded to adopt and hold to a certain 'optimum' rate of overall expansion in public expenditure the strategies employed by individual ministries could merely determine their *share* of the cake not its absolute size. Therein lay the essence of the strategy.

As comments made by the proponents of the new system have made clear subsequently, its success or failure could be judged, at least in part, by whether it checked the growth of the public sector. Such then was the emphasis on constraint in the British reforms.

The second objective outlined in the original Plowden report was to seek the greatest possible stability in public expenditure decisions – to prevent the sudden cuts in school or house-building projects that had recurred several times in the 1950s. To stop and start capital projects was a costly business, and to be avoided as far as possible. Valid as the point was it has the appearance of being something of a cover for the essential purpose of the new system. The last two objectives were to improve the statistical tools for controlling expenditure and to improve the arrangements which would enable ministers to 'discharge their collective responsibility for the oversight of public expenditure as a whole'.[15]

There is at this stage little emphasis on choice, so long as constraint is secured. Even the final reference to ministers 'discharging their collective responsibility' was a veiled way of suggesting that the spending ministers should be put in their place and that a committee of non-spending ministers be given the task of vetting departments' bids. There was, in short, a substantial difference in the motivation and the tenor of these proposals compared to those we considered in the last chapter.

Even more noticeable was the manner of their coming. The apparatus was gradually assembled, growing in detail and sophistication as the years passed. Its significance and impact came to be felt gradually, as did public knowledge of its operation.

The Treasury was reorganised to carry through the changes. The existing supply divisions each kept a close watch on spending departments. They were retained and renamed 'expenditure' divisions to indicate that their proper concern extended beyond a single year's 'supply cycle'. The real innovation was the creation of two new divisions, one to oversee the Nationalised Industries and the other to handle the new long-term Public Expenditure Survey.[16] Further changes have followed but the broad organisational outlines remain. There are now (1974) three Permanent Secretaries of the Treasury (the senior rank in the British Civil Service) one of whom is responsible for 'the Public Sector'. Beneath him are two Deputy Secretaries each responsible for a group of divisions: Public Sector A and B. There are seven of these altogether and one has the task of overseeing the whole area of social service expenditure. Thus the peak of the pyramid is very small. The work of the social services division is undertaken by three Assistant Secretaries and their principals.[17] The reorganisation of the Treasury was accompanied by the creation of a new political post: the Chief Secretary. He assumed responsibility for the whole survey system. Within the spending departments the responsible official was and still is their Principal Finance Officer. These individuals are Under Secretaries in charge of the Finance Divisions of the Departments. The results are reported to the Public Expenditure Survey Committee. It is popularly known by its initials – PESC – and the whole process is often referred to as the PESC system.[18] This committee has the task of agreeing on a document that can be presented to Ministers showing how much it would cost to maintain current policies over the coming five-year period. These expenditure forecasts can then be compared with the medium term assessment of the country's economic growth potential for the same period. The Cabinet must decide on the appropriate growth rate in public expenditure for the period in the light of these two pieces of information. The process of control is not confined to this 'single cosmic operation'. From time to time economic crises require sudden reassessments and emergency cuts. Moreover, there are monthly reviews of the way the expenditure figures are developing within each department as well as day-to-day contacts between those in the Treasury and their opposite numbers in the spending departments. But the strategy is broadly decided in these summer exercises and what is more that cycle of events has broadly held ever since the Plowden changes were formalised. It is in content and sophistication that the whole process has developed to such a remarkable degree. One enormous technical task has been to produce a consistent set of statistics where so many different sources and categories are involved – local authority grant returns, the House of Commons Estimates, the National Income accounts, none of which agreed with one another at the outset. The first surveys only included the next year's expen-

Table 7.2 The Public Expenditure Survey Timetable

Month	Survey Procedure	Economic Assessment	Parliamentary Timetable
December	Instructions on the conduct of Survey sent out by Treasury giving guidelines for expected growth.		
End February	Departments send to Treasury estimates of the cost of existing policies for next five years and possible additional programmes.		
March/April	Discussion between Treasury and Departments to agree policy assumptions and statistics. Draft report drawn up by Treasury agreed by PESC.		
June	Report to Ministers.	Medium term assessment drawn up on prospects for the economy. Report to Ministers.	
July–October	Decisions on total public expenditure targets over the next five years; and on functional split.		
November/December	White Paper including the basis of agreed figures published.		
February			Discussion by the House of Commons Expenditure Committee of broad principles. Debate in Parliament on White Paper.
February/March			Publication of Estimates which relate to the next year's expenditure.
April–July			Debates on Estimates by the House of Supply Days.
End July/August			Appropriation Act passed giving Crown Authorisation to spend sums requested.

diture and the figures for five years hence. By the end of the sixties figures for each of the five years were included. The first three are relatively firm estimates, the last two more speculative. An elaborate series of conventions has been adopted to measure the impact different programmes have on effective demand in the economy. A whole treatise could be written on the adoption of an appropriate price basis for the forecasts. The surveys began with the use of a simple constant price concept. But as real incomes rise in the rest of the economy so will public sector salaries. In labour intensive social services raising real salaries means raising costs relative to less labour intensive services or industries. To look at the same point another way, even if the amount of education or health provided increases at the same rate as the economy expands they would still end up taking a larger share of the GNP because their relative prices rose. Hence, the Treasury began to add on a 'relative price effect' first to expenditure overall, then to individual programmes and then to parts of programmes.[19] It is a sophistication which works to the detriment of the social services in particular. It makes social service spending appear to increase at a faster rate than hitherto. One further development began at least in part response to the complications of trying to cope with the longer term consequences of building programmes and policy developments in the social policy field. It became obvious that five years was too short a period to consider the impact of many new policies especially social policies. The Hospital Plan of 1962 was, even at that stage, concerned with plans for ten years ahead. The Committee on Higher Education made recommendations for student numbers twenty years ahead, so did the advisory committee on teacher supply and the Royal Commission on Medical Education. Although none of these recommendations were accepted in detail that far ahead, once the principles on which they were based became accepted they did have very long term implications. Even more difficult was the Labour Government's National Superannuation Scheme. It would take over twenty years to come to fruition. Hence the Treasury came to see the need to forecast the impact of current policies even further ahead. Long term surveys covering the next fifteen years are now conducted from time to time.

One measure of the growing sophistication that has taken place can be gained by comparing the White Paper the Conservative government issued in 1963 with its latest counterpart. The 1963 document contained the outcome of the PESC exercise of that year.[20] It amounted to eleven pages and contained essentially two columns of figures. The Conservative Government's White Paper of

December 1973[21] amounted to 160 pages and a huge array of tables. As someone involved commented: 'No one understands it all now except the Treasury'. More important still is the growing rigour with which the control is exercised. In the first White Paper the five year projections purported to show that the growth of public spending could be sustained if a growth rate were realised without increasing taxation. The figures were merely 'guidelines' for the Departments. After 1968 the survey laid down a firm growth path – a year by year indication of the Department's limits. These all appear in the White Paper.

If the process is now more complex it is also more public. How did this come about?

More Public
Plowden had argued:

'It is therefore doubtful whether any government will feel able to place these surveys before Parliament and the public. To do so would involve disclosing the Government's long-term intentions for a wide range of public expenditure; and also explaining the survey's assumptions about employment, wages, prices and all the other main elements in the national economy. It would be surprising if any Government were prepared to do this.'[22]

However, in 1963, in response to a pre-election challenge by the Labour Opposition, the Government published a summary of the results of the PESC survey that was mentioned earlier. In September 1965, the Labour Government published a much more detailed account as part of its *National Plan*.[23] Chapters 18 to 22 of that document were devoted to a discussion of the new Government's public spending plans up to 1969–70. In 1966 the White Paper *Public Expenditure: Planning and Control*[24] not only outlined the forecasts in more detail but also gave an account of the Survey process as it had then evolved. It was only when devaluation caused the Government to rethink their programme in January 1968 that another White Paper was produced covering the last two years of the cycle – up to 1970.[25] It was a very slim document, comprising no more than the same basic table of figures that the 1963 White Paper had contained. However, by this time the Treasury officials seem to have concluded that publication of the forward plans, and some Parliamentary scrutiny of them, might help to hold the line against the spending departments more effectively. During the session 1968–9 the House of Commons Select Committee on

Table 7.3   *The Basic Programme Categories*

As in 1972/73

	£ millions	1963 categories
Defence and external relations		
1 Defence budget	2,842	Defence
2 Other military defence	75	
3 Overseas aid	275	Aid and other overseas
4 EEC and other overseas services	198	
Commerce and Industry		
5 Agriculture fisheries and forestry	572	Assistance to industry
6 Research Councils etc.	137	Transport and agriculture
7 Trade, industry and employment	1,615	
Nationalised Industries		
8 Nationalised industries' capital expenditure	1,741	Investment by nationalised industries
Environmental Services		
9 Roads	971	Roads
10 Surface transport	283	
11 Housing	1,417	Housing and environment
12 Miscellaneous local services	1,159	
13 Law and Order	818	Police and prisons
14 Arts	41	
Social Services		
15 Education and libraries	3,375	Education
16 Health and Personal Social Services	2,814	Health and welfare
17 Social Security	5,050	Benefits and assistance Children's services
Other Services		
18 Financial Administration	431	Administration and
19 Common services	298	other services
20 Miscellaneous services	97	
21 Northern Ireland	694	
Total programmes	24,903	

Source: Public Expenditure Handbook (1972) and Cmnd 2235 (1963)

Procedure discussed Parliament's scrutiny of expenditure. This had become little more than a charade. The House only considered expenditure estimates for the year ahead, like Congress. But unlike Congress it did not examine them in detail, it merely rubber stamped them. Supply days were used by all Oppositions to debate issues having nothing to do with the estimates. Even the few days of debate set aside to discuss the estimates themselves were, and still are, debates on general issues not the details of spending. The Select Committee on Estimates had concerned itself with intensive studies of very narrow topics – such as school building controls – one per year. The development of the new long term control system within Government had not been paralleled by any comparable changes in Parliamentary procedure. As a result:

'The House has no machinery for scrutinising this complicated process and has had little opportunity to debate the forward projections of expenditure produced during recent years.' (Para. 9, H.C. 410 1968–9.)

In evidence to the Committee, the Government announced that it intended to publish annually a White Paper giving the results of the survey together with projections of tax revenue and an assessment of the prospects for growth in the economy, which provided the rationale for the limits imposed.[26] Beginning in December 1969 that government and its successors met the first of these promises. A White Paper outlined spending plans.[27] Latterly, White Papers have given some indication of growth prospects but have not yet found it possible to produce projections of tax revenue.

The Select Committee recommended that the House should debate the White Paper as a whole House and that the old Estimates Committee be abolished and a new Expenditure Committee be set up to consider the White Paper as a whole in more detail. To do this it should have sub-committees paralleling broad areas of Departmental responsibility and a General Sub-committee. This recommendation was carried through in 1970 and has been operating ever since. The General Sub-committee, at least at the beginning of its life, had gone a long way to prising out the assumptions that are made in drawing up the surveys and in illuminating the whole process. The 'functional' sub-committees have disappointingly spent most of their time on small scale issues. They have, for example, produced reports on probation and aftercare, NHS facilities for private patients, planning the scale of further and higher education, urban transport planning, and several more. They have not sought to delve deeper into the separate sections of the White Paper, perhaps because they would raise too many sensitive party political issues.

American Influence

So far we have seen a sharp contrast between the rather unsuccessful history of government-wide expenditure planning in the US and the apparently more successful and gradual British developments. Yet when the PPB reforms hit Washington some inside and outside the Treasury thought that they had something to offer Whitehall too. Following the American model a programme budget and planning review procedure was introduced into the British Ministry of Defence after 1964 with rather similar purposes. In both cases it was hoped that the new procedures would produce more effective inter-service planning. However, Healy had a more difficult task for he had to preside over first a stable and then a declining budget in real terms. MacNamara had presided over a rapidly rising budget. Defence expenditure did stabilise after 1964 and this must have been an encouraging sign.

In 1966 the Treasury concluded that they would like to see how far a similar approach could be adapted in other fields. Feasibility studies were undertaken in the Home Office and the Department of Education but the pace was very gentle.

Outside a group of Conservatives who were advising Mr Heath had grown far more enthusiastic. Supported by a group of businessmen they concluded that corporate planning and business management methods were what government needed. From the end of 1968 on, they prepared ways of introducing this new approach into government.[28] Their conclusions were reflected in the new Conservative Government's White Paper on *The Reorganisation of Central Government* published shortly after they reached office in October 1970. The precise proposals had to await the outcome of work being done by 'a team of businessmen based in the Civil Service Department'. But, the White Paper stated, there would be a system of reviews which 'will certainly involve a greater emphasis on the definition of objectives and the expressing of programmes so far as possible in output terms'.[29] It is fairly clear that what was envisaged was something pretty close to the pure milk of PPB with a programme budget and large-scale programme memoranda.[30] In 1969, the House of Commons Select Committee on Procedure had already argued that output budgeting should be more widely adopted and used in the presentation of the Estimates to the Commons.[31] The advisers' other main recommendation had been

I

the creation of a powerful central capability unit which would advise on government priorities and serve the Prime Minister and the Cabinet. As we now know things did not work out quite as intended. The Treasury too had been developing its own ideas. What emerged ultimately was the Central Policy Review Staff, 'a small multi-disciplinary-staff in the Cabinet Office',[32] and the system of Programme Analysis and Review. It is the latter that primarily concerns us here. Its interest lies in the way the Civil Service had sought to avoid some of the pitfalls of the early American experience. They did not see the need for elaborate output-oriented programme structures. They did not seek a detailed analysis of options in each programme area. They went instead for the selective analysis in depth of one or two issues or areas of policy, by each department each year. It was much nearer the approach the Americans came to rely on in the early 1970s. Though the original intention was to integrate the analyses into the PESC time table, in the end those concerned adopted a 'two track' system very similar to that advocated by Wildavsky in his evidence to the Congressional Committee in 1969. A separate parallel set of procedures was created. Alongside PESC there was now to be PARC – the Programme Analysis and Review Committee. Both committees had the same Chairman and many of the same members. PARC included in particular those from the Central Policy Review Staff and the Civil Service Department, but after an initial tussle major responsibility for the operation is firmly within the Treasury and it is serviced by the expenditure divisions who are also involved in PESC work. There was to be an annual cycle of policy reviews on a selected number of issues chosen after discussion between the spending departments, the Treasury and the Central Policy Review Staff. There were to be two kinds of review. The first, and least numerous, were to cross departmental boundaries and were to be undertaken with the help of the small CPRS staff. The second and most usual type were the responsibility of a single department. Their studies were typically to last a year, though longer term ones were possible. When completed a report was to be submitted to the PARC committee and to a committee of ministers. The links with the expenditure process came not, as in HEW, through some time tabling process, but by virtue of the fact that the central actors are the same. The Treasury essentially controls the system. The same Under-Secretary (civil servant) and Chief Secretary (politician) are in charge. If Ministers agree that policy conclusions should follow one of the PARs then these can be automatically fed back into the PESC system which is there to cost accepted policy.

The whole PAR enterprise had been clouded in a great deal of secrecy. Government have consistently refused to say even which policy areas are, or have been, considered. The general procedure appears to differ somewhat between departments but it is said to comprise four elements:[33]

(a) Discuss the objectives of the programme in detail and discuss ways in which progress towards them could be quantified;

(b) Examine trends in the scale and kinds of resources used, determine the factors which have been associated with past changes.

(c) Discuss how far these trends are immutable.

(d) What impact is the programme making? What information is there on needs and future trends in demand? Identify options for policy change.

Clearly studies of this kind have always been part of social service departments activities. What is new is that the topics for study have to be discussed with the central departments and may even arise from suggestions made at the centre. Moreover, the results have to be discussed with the Treasury. It is above all a way for the Treasury to get more deeply into the policy promotion process and to get at more departmental knowledge. It may therefore be able to influence the outcome more powerfully.

The development of programme budgets appears to be progressing as a separate activity which may eventually change the categories used in the annual PESC return and may also give a more helpful quantitative base upon which the PARs can be built as well as throwing up issues for study.

The originators of the system in the Treasury and outside had been critical of the survey system for helping to perpetuate the general growth of public programmes beginning with the previous year's base lines. They hoped that this new system would provide the opportunity to question the very existence of some programmes and certainly to question whether any might be substantially curtailed. This view seems to have generated much of the impetus for change. 'The people at the centre tend to keep asking "do you need to be doing this at all?" '

We can see from this brief description that the Treasury had learned a good deal from the 'mistakes' across the Atlantic. What they or the spending departments have been slower to learn is that to be at all useful such analyses must draw upon a very substantial body of on-going research work about the way the programme is being delivered, what impact it is having, what the needs of its recipients are and much more that we discuss later. The system is there, but the building material to use in it is sparse. Before looking more specifically at the way these new systems have affected social service planning we must pause to ask what they have achieved in broader terms.

The Achievements

There is no doubt that those who invented the system and those who are currently operating it are very proud of their handywork. Sympathetic observers too are convinced that the British Treasury has produced perhaps the most successful expenditure management systems in the world. In purely logistical terms this is probably true for the reasons we have just elaborated. In psychological terms too, PESC has bitten deep. Not only civil servants in spending departments but ministers and ex-ministers tend to think in terms of a given allocation within which they must work. Even the Labour Opposition in 1973 conducted its own amateur PESC exercise on its election manifesto proposals. Without doubt decisions about expenditure priorities have to be taken far more explicitly than ever before. The implications of these decisions are also more public and therefore debateable than they were. So far so good. But how would PESC stand up to a PAR? How far has it met the objectives set out originally in the Plowden Report? How appropriate were these anyway?

It will be recalled that Plowden had four aims:

(i) Planning public expenditure on the basis of five-year rolling programmes so that the long-term rate of expansion was 'properly aligned with prospective resources'.
(ii) Achieving greater stability in public expenditure decisions.
(iii) Improving the tools for making choices.
(iv) Improving the collective responsibility of ministers.

The first was the central objective, but in assessing it a great deal turns on the interpretation of the words 'properly aligned'. It is absolutely clear from the context within which Plowden used the phrase, from the Chancellor's speech in 1961,[34] from the comments of ex-Treasury men like Sir Richard Clarke[35] and from statements made to the Expenditure Committee, that 'aligned' with economic growth meant 'equated with' or 'slower than'. One test of success may therefore be total public expenditure expressed as a percentage of GNP. If this percentage rises then on its original terms the system is failing. If it is static or falling the system is succeeding.[36] It has already been argued that as an indicator it is an economic nonsense, including as it does resource costs and transfers in the numerator and resource costs alone in the denominator. Its only virtue is that it shows whether, other things being equal, more taxation will be required or less. In the light of all this the actual post 1961 record comes as something of a surprise. The rate of increase in public spending after Plowden was significantly faster than the scale of the increases which had been the very reason for its creation. Moreover, the subsequent increases were far bigger than had been permitted in the 1950s without any such sophistications. By 1968 the ratio of public expenditure to the GNP was a full 10 per cent higher than ten years earlier. However, the figures also illustrate why Treasury officials explained to Heclo and Wildavsky that the system really only began to 'work' after 1968 for it was only then that the growth was virtually halted. 'By early 1970' Goldman writes 'the system had reached full maturity, and shown a capacity, in determined hands, to deal with widely varying situations.'[37]

What went wrong? Goldman produces two reasons: First, 'indicative planning', i.e. the attempt to set a target or a hoped for growth rate for the economy. Public expenditure was hitched to that target which in the event proved unobtainable. Second, he blames the stupidity of politicians, or as he more delicately put it 'the dominance of the political over the intellectual factor'.

The whole survey procedure had the misfortune to begin in the run up period to a general election, when the Government of the day

Table 7.4 *The Growth of Public Expenditure* 1952–74*

	1952	1958	1960	1965	1968	1970	1974
Public Expenditure as a percentage of GNP at Factor cost	47·0	41·6	42·2	45·9	51·7	49·8	50·5

	1952–8	1958–60	1960–5	1965–8	1968–70	1970–74
Average annual growth in total Public Expenditure per cent	0·4	4·6	5·2	5·2	0·1	6·5

* With relative price effect attributed

Source 1952–70: Sir Samuel Goldman, KCB, *The Developing System of Public Expenditure Management and Control*
1970–74: Cmnd 5879 (1975) and *National Income and Expenditure 1963–73.*

was in real political trouble, and when the Opposition had made its main election plank the Galbraithian theme – 'public squalor amid private affluence'. It was also a period dedicated to achieving a high growth rate or bust – the 'take off' or 'Maudling' strategy. The consequence was that as the 1964 election approached more and more large scale public expenditure programmes were entered into. The December 1963 White Paper made it clear that the Conservative Government had gambled on being able to attain a 4 per cent growth rate. Total expenditure was to rise at this rate in the long term. Yet between then and the election even more commitments were entered into. The new Labour Government, whose policies entailed even higher public spending, was also faced with a large balance of payments deficit. A major review of the previous government's commitments was undertaken. As a result the Cabinet agreed that the total growth of the public sector (excluding the nationalised industries) should be limited to $4\frac{1}{4}$ per cent per annum rate of increase between 1964–5 and 1969–70. Again, like its predecessors, the new Government was pinning its hopes on achieving roughly a 4 per cent growth rate and basing its expenditure limits on that. What the Chancellor actually said was:

'Meanwhile the government have decided that the growth of public sector expenditure between 1964–5 and 1969–70 will be related to the prospective increase in national production, which in our present judgment means limiting the average increase in public sector expenditure, taking one year with another, to $4\frac{1}{4}$ per cent a year at constant prices'. (Hansard 22 Feb. 1965.)

This sounded as if they hoped the growth rate in the economy would be $4\frac{1}{4}$ per cent, but it preceded the detailed work in the new Department of Economic Affairs on an appropriate growth target. When this was produced it was rather less optimistic. The National Plan aimed at an *eventual* 4 per cent target with an average of 3·8 per cent per annum in the whole five year period. The government did not, however, alter their public expenditure target. As a result the National Plan propounded the government's judgement that the public sector should grow slightly faster over the whole period than the whole economy – 4·25 per cent compared to 3·8 per cent per annum. The White Paper in 1966 stated that the rate of expansion in the public sector was to be even faster than $4\frac{1}{4}$ per cent in the first few years, before the proposed cuts in defence spending could take full effect.

What actually happened was very different. The balance of payments failed to go right. Emergency measures in July 1965 and especially in July 1966 finally made the attainment of even the average 3·8 per cent growth impossible. The hoped for target for output was reduced to 3 per cent per annum, and the eventual outcome for the whole period was nearer 2 per cent. Nevertheless, the Government did not, for a long time, make any drastic changes in its strategy for the public sector until forced to do so by the November 1967 devaluation. Now it is possible to argue that such stubbornness merely proves how stupid the Labour politicians were. On the other hand these decisions represent a series of deliberate political choices. They meant that the Government's social programmes were to be sustained and that the consumer would have to bear the major consequences of the failure to achieve a faster growth rate. They ensured that the share of the public sector in the economy grew faster than had been intended in 1965. These planning decisions were entirely legitimate and for many people laudable political stances.

Goldman and other Treasury critics are possibly nearer the mark when they criticise the actual trend of expenditure between 1965 and 1968. Compared to the average rate of expansion laid down in the National Plan – $4\frac{1}{4}$ per cent up to 1969–70 – the actual rates of increase were higher, double those forecast in 1967–8. Finally when public expenditure was cut back after 1968 and PESC really began to bite, it did so only because the Cabinet had been convinced by the severity of the economic crisis that resources had to be forced into exports. This, too, is an illustration of the fact that the system depends for its success not on its sophistication but upon political support. In short the Treasury only succeeded in its public sector strategy through the failure of its economic management. There must be a temptation, to put it no higher, for the Treasury to exaggerate the impact that savings in public expenditure can make to help resolve an economic crisis. Nevertheless after the 1967 crisis the Treasury finally managed to convince Labour ministers that in the long term the growth rate for public expenditure should be *equal* to the likely increase in national output – about 3 per cent a year. The average rate of expansion agreed for public expenditure between 1968 and 1972 was indeed 3 per cent per annum. The Conservative Government revised this target downwards in each of their expenditure reviews, first to 2·6 per cent, then 2·2 per cent, then 2 per cent. In the outcome public expenditure rose faster in the seventies than for many years (Table 7.4).

Whether the survey system should have 'succeeded' in reducing public expenditure growth after 1968 raises what is or ought to be the major issue in British politics. The experience of the period between 1952 and 1957 suggests that services cannot be held back below the general economic growth rate for very long without serious political repercussions. International experience suggests that nations have tended to spend a higher proportion of their resources on the social services the more their incomes rise.[38] Indeed the relative price effect alone makes this probable. To a limited extent, and for a finite period, the circle can be squared by reducing foreign and defence commitments but sooner or later the issue has to be faced. To hold down the percentage of resources devoted to the public sector either means holding back a well-established historical and international trend towards higher social service spending or it means the services must be 'reprivatised'. The justification for either course of action is contentious to say the least.

What of the second of Plowden's objectives – *stability* in expenditure decisions? The period since 1961 has not been noticeably freer of the kind of emergency economy cuts of which Plowden was so critical. The January 1968 cuts were as damaging as anything which occurred in the 1950s. The early seventies saw an even more serious break with the Plowden tradition. The new Conservative Government in October 1970 had proposed spending £330 million less in 1971–2 and £1,500 million less in 1974–5 than the Labour Government had been proposing to do. Yet within a year, clearly frightened by the prospect of a million unemployed, the Government once again *increased* its spending plans, replacing in cash terms over a half of the cuts it had imposed so recently. A year later (December, 1972) the Government's White Paper showed that it had raised its limits once again. By now the total spending in real terms was to be higher in 1974–5 than it would have been under Labour's plans.[39] Then six months later the Chancellor announced *cuts* of over £90 million in that financial year and more the year after. The White Paper which came out in December, 1973, showing moderate cuts was followed the same day by announcements of further cuts amounting to over £1,000 million in the following year.[40] A few months later the minority Labour Government raised the targets once more. Nothing remotely like this bedwildering set of changes had occurred in the 1950s. What had happened was that the Treasury decided both to introduce some short term measures to boost employment in the form of capital expenditure for the regions and to revise its judgements about longer term programmes too.

The former were to last for only two years, the latter were more difficult to fit into that time span. It is not our purpose to discuss the appropriateness of these measures for the economy – The House of Commons Expenditure Committee was 'strongly critical of these decisions taking them as a whole'.[41] But it is quite clear that the Treasury was now using the expenditure control system as a demand management tool in a way that is quite contrary to what Plowden recommended. Plowden essentially argued that if public expenditure were linked to the long run growth rate of the economy it could avoid being used as a short-term regulator. This has proved unduly optimistic. The last six years have two lessons. First, that now the Treasury has forged an effective mechanism of control it will not be able to resist the temptation to use it for medium and short term demand management with all the diseconomies that are involved. Second, economic crises will interfere with forward planning whatever the good intentions of the planners, just as political pressures will. This is also clear from the replies which Sir Douglas Henley gave the House of Commons Committee on Expenditure:

'Recent experience has shown that if sufficiently clear action is taken public expenditure can be used to an extent to effect demand control. I would not say that this was done without some measure of disruption . . . but given the necessity I think it is clear that you can use public expenditure . . . perhaps somewhat more than would have been thought two or three years ago.'[42]

Despite the optimism that the Treasury spokesman showed here the fact is that in the outcome the boost which these temporary measures were expected to bring did not materialise quite as intended. Other people's programmes are easier to cut than they are to stimulate in the short run. On a longer term perspective Table 7.5 matches actual and planned increases in the other social services. It takes first the 1964 Labour Government's National Plan and second its 1968 revisions, and thirdly the Heath Government's proposals on reaching office and compares them with the outcome. They all three illustrate the disheartening life planners would lead if only they looked over their shoulders.

Housing has proved particularly difficult for central government to forecast, and so has social security. The manpower intensive services like education and health have been nearer the mark.

Table 7.5   *Relative Growth Rates in Social Service Programmes*

(i) *Planned average annual growth rates in constant prices*

		Volume Terms			
	Conserva-tive Plans	Labour Government Plans		Conservative Plans	
Service	1963/4–1967/8	1964/5–1969/70	1968/9–1971/2	1970/1–1974/5	1972/3–1976/7
Housing	3·8*	7·1	3·2	−0·4	−4·4
Education	5·7	5·7	3·8	3·3	3·4
Health and Welfare	3·0	4·8	3·8	3·3	3·4
Social Security	4·8	6·6	5·1	2·1	1·3
Roads	6·9	7·2	7·5	6·1	5·15
Defence	2·7	0·0	−1·9	−0·9	1·4
All public expenditure	4·1	4·2	3·0	2·6	2·2

* Includes Environment

(ii) *Actual as against planned growth rates in constant prices*

	Volume Terms					
	1964/5–1969/70 (Cmnd 2734)		1968/9–1971/2 (Cmnd 4234)		1970/1–1973/4 (Cmnd 4578)	
	Actual	Planned	Actual	Planned	Actual	Planned
Housing	3·8	7·1	−1·6	3·2	5·9	0·0
Education	4·9	5·7	4·0	3·8	4·9	3·5
Health and Welfare	3·4	4·8	3·2	3·8	5·2	3·2
Social Security	6·5	6·6	9·7	5·1	4·0	2·5
Roads	5·7	7·2	5·5	7·5	3·9	6·2
Defence	−2·4	0·0	−3·1	−1·9	−0·8	−1·4
All public expenditure	4·1	4·2	1·4	3·0	5·5	2·0

NOTE
The figures show increases in the amount of services provided, not their cost.

Sources: Cmnd 2235 (1963), Cmnd 2764 (1965), Cmnd 4234 (1969), Cmnd
4578 (1971), Cmnd 5178 (1972)
1964/5–1969/70: National Income and Expenditure 1973 (Tables 14
and 49) (1964–1969 UK Basis, 1970 prices)
1968/9–1971/2: Cmnd 5519
1970/71–1973/4: Cmnd 5879 (1975)

Table 7.6 *The impact of demand management on the Social Services (1971–3)*

The effect of policy changes on 1974/5 expenditure levels
Total changes proposed £ millions (1973 prices)

	From Labour's 1970 plans to Cmnd 4578 (Jan. 1971)	Cmnd 4578 to Cmnd 4829 (Nov. 1971)	Cmnd 4829 to Cmnd 5178 (Dec. 1972)	Cmnd 5172 to Cmnd 5519 (Dec. 1973)	Cmnd 5519 to 17 Dec. 1973 Statement	Total
Housing	−182	+98	+76	+103	—	+95
Education	−55	+15	−29	−59	−182	+310
Health and Personal Social Services	−64	+68	+12	−1	−111	−96
Social Security (excluding increases due to restoring purchasing power)	+6	+154	+246	+189	—	+595
All public expenditure	−984	+597	+1051	−306	−1087	−729

Source: House of Commons Expenditure Committee (General Subcommittee) Session 1973/4, Minutes of Evidence 28 January, 1974 H.C. 143 (1973/4).

So in retrospect it appears that neither of Plowden's major objectives have yet proved attainable – over the long term – restraining the growth of the public sector or insulating it from sudden changes of course. The third goal of more 'rational' choice we shall return to in Chapter 10. The fourth, 'improving' ministerial responsibility, proved equally elusive. The Treasury clearly felt in 1961 that the Chancellor needed 'a greater measure of support' in Cabinet. One answer was the creation of a new cabinet post – Chief Secretary – and in an unpublished section, the report had proposed that the expenditure survey should be discussed by a Cabinet Committee of ministers from non-spending departments chaired by the Chancellor. The Conservative Government rejected the idea but in its early years the 1964 Labour Government adopted it. 'Spending' ministers were called before it one by one. This did not last long. The system of control will only work if the Chancellor, backed by the Prime Minister, can convince the Cabinet of the need to hold to a particular growth target. If they agree then the Treasury's hand is enormously strengthened. It means that the game played between the spending departments and the Treasury cannot increase the total prize money. Only if a majority of Ministers can agree on some 'sacrificial department' preferably a large spender who can be forced to contract, will most be able to gain much above the norm. In the 1964–70 Labour period this is quite clearly what happened to the defence programme. More recently it looks as if it has been the roads programme that has had to suffer.

Despite the limitations we have discussed PESC is now an immensely powerful system. It has had a profound impact upon the planning of social services.

Social Services Departments
The Overall Strategies
The overall social priorities which the different parties have set in government appear fairly clearly from a retrospective look at the planned growth rates in social programmes (see Table 7.5 (i)). The 1964 Labour Government accepted the Conservatives' plans for education adopting an identical growth rate. They did go for a rather higher growth rate for the Health Service and a considerably higher one for housing. This was to be 'paid' for by stabilising defence expenditures. When that Government was forced to recast its spending strategy in 1968 all the social programmes were pulled back and there was to be a more even pattern of growth between them. Indeed it was in that year that we see education and health given *equal* growth targets compared to the much higher rate that

education had enjoyed in the 1950s and early 1960s. It is no accident that in the later White Papers these two growth rates have been identical. It does not reflect any sophisticated, or perhaps one should say spurious, attempt to judge different 'needs' between the two services. The demographic factors affecting each are quite different, for example. What it does illustrate is that the political weight of these two departments, the DES and the DHSS, is now roughly equal and that during this period they agreed to play for a draw. This balance of power held under both the Labour and Conservative Governments. However, the Conservative plans did differ sharply when it came to housing and social security policy. Housing expenditure, on new building and subsidies, was to fall slightly and then very sharply after 1972 compared to the steady increase Labour had planned. The Heath Government was also planning for a far slower growth rate in social security expenditure. In short, an explicit and quite coherent set of priorities can be traced in social spending intentions since the mid-sixtes. They were not as muddled or incoherent as some commentators have suggested. What happened was not entirely what was intended as can be seen from the next part of Table 7.5. The Conservative Government's housing subsidy policy went seriously wrong. Also the exceptionally high level of unemployment meant that far more went on unemployment benefit than had been anticipated. On other counts the economic climate was partly to blame for the divergence between plan and outcome.

Finally, the intended impact of the government's 'boosters' and 'dampers' on social service spending is illustrated in Table 7.6. Clearly as economic difficulties grow the shocks which the social services are going to have to absorb will be more frequent and more painful. We may soon come to look back on the past decade of 'planned growth' with a strong sense of nostalgia. We turn now to the evolution of planning within the separate departments.

The Department of Education and Science
Capital Planning

As we saw earlier one of the few direct financial controls the Ministry of Education, or later the DES, has had over the education system has been its power to approve building projects. This power extends to all local authority building for education purposes – not only schools, but colleges of further education and polytechnics. Probably the first piece of post-war capital planning was the emergency building programme mounted to house the extra children who would be staying on at school until fifteen in 1947. The 'hutted operation for raising the school leaving age' (HORSA) – a name which evokes memories of D-Day and post war emergency restrictions.

After 1949 the Ministry introduced a system of cost limits under which all school building proposals from local authorities had to cost less than a specified sum per place. However, it was not until the mid-1950s that the deliberate forward planning of building programmes began. The White Paper 'Technical Education' proposed not merely that a series of new Colleges of Advanced Technology should be created but, in some ways more important, it announced a five-year building programme for the whole of Technical Education.[43] Then two years later came another White Paper, this time on school building.[44] It set out a five year programme from 1960–1 to 1964–5 which was designed to eliminate 'all age' schools – the old elementary schools which took children from the ages of 5 to 15 and which the 1944 Act had said all local authorities should replace by separate primary and secondary schools. Science facilities too were to be improved – another post-Sputnik response. The Government announced, in effect, that it would accept bids from local authorities under these two headings up to a total value of £60 million a year. In 1963 a new three-year programme was announced,[45] and authorities were asked to submit all their school building proposals covering the years 1965–8. Once again indications were given of the criteria that would be applied in judging the requests. Most of the allocations, the Treasury had agreed, would go on new school places to meet the rising birth rate, and on sixth form places to meet the larger numbers who were staying at school. These programmes were then rolled forward.

In 1968 the control system was made even more elaborate. The Department introduced a system of 'programming'.[46] It was to have three distinct phases. First, authorities must submit a 'preliminary list' of projects which they would like to have permission to begin work on – securing sites and gaining planning permission. The proposals must conform to criteria set by the Secretary of State. In the early 1970s, apart from new population needs, this mainly meant the replacement of pre-1902 primary schools. The lists were approved seven to five years ahead of actual building, but even this is not far enough ahead for a large urban authority like the Inner London Education Authority. One year before the authority is ready to start building it must submit a 'design list' with most of the design complete and with costs. Even then the DES only gives an amber light. A project next has to get on to the 'starts list'. Only then can building begin. At each stage the Government can hold the process up or defer permission on all or some of the projects if the Treasury demands cuts in the total capital programme that year.

In short, the loan sanction procedure has been developed so that the Central Department aims not merely to promote economy and ensure minimum standards, but also to set a limit to the size of the programme well into the future, to determine priority needs it will meet, and to keep a close and continuing control over each stage of the process from site acquisition to the laying of the foundations.

Informal Promotional Planning

The mechanism of the advisory committee has been important in the formation of British education policy for more than a century. The 1870 Elementary Education Act which created a comprehensive pattern of state education had been preceded by a series of committees of enquiry which also prompted reforms in the private sector. A series of famous reports by the Consultative Committees on Education between the wars laid the intellectual foundations for the 1944 Act and, perhaps even more important, for the way it was administered. But it was in the decade between the mid 1950s and the mid 1960s when the practice reached its peak. It was used as vehicle for a series of separate investigations on different sections of the education system. The growth rate in education expenditure during and immediately following this decade is a partial testimony to its success. There were three types of advisory committees operating at this time. The statutory advisory council, the specialist National Advisory Council on the Training and Supply of Teachers and *ad hoc* committees set up for particular and limited purposes.

Under Section 4 of the 1944 Act the Minister, now the Secretary of State, is required to appoint two central advisory councils, one for England and one for Wales. Although they began with a general overview function, after 1951 the strategy changed and the members were to be appointed for three years to study specific areas of concern identified by the Minister. All the subsequent reports did this. Early Leaving (1954), Crowther (1959), Newsom (1963) Plowden (1967).[47] Crowther and Plowden especially were important planning documents. The first discussed the educational needs of the 15–18 age group. Apart from the impact made by its social surveys, it drew attention to the steady upward trend in voluntary staying on which was to have important repercussions on the planning of higher education. Above all it marshalled economic and social arguments for raising the school leaving age to sixteen. It estimated the additional demands for teachers and it recommended a time, seven to nine years afterwards, when the demographic trends would be favourable. It recommended an early announcement of the government's intentions and the laying of plans for buildings and teacher supply well in advance. Yet another report (Newsom) was needed to finally tip the political balance four years later. In the pre-1964 election period the Minister Edward Boyle did make such a declaration of intent. The staff work for this committee and all the statistical and planning work was undertaken in the Ministry of Education.

Plowden is in many ways an even better example. The period when it reported was one of recurrent economic crisis rather than the days of heady optimism in which the Crowther report was drafted. Consequently Plowden was very modest in its proposals all of which were carefully costed. The priority area proposals are the ones for which it is perhaps most remembered. Yet more important in resource terms were its proposals for introducing universal part-time pre-school education. Plowden's planning assumptions here were accepted largely unaltered once the principle was agreed nearly six years later. For example, the government incorporated Plowden's assumptions about the proportion of children whom parents would wish give part time schooling, and the numbers of fulltime places that would be needed for working mothers. Yet the figures had been made on the most flimsy and out-dated social survey evidence.[48] They were all Plowden had, yet they became enshrined in the Government's 1972 White Paper.[49]

Perhaps the best known and the most important report was that of an *ad hoc* committee appointed to examine higher education under the Chairmanship of Lord Robbins.[50] The methodology that the committee's advisers, with DES help, evolved for forecasting the demand for higher education, and the rationale it used for deciding on the total number of places that were needed, has been adopted by governments ever since as the basis for planning and financing higher education.[51] Other *ad hoc* committees have contributed to the debate about policy and organisation – most recently the Public Schools Commission (1970), the James Report on teacher training (1971) and the Russell Report on Adult Education (1973). The third type of committee, an on-going specialist committee on the supply of teachers, played a very important part in expanding teacher supply in the 1960s. The detailed projections and the assumptions about 'demand' largely derived from the Department, but they were discussed on the Committee by representatives of the teaching profession, and local authorities, and they were public knowledge. Their recommendations were the subject of fierce tussles with the Treasury and the professional and public support that the reports gained certainly helped in these battles.[52]

This series of reports illustrates both the strengths and the weaknesses of this kind of 'disjointed' planning. Its strengths were that the committees educated and informed their specialist, interested publics as they worked. They called for evidence. About 110 different bodies gave evidence to Plowden as well as about 200 individuals in key positions. As all these bodies held their own meetings and did their own background reading and research in order to write their evidence so they became increasingly well-informed about the issues. Then, having completed it, these organisations would typically publish their evidence and this would be used as the basis for discussions at local NUT or AUT branches, at meetings of local parents who were members of Committees for the Advancement of State Education and so on through all the network of educational interest groups. Each committee was carefully balanced to include representatives of all the many interests and organisations within the education system. Many came with clearly formed views. Some went away with the same ones afterwards, but for most membership itself was an enormously educative process. Members became aware of information, arguments, and attitudes they may have barely perceived or even knew existed. Even the DES observers or 'assessors' sometimes found themselves in this position. Moreover, the committees generated much original research. As a consequence a kind of feed-back process operated and the members in turn educated their own 'constituencies' both before the reports were published and afterwards as they went round the country explaining and justifying the report they had signed. These reports themselves had astonishingly high sales,[53] especially considering their length. Their contents were summarised and discussed particularly in the specialist press. In short, an elaborate educative process took place during and after the time the reports were published. Opinion within the universities on the desirability of expansion moved a long way while the Robbins committee was actually sitting, for example. The interested parties were not only educated, they were mobilised; if some degree of consensus emerged this put the Minister in a far stronger position with his Cabinet colleagues when it came to arguing with the Treasury.

If these were the strengths, there were also weaknesses. They became particularly obvious after the Robbins report had been accepted. If there were to be any constraints on education expendi-

K

ture at all, the commitments made by the Conservative Government to expand higher education on demand pre-empted funds on an unprecedented scale. It meant that other options were effectively closed – for example the option to devote significantly more resources to primary education or to expand nursery education or to go ahead with comprehensive reorganisation. Certainly from the Treasury's point of view they were an embarrassment. It could also be argued that education was beginning to pre-empt too large a share of resources which the social services as a whole were likely to gain. None of the other Ministries had used their advisory councils to such effect. But in the mid-sixties Departmental and Ministerial opinion ceased to favour the advisory committee approach and turned instead to internal planning arrangements. It is not entirely clear why this was so. The factors we have mentioned no doubt played some part. There was the view that they slowed up the decision making process, they took time and resources, and there was a feeling that, as Crosland put it, if the Department could not do its own planning it ought to pack up.[54] But more than this the Department was probably unhappy with many of the Committee's proposals. This was certainly true of Robbins thoughts on the public sector of higher education and on Ministerial responsibility. The DES fought both and won. It was by no means enthusiastic about Plowden's priority area proposals and differential salaries for teachers in stress schools. With teacher supply the officials in the Department were feeling their way towards an unpopular as well as an important shift of policy, and probably did not welcome the idea of having it exposed to public gaze. Perhaps the Treasury had had enough. Whatever the precise reasons the change of approach is very clear. After Plowden no new Central Advisory Council was appointed for over seven years, contrary to the Secretary of State's clear statutory duty to keep one in being. The National Advisory Council on the Training and Supply of Teachers, too, was disbanded and not reappointed throughout the period when the Department was formulating its proposals to cut back the number of teacher training places and close many Colleges of Education. Only when this had been decided was the Committee reconvened and then all the statistical reasoning that lay behind the Departments conclusions on the future supply and demand for teachers was presented as confidential documents and no report was published. When Mrs Thatcher did appoint a committee with instructions to produce a rapid report on the education of teachers (James 1972)[55] it proved to be the very antithesis of what had gone before. No research, nothing on resources, no costs of its proposals, an after-dinner-speech kind of a report. A period of openness in educational planning had been replaced by baffling silence, secrecy and evasion.

Only in 1974 with the appointment of the Warnock committee on special education and the reconvening of the Teacher Supply Committee did the older tradition appear to be returning.

Formal Departmental Planning – Model 1

In the mid-sixties various people had called for a National Plan for education, and Crosland as a new Minister had set up a Planning Branch within DES and some saw this as the body to formulate such an overall set of proposals and priorities. This never happened. The Branch was set up against strong opposition from senior officials in the Department. Crosland's own account illustrates this. The Department argued that 'it did not need a central planning division because the planning function was already being carried out in the separate operations branches – teacher supply, school building, further education and so on. I didn't agree.'[56] He had to insist on his proposal. 'I sent a polite minute to Herbert Andrew saying "I would be grateful for your final advice on this matter as I propose to make a public announcement in a fortnight's time." An experienced civil servant can always tell when the argument is over and he's lost the battle.'[57] However it is far from clear that Crosland had won. The Branch was never given the resources or the status to perform effectively. It was in quite a different position to the Planning, Evaluation and Budgeting teams we have described in the American context. It was not a unit superimposed above the other branches which were responsible for schools, or teacher supply or further education. It could not give advice on the respective merits of these other branches' claims on resources. Such an innovation would have run counter to the structure and traditions of the whole of the civil service. Instead it was created as a parallel branch and a weak one too. The statisticians were brought within it but they continued to do broadly what they had done before – produce a comprehensive series of historical statistics and make projections. Then two economists were brought in – the first the department had ever employed. The branch serviced the needs of other branches and conducted two major exercises that were published – a feasibility exercise for the programme or output budget and the other a paper outlining the trends in demand for higher education.[58] The Branch was never allowed to compete with or in any way challenge the specialist or 'policy' branches.

Formal Planning–Model 2

When the Conservative Government came to power in 1970 and the new PAR arrangements were being discussed, the Planning Branch was abolished and a new arrangement was introduced in 1971 called the Departmental Planning Organisation. It was officially said to consist of a 'flexible network of committees and working groups'. The first principle upon which it rested was that 'planning must directly involve those who must administer the policies that have to be planned.' What this meant was that the policy branches were officially included in the planning system. Nor were they to be dictated to by a separate breed of 'planners'. 'Specialist skills must be built into the machinery in such a way as to ensure that they can make a creative contribution to policy formation without being able to determine it single handed.'[59]

The Planning Organisation since then has consisted of:

1 A Policy Steering Group under the Chairmanship of the Permanent Secretary which includes the heads of the most important branches. It determines the planning programme in consultation with Ministers. It sets particular studies in motion and receives the reports when they are complete, before submitting them, if they are accepted, to Ministers.
2 Beneath this are specialist policy groups each chaired by a Deputy Secretary covering a particular programme category or field of activity, e.g. schools or further education. On these groups will be Under-Secretaries, HM Inspectors, specialists like architects and statisticians. It may well break down into small subgroups.
3 To service these groups is a Planning Unit to ensure that consistent planning, population and cost data are used.

It was this machinery that was employed to conduct a comprehensive assessment of resource priorities and plans for the 1970s. The results eventually emerged as the White Paper: *Education a Framework for Expansion* in December 1972. The review took the form of two separate PARs within the new government wide machinery described earlier in the Chapter. Thus from the earliest stages the Treasury and the Central Policy Review Staff were involved. The results were put before the appropriate PAR committees and then fed into the PESC machinery. The whole exercise was dominated by the need to keep education expenditure within the new constraints that were being applied to public expenditure overall.

The White Paper does even so represent an attempt to view the system as a whole and to make explicit decisions about priorities between the different sectors of education – pre-school, primary, secondary and higher education. The declining birth rate made it possible to consider realistically alternative strategies and the White Paper proposed tipping the balance more towards the pre-school/primary school sectors and away from higher education in the next decade. Part time nursery education for all children by the early 1980s was balanced by a reduced expansion in higher education. The way the proposals were evolved indicates very clearly how the whole planning process has now become subordinated to or contained within the public expenditure control process we have described. The informal pluralist system of advisory committees was at least temporarily abandoned. An open system had been replaced by a more closed one. A diffuse system by a more centralised one.

Health and Welfare
A brief look at the Health and Welfare services shows that similar trends have been at work there too. The Secretary of State for Health and Social Security has had direct responsibility and control over a larger part of the health sector than his or her education counterpart. Until 1974 only a small part of total health expenditure was undertaken by locally elected health authorities. Since the reorganisation the whole budget is ultimately the responsibility of the Secretary of State. Only the personal social services remain in the hands of the local councils. In this respect the old Ministry of Health (pre-1968) and its successor have had more opportunity to undertake forward planning than the education counterpart. Yet until the last few years the Department of Health has never taken as active a role. This has something to do with the strongly independent medical profession and the powerful part it plays in the administration of the regional and local levels of the service. It also reflects the low financial priority which health was accorded in the 1950s and that had to do with the political conflict within which the service was created. Once again technical logic and political pressure combined to make capital planning the most important, indeed almost the only form of forward planning the Ministry undertook until recently, apart from one disastrous decision to cut the entry to medical schools in the mid-1950s.

Capital Planning
The Guillebaud Committee had been set up by the new Conservative Government in 1952 to suggest ways of limiting the cost of the

Health Service. Its report, instead, suggested that the service was under-financed, notably its capital programme which was running at a third of the pre-war level. As we have seen the lack of new hospital building became a political issue between the two main parties and this led ultimately, after the 1959 election, to the Ministry asking Regional Hospital Boards to prepare a 10-year building programme for their regions, with the main aim of replacing the very oldest. Nearly half of the hospitals had then been built a century before. The Boards were given guidelines showing how many beds per 1,000 population they ought to seek to provide under five different headings – acute, geriatric, maternity, mental illness and mental subnormality. The 'scientific' bases for most of these guidelines were very thin and most showed relatively little change on the existing levels, but there was one very important change – a projected drop of more than a third in the number of mental illness beds per 1,000 population (3·3–1·9). The reasons for this are now well known. The changing pattern of treatment, more outpatient work, short stay units and above all the increased use of tranquillisers first introduced around the spring of 1954 had caused a steady fall in the mental hospital population. The General Registry Office began to make a study of the changes. In 1954 it took a sample of all entrants to mental hospitals in that year and followed it up with another sample cohort in 1956 and 1959. It was possible to build up a picture of how many patients were being discharged within three months, six months and so on. Largely using the results from the 1956 cohort statisticians at the Ministry and the General Registry Office produced a paper arguing that bed requirements could fall to about 1·8 per 1,000, in other words virtually the level that was eventually adopted for planning purposes.[60] Since about a third of all hospital beds were for mental illness such a reduction would have a very significant impact on the size of the building programme. It is not our purpose to follow the disputes that arose about this planning target or the validity of the statistical assumptions. They were in fact revised later. What we must emphasise here is that as a result of this whole exercise the government published a White Paper in 1962,[61] which committed that government, and in effect suceeding governments, to a programme of building which must be the largest the country had ever undertaken. From a regular £10 millions a year on hospital building in the mid 1950s, mainly devoted to extensions and patching-work, the total sum to be spent rose steadily to well over £100 millions in 1970. Ironically, the politician to carry through this *coup* was one of those three Treasury Ministers who had resigned in 1957 because they were unable to check the rise in public spending – Enoch Powell. Until recently planning in health service terms has been dominated by this huge building programme.

Planning from Behind

If community care for patients not catered for in hospital was to become a reality the local authorities responsible for the domiciliary services and for intermediate care had to respond. The Ministry therefore asked local councils to review their services and draw up a ten-year development plan. They were to be prepared on the assumption that loan sanctions ran at about the same rate as before and they were to think in terms of current expenditure growing in the next four years by about $2\frac{1}{2}$ per cent a year. This figure came directly from the new PESC exercise. No guidelines for planning were set. The consequence was a very wide variation in the proposals the authorities produced. They regularly extrapolated forward previous trends in their authority and if anything the plans showed that there would be even more variation at the end of the ten-year period than there were at the beginning. The Ministry put these proposals together in a single document and published it as a White Paper. In the document and a later circular the Ministry commented on the proposals.[62] It was mildly critical of some aspects. It thought more residential accommodation was needed for the elderly and handicapped and probably more domiciliary staff. Authorities were asked to submit revisions rolling the programmes forward a year.

This polite and tentative criticism was very much in tune with the Ministry's whole approach to the local health and welfare authorities during the previous fifteen years. Gentle pressure and persuasion continued. But at the end of the sixties came the upheaval caused first by reorganisation of the personal social services and then the reorganisation of the whole National Health Service. Very soon after their creation the new Social Service Departments were asked to submit ten-year plans though this time guidelines were suggested by the central department for particular services and a 10 per cent figure for overall expansion was mentioned. It is these plans that have suffered particularly badly in the successive round of cuts since 1972.[63]

Informal Promotional Planning

In contrast to education the Ministry of Health did not use advisory committees to produce forward plans, although the Guillebaud committee gave rise to some development as we have seen and the Cranbrooke committee[64] on the maternity services made proposals for increasing the number of hospital confinements. The Royal Commission on Medical Education is the only committee to have made long term proposals to increase the intake to medical schools.[65] The long term view has been dominated by the hospital capital programme with a separate and very tentative process carried out by local authorities. In short until the late 1960s forward planning, in so far as it existed, was exclusively institution dominated, as opposed to beginning with the needs or demands of particular groups in the population.

Systematic Forward Planning

Planning for particular groups, on a national scale really began with Crossman's reactions to Ely and the attempt to plan services for the mentally handicapped – responsive planning. Then as a pure accident of timing the reorganisation of the Health Service took place while the emphasis within Central Government was upon introducing managerial principles into public administration. It coincided exactly with the elaborations of PESC and PAR. Arising out of a proposal in the Consultative Document a study group was set up under a Steering Committee with Departmental representatives and outsiders, to consider the management structure of the service. We are not concerned here with the structure but with the planning system that was proposed in Chapter Three of their report. (The Grey Book).[66] It bears a close resemblance both to a PPB system and to HEW's Master Calendar approach we discussed in the previous chapter. The Department is now experimenting with a planning and programming approach that follows the broad outlines of what the 'Grey Book' proposed, though it differs significantly in detail. Taken together with the PAR and PESC changes the planning apparatus has now taken a sharp turn towards the systematic managerial form though, as we shall see, this applies most to the programming element.

As a result of the PAR reorganisation the Department emerged in January 1972 with a small Central Planning Unit for the whole department and a separate policy unit for the two sides of the Department – Health and Social Security. The Secretary of State and senior staff can arm themselves, before the major PESC battle is joined in the summer, with an overall briefing discussion of the Department's possible priorities, and these will evolve not only with changing political pressures but in part as a consequence of regular PARs. From the PESC exercise will emerge the rate of growth for the Health Service in the next five-year period and in firm terms for the next three years. This must then be translated into the guidance given to the regions and via them for the areas and districts. It will provide the constraints for their short-term plans, and in particular next year's budgets. The building programme demands a longer perspective, but the Department wants this perspective to apply to all resources, not merely buildings. Hence the DHSS will, in future (post-1974), ask Regional Health Authorities for ten or fifteen-year plans. The Central Department will offer broad guidance on priorities and constraints. Each Regional Authority will then draw up its own list of priorities within its region and these will in turn be passed to the area authorities to produce more detailed strategic plans for their areas on a district by district basis. Clearly the lower tiers are not necessarily going to agree with the proposals from above and will argue with them. In the end a regional plan will be drawn up summarising the outcome of these discussions and will cover a ten to fifteen year period. This will be submitted to the Secretary of State. It is only envisaged that these plans will be revised every 3–5 years. They will set the targets towards which the areas will work with their rolling three-year plans and they will set the rationale for capital allocations.

The Department is drawing up a complex information system setting out what data each district will need to collect in order to make the plans and which it must submit to the area as a justification for its proposals. As in the Grey Book this will involve a consideration of the needs of each 'care group' in the community.

What we then see emerging for the National Health Service is the most managerial and the most hierarchical of planning systems we have encountered either in America or the UK. Yet, as we shall argue in later chapters, it is still almost exclusively concerned with planning resource inputs and to that extent is still far removed from the pure PPB model.

Social Security
Social Security provides a contrast not only to the other Departments we have discussed in Britain but to its counterpart in Washington.* It has had complete financial and administrative res-

---

* It has undergone various metamorphoses. From 1948–66 the Department responsible was the Ministry of Pensions and National Insurance (MPNI). Assistance Benefits were administered by a semi-independent body, the National Assistance Board (NAB). From 1966–8 the MPNI became the Ministry of Social Security. Day to day administration of assistance benefits was to be controlled by a separate Commission, the Supplementary Benefits Commission. Then in 1968 this Ministry was absorbed into a new joint Department of Health and Social Security which continues to date.

ponsibility for its programmes, unlike education and unlike the pre-1974 Health Service. Yet it has also been less intimately bound up with the PESC routine since only about 18 per cent of its expenditure is financed out of general taxation. PESC especially in its early days was primarily concerned with levels of general taxation. To most economists the distinction between insurance contributions and general taxation is something of a nonsense but the political differences are real. Then it has had virtually no capital planning. Nor has the Ministry used its advisory committee procedure in the way education was able to do. The National Insurance Advisory Committee (NIAC) has confined its activities to fairly narrow technical questions. Since pensions especially have been such a contentious area of party political debate, the Ministry could scarcely get involved in the freebooting promotional activities of its American counterpart or indeed of its educational colleagues in Curzon Street. The only important example of an external committee in this field is the Philips Committee (1954).[67] This was set up as a twin to the Guillebaud Committee by the then Conservative Government to investigate ways of cutting the Exchequer contributions to national insurance. This time the committee relied on departmental actuarial advice. It came out with answers the Government must have been hoping for. In the light of demographic trends it argued it would be too costly to seek to provide subsistence level old age pensions and other benefits. The Exchequer contribution from general taxation to the Insurance Fund should be kept to a minimum. As we have argued previously the graduated pension scheme of 1959 was devised within the Ministry partly to counter Labour's National Superannuation proposals prior to the 1959 election but mainly as a way of finding a politically acceptable way of raising insurance contributions to avoid what otherwise would have been a steady increase in the 'subsidy' from general taxation. From 1965 onwards the Ministry and its successors have been heavily engaged in replanning the whole social security system first along lines laid down by the incoming Wilson Government.[68] It was a scheme that had been worked out in some detail in opposition. Then after 1970 another complete 'recasting' was undertaken along lines laid down by the new Conservative Government.[69] Both schemes and particularly the Labour Government scheme involved planning over a period of forty years, and in particular over the next twenty.

To undertake the 1965–9 exercise the Department, really for the first time, had to set up a special policy planning unit to work through the immensely complex consequences of going over from a largely flat rate insurance scheme to a graduated one that would cater for most of the pension needs of most of the population. The task fell to a small, in restrospect a far too small, group. There is no space, nor is it relevant, to tell that particular story. The outcome of their labours was at least temporarily lost when the 1970 election returned a government committed to a very different scheme. This time a much larger group was set to work on the new legislation which was on the statute book in three years. At the same time the PAR changes were taking place and the policy analysis section that was undertaking the review also assumed the task of undertaking regular PARs. Those involved felt with some justice that they knew most of the available options backwards. They could reasonably claim that the insurance system had been under continuous PAR review for nearly eight years, but there were still plenty of smaller issues to investigate. The aim was to take each of the major 'programme' areas – there were about ten in social security – and undertake one PAR each year.

In this case then the impact of the PESC and PAR exercises have not been as traumatic or far-reaching as in the two previous cases, if only because the period since 1964 had been traumatic enough in any case.

In Brief

The contrasts with the American attempts at the forward planning and control of public expenditure are important. The British reforms, prepared in outline in the 1961 Plowden report, were introduced relatively quietly and tentatively. They have evolved steadily ever since in technical sophistication. Initially the reforms laid little stress on choice or analysis but as the sixties passed American ideas made their impact and the two traditions drew closer together. Yet the Treasury learned from the main errors of the American experiment even if the more enthusiastic outsiders and politicians did not. What resulted was a 'two track' system, one the forward planning of public expenditure, the other a selective in depth review of policies and programmes. The central departments formed the link playing the leading role in both performances.

What emerges fairly clearly from considering the impact of these changes on three separate areas of social service planning, is the way in which all the disparate and informal systems of planning have, to a very large degree, been incorporated within or contained by the new public expenditure control system. It is a contrast to the outcome of similar attempts in the United States, but above all it illustrates the fact that it has been possible for social service planning to become both more 'comprehensive' and to have a longer term perspective than was the case fifteen years ago. It has also become dominated by the need to keep within resource constraints and hence to consider opportunity costs – the possible alternative use of resources. These elements in the synoptic method have become accepted as of political necessity, and in consequence organisational forms have been developed to cater for them. This is not the same thing as saying that 'the Treasury has won' for the PAR system provides the spending departments with a continuous opportunity for feeding new proposals into the system although its originators clearly hoped that it would be primarily used for the opposite purpose. Most important of all, the whole process depends crucially on the attitudes to spending and tax levels within the Cabinet. It depends on how far ministers wish to 'relate' public spending to economic growth and how far they wish to 'equate' it. In the 1960s PESC could be said to have been the means of achieving faster growth in social spending. If it is still unclear what the long-term impact of the new procedures will be, it is clear that the new 'systematic' control procedures have tended to 'close' the decision making process. Despite Fulton's injunctions, social policy planning since 1968 became more secretive and more obscure. That was most noticeably the case in the education sector which had previously been characterised by a remarkable degree of open debate and informal planning. So in this respect Linblom's fears have been borne out, comprehensive planning is also more centralised and less open planning. At the same time it is apparently no less 'political' or value laden, nor has it been any less 'incremental'. Indeed in some respects the system has become dominated by the concept of an average annual rate of increase, with each department fighting for its 'fair' share of this increment.

REFERENCES

1 Sir Samuel Goldman, *The Developing System of Public Expenditure Management and Control*, Civil Service College Studies No. 2, HMSO, London, 1973, p. 73.
2 Enquiry into the Cost of the National Health Service, Cmd 9663, 1956.
3 D. V. Donnison, *The Government of Housing*, Pelican, 1967.
   Exchequer subsidies for 'general need' annually per house:

February, 1952	£26 14s
April, 1955	£22 1s
November, 1955	£10
November, 1956	Nil

4 Circulars 10/56–11/56	February, 1956
54/57	November, 1957
4/58	January, 1958

5 *Local Government Finance* Cmnd 209, 1957.

See also Enoch Powell's speech to the Conservative Party Conference in 1957: 'By the new financial arrangements between central and local government we shall provide encouragement for thrift and responsibility in local expenditure ... only thus can be got the elbow room that is needed in the economy, room to fight inflation and room to reduce taxation.' Powell was at that time a Treasury Minister.

6 'The main feature of the scheme, in some ways its whole essence, is that it is expected to save the Exchequer £99 million in its first year of operation rising to no less than £428 million in 1981/2.' *Economist*, 18 October, 1958.

7 H. Heclo and A. Wildavsky, op. cit.

8 Committee on the Cost of Health Service, op. cit.

9 The Crowther report showed that the sixth form population was likely to double between 1958 and 1964. *15 to 18*, Ministry of Education, HMSO, 1959.

10 The Labour Party produced a series of policy documents in these years: *Homes for the Future, Learning to Live, National Superannuation, Members One of Another.* For a philosophical justification for the shift of emphasis see C. A. R. Crosland, *The Future of Socialism*, Cape, 1956.

11 Heclo and Wildavsky, pp. 167–8.

12 Ibid., p. 203.

13 Ibid., p. 208.

14 *Control of Public Expenditure*, Cmnd 1432 (1961).

15 Ibid., para. 31.

16 Lord Bridges, *The Treasury*, George Allen & Unwin, London, 1966 Chapter XIV.

17 Heclo and Wildavsky, p. 38.

18 For official accounts of the process in broad outline see First Report from the Select Committee on Procedure, Session 1968/9. *Scrutiny of Public Expenditure and Administration*, HC 410 (1968/9). Evidence from the Treasury 26 February 1969. Or again in H 549 (1970/71), also HM Treasury *Public Expenditure White Papers Handbook on Methodology*, HMSO 1972. For a series of official accounts see Sir Richard Clarke, *New Trends in Government*, Civil Service College Studies No. 1, HMSO, 1971, p. 42–7, and more fully Goldman, op. cit. For an American view see Heclo and Wildavsky, op. cit., Chapter 5.

19 For a technical description of the principles see P. M. Rees and F. P. Thompson, 'The Relative Price Effect in Public Expenditure, its Nature and Method of Calculation', *Statistical News*, August, 1972.

20 Cmnd 2235, December, 1963.

21 Cmnd 5519, December, 1973.

22 Cmnd 1432, para. 17.

23 Cmnd 2764.   24 Cmnd 2915.   25 Cmnd 3515.

26 Cmnd 4017.

27 Public Expenditure 1968–9 to 1973–4, Cmnd 4234 (1969).

28 Heclo and Wildavsky, op. cit., pp. 271–2.
29 Cmnd 4506, para. 52. Shortly after the Conservatives came to office in June 1970 two issues of the Treasury's *Economic Progress Report*, August and October, 1970, were devoted to a description of PPB in theory and as it was being applied in practice in the Department of Defence, the Home Office and Education.
30 The White Paper, Cmnd 4506, stated: 'These reviews would be a natural extension of the public expenditure survey system and would support present departmental submissions in the public expenditure survey cycle.'
31 HC 410, para. 22.
32 Cmnd 4506, para. 46. See Pollitt, C., in *Public Administration*, Winter, 1974.
33 This is an amalgam of slightly different descriptions produced by various civil servants in different departments. An early description of what the Treasury hoped for is described in evidence to the House of Commons Expenditure Committee. HC 147 (1971–2).
34 House of Commons, 17 April, 1961.
35 See Clarke's article in *Taxation Policy*, Ed. W. A. Robson and B. Crick, Penguin, Harmondsworth, Middlesex, 1972.
36 *Public Expenditure: Management and Control*, op. cit., p. 12.
37 Op. cit., p. 9.
38 See F. L. Pryor, *Public Expenditures in Communist and Capitalist Nations:* George Allen & Unwin, London, 1968 (especially Chapters IV and V) and on a more general level see: H. L. Wilensky: *The Welfare State and Equality: The Structural and Ideological Roots of Public Consumption Expenditures.* University of California Press, Berkeley, 1974.
39 *Public Expenditure to 1976–77*, Cmnd 5178.
40 *Public Expenditure to 1977–78*, Cmnd 5519 and the Chancellor's Statement 17 December, 1973.
41 Fifth Report from the Expenditure Committee Session 1972/3, HC 149 (1972–3), para. 11.
42 Expenditure Committee (General Sub-Committee) evidence given on 28 January, 1974. HC 143 (1973–4), p. 29.
43 Cmd 9703.
44 Cmnd 604.
45 Ministry of Education, Circular 12/63.
46 Department of Education and Science, Circular 13/68.
47 Central Advisory Council for England: *Early Leaving*, 1954; *15–18*, (Crowther), 1959. *Half our Future* (Newsom), 1963; *Children and their Primary Schools* (Plowden) 1967.
48 See the review article by the author in *Journal of the Royal Statistical Society*, Series A., Vol. 132, Part 2, 1969.
49 *Education: A Framework for Expansion*, Cmnd 5174.
50 *Higher Education*, Cmnd 2154 (1963).
51 See for example DES, *Education Planning Paper No. 2, Student*

Numbers in Higher Education in England and Wales, HMSO, 1970.
52 See Boyles's comments to Kegan in E. Boyle and A. Crosland (Ed. M. Kogan) *The Politics of Education*, Penguin Books, Harmondsworth, 1971. The last report published by this body was the ninth report, *The Demand and Supply of Teachers 1965–86*.
53 Kogan, M., in *The Role of Commissions in Policy Making* (Ed.) Chapman, R. A., George Allen and Unwin, London, 1973. This also gives a vivid account of such a committee at work and its impact. See also R. Layard, *et al.*, *The Impact of Robbins*, Penguin, Harmondsworth, 1969.
54 Boyle and Crosland, op. cit., pp. 173–4.
55 *Teacher Education and Training*. A Report of a Committee of Enquiry appointed by the Secretary of State for Education and Science (under the chairmanship of Lord James of Rusholme), HMSO, 1972.
56 Boyle and Crosland, op. cit., p. 177.
57 Ibid., p. 183.
58 DES Education Planning Papers Nos. 1 and 2.
59 Pyle, Sir W., *Public Administration*, Spring, 1974.
60 G. C. Tooth and E. M. Brooke, 'Trends in the Mental Hospital Population', *Lancet*, 1 April, 1961.
61 Cmnd 1604.
62 Cmnd 1973 and Ministry of Health Circular 6/63.
63 Webb, A. and Falk, N., in *Policy and Politics*, December, 1974.
64 Report of the Maternity Services Committee, 1959.
65 The Report of the Royal Commission on Medical Education 1965–68. Cmnd 3569 (1968). The only other attempt to plan entry to medical schools by a departmental committee in 1956 (the Willinck Committee) proved disastrous. It recommended a cut in the intake of 10 per cent just at the point in time when the birth rate began to rise as we now know with hindsight.
66 Department of Health and Social Security, *Management Arrangements for the Reorganised National Health Service*. HMSO, 1972.
67 Committee on *Economic and Financial Problems of the Provision for Old Age*, Cmd 9333 (1954).
68 *National Superannuation and Social Insurance*, Cmnd 3883 (1969).
69 *Strategy for Pensions*, Cmnd 4755 (1971).

Further Reading

Heclo, H., and Wildavsky, A., *The Private Government of Public Money*, op. cit. (Chapters 5–8).
Clarke, Sir Richard, *New Trends in Government*, Civil Service College Studies, No. 1. HMSO, 1971.
Goldman, Sir Samuel, *The Developing System of Public Expenditure Management and Control*, Civil Service College Studies, No. 2. HMSO 1973.

Chapter 8

Output Budgets
Out?

The previous two chapters have been concerned with the planning *process*. This is more narrowly concerned with one tool of analysis: the presentation of expenditure figures and in particular the concept of programme or output budgets. It begins by referring back to the original American proposals, goes on to discuss the inherent difficulties, examines some of the outcomes in the US and the UK and finally draws lessons from the different experiences.

Original intentions
It will be recalled that the American reformers had laid great store by the presentation of the budget. The characteristics of a useful budget structure were seen to be:

the allocation of money costs to defined objectives;
the presentation of accounts in such a way as to facilitate comparisons between different ways of achieving the same objectives;
the inclusion of output measures to accompany each programme or sub-programme;
the categorisation of expenditure and outputs into sufficiently discrete activities to enable cost effectiveness studies to be made.

Taken together this entailed the creation of a logical hierarchy of distinct programmes. Taking health as one example, it had been argued that five basic programmes could be distinguished, each related to the following five health goals: [1]

Prevention and control of disease
Treatment of illness and injury

Long-term care for the chronically sick, the disabled, the aged
Training
Research (not clearly allocable to the above)

Each of these broad programmes could in turn be sub-divided by
type of disease. Thus 'prevention and control' could be divided
between.

Communicable diseases
Neurological, metabolic and degenerative diseases
Mental diseases
Chronic diseases
Occupational health
Environmental hazards
Other

'Prevention' could also be sub-divided between certification, care
and detention, technical laboratory services, research, etc.

Within each grouping it was further desirable to cross classify by
type of institution, the source of funds, the beneficiary group –
children, old people, etc. The sheer volume of data necessary to
undertake such an analysis would have been vast. Yet before any
technical difficulties were encountered those who sought to apply
this 'top to bottom' approach to social service budgets ran into more
fundamental logical and indeed ideological problems. They went
beyond the issues of general principle raised in Chapter Two.
Lindblom and others had emphasised the lack of consensus which
exists in many areas of policy. This proved particularly true of
social policy. Yet this difficulty has been compounded by the degree
of professional independence that is often considered appropriate
and beneficial to these services.

At least seven major difficulties have been encountered in trying
to create new budget structures for the social services.

1 Disputed Objectives

The first and most basic difficulty has been that the objectives of
social policy, in general and in particular, are in dispute. The literature of social policy is largely concerned with disagreements about
the appropriate boundaries and rationale for social intervention.[2] It
is the very stuff of political debate. Nor can it be argued that disputes only occur about marginal changes. Recent policy debates on
housing finance, social security and secondary reorganisation have
concerned issues of central importance. Each has arisen because the

L

two political parties hold sharply conflicting views about the appropriate role or purpose of council housing, social security and secondary schools.

Thus social services are typically concerned with areas where either final objectives are in dispute or where there is disagreement on what weight to attach to the several outcomes. Where agreement does exist it usually focuses on means not ends. The recent proposal to introduce universal part-time pre-school education is a case in point. It was supported by those who hoped that it would help to break a cycle of multiple deprivation, and by others who believed that this was a profoundly mistaken belief. It was supported by those who wished to see more mothers go out to work, and by those who thought that such an outcome would be socially damaging, it was supported by those who hoped for a more equal society and by those to whom this was an anathema. It was supported by parents who wanted social benefits for their children and by those who wanted them to learn to read earlier and do better academically. This is typical of most extensions in social welfare. Nor is it the case that in an *established* social service the 'providers' – social workers, local housing officials, or teachers, are agreed about their objectives or the values they see embodied in the activity they are performing. Nor, where a service is locally provided, are the local authorities of the same mind. Looking in retrospect at the actual resource decisions taken by local authorities, Byrne and Williamson[3] have argued that it is possible to distinguish authorities that have pursued élitist strategies and those who have devoted more resources to a more egalitarian approach, e.g. funding primary schools more generously. They argue that these strategies do reflect a different philosophical approach to education which is in its turn related to the social class composition of the areas.

Now, in theory, there is no reason why a dispute about objectives should not be resolved by creating a whole series of quite different strategies. It would be possible to argue that one of the two or three central objectives of the education system is to educate to the maximum feasible extent a small number of people who would constitute an effective ruling class. Alternatively it might be postulated that the education system should aim to make possible the maximum possible participation of all citizens in every kind of decision. Both views are firmly held within the world of education, and to accept one objective, as opposed to the other, would have profound consequences for resource allocation. Another central objective might be to pass on to the next generation our common culture and heritage. It could be contrasted with the aim of diversifying or even transforming our culture. All these views would gain support.

A fourth objective might be to train an appropriately skilled labour force to ensure maximum growth of the economy. It could be contrasted with one that sought to educate children in such a way that they were weaned from a desire to acquire possessions and sought instead a peaceful rustic existence.

This may seem rather far removed from the process of public expenditure control but to take the construction of an output budget seriously raises such issues. Once raised how can such disputes be resolved by those who would construct a budget framework? Clearly one theoretical solution is to analyse the budget from numerous perspectives and compare the results. Moreover if the intention is merely to present different analyses of total expenditure broken down in different ways it is not only theoretically possible, it is a practical possibility too.

However, that was not what the original theory entailed. For the budget to be the basis for forward planning, expenditure control and analysis of comparative effectiveness there has, for all practical purposes, to be one budget framework. It is important to understand why this is so. It was argued that if budgets were to work effectively the administrative divisions should match the programme categories. There could not be multiple administrative hierarchies. Similarly if the purpose is to conduct discussions with the Treasury on the future public expenditure strategy there has to be a single agreed set of expenditure categories. Above all the data requirements for a *set* of different budget programme structures would be excessively costly. As it is Parliamentary or Congressional appropriations usually run parallel to the new programme budgets.

However, if it were necessary to produce *one* budget structure this would mean embarking upon a long and bitter battle about basic philosophical or political values which no Finance Officer or Comptroller is going to relish. In many areas of social policy individuals and organisations only continue to work together because they agree to differ about aims and objectives. Output like beauty lies in the eye of the beholder.

2 Professional Providers

Not only are objectives disputed but the responsibility of deciding what these objectives should be in any situation are devolved to quite a remarkable degree in social services. This reflects not merely the professional status or semi-professional status of those who actually perform the services but a widely held view that these professions ought to have a high degree of autonomy. This is true of both Britain and America but the professional freedom is perhaps greater in many respects in Britain. Certainly school teachers and social workers in the public service are freer from administrative oversight in Britain, while the medical profession defends its rights to 'clinical freedom' as vigorously and successfully as ever. A head teacher and his heads of departments in a British school can decide what is taught, who teaches and how it is taught. Indeed the individual class teacher usually has a substantial degree of freedom. We emphasised the general importance of this in Chapter Two. The peculiar difficulty it presents in this context is that society deliberately leaves many of the most difficult value conflicts to be resolved by the individual professional. One set of values will be held by one worker, a different set by another, and especially in the case of education the very health of the democracy depends on that being so. Indeed, it could be said that the one objective on which most of those in the education system agree is that it should not pursue any one set of objectives or hold to one set of values. Even that is in dispute.

Education may seem an extreme case, but decisions about life and death are left to doctors on precisely analogous grounds. So too are the tensions between 'social control' or 'befriending the client' in social work.

Once again taken at its face value the concept of an 'output' or 'objective' oriented budget raises issues of the profoundest importance, and runs the risk of causing the bitter resentment and hostility of the professions. It may be right to bring the professions to account in this way but there is clearly more at stake here than a piece of financial book-keeping.

3 The Views of the Consumers

In all the massive literature on output budgeting one rarely if ever finds the budget official advised to build his budget on the expressed preferences of consumers. Users of services may have very different views about its objectives.

In their evidence to the House of Commons Expenditure Committee DHSS officials explained how difficult it was to set aims or objectives for services to the elderly.[4] They said:

'General aims for the services can be formulated in such terms as "to enable the elderly to maintain their independence and self-respect"; "to enable them so far as they are able and willing, to take part in and contribute to the normal range of social life of their community";

"to enable them to live in their own homes as long as they wish and are reasonably able to do so"; "to provide for essential needs which the elderly, with the support of their friends and families, cannot meet for themselves"; "to provide treatment and care of an appropriate standard for those suffering from chronic disabilities", "to restore patients with illness or disability to as healthy a state as possible", etc. Even at this level of generality the possibility arises of conflicts between the ideals embodied in different aims. Thus a chronically sick old person may wish to stay in his own home though he could be looked after better (in a technical sense) and more economically in a residential home or hospital. It is necessary to have regard to the welfare of the old person's family when setting aims, and this can be in conflict with what is best for, or desired by, the old person himself.'

4 *Multiple Objectives*

Even if the objectives of social services were not in dispute, even if the professional were a passive agent, or the consumers' views were known and consistent, even then analysts face the most difficult technical task of deciding how to create a budget structure for a single activity that has a multiplicity of outcomes. For example: the one professional activity we call 'general practice' encompasses or can encompass all the five major programme areas previously listed – prevention, treatment, long-term care, even training and research. Nor is it enough to argue that the GP's time can be allocated out between these different headings and costed. Quite apart from the sheer technical difficulty and the probability that individual returns would not be comparable or even correct, the basic problem is that a great deal of a GP's work contributes to several objectives. Seeing a mother and a child, who almost certainly has no more than a temporary stomach upset, may be counted as a totally unproductive contribution to the treatment of illness. But it could also be counted as prevention since the child might have had something more serious. Probably much more important, willingness to see such a case means that the mother and others like her will bring their children much more readily on other occasions. A brisk assurance by the receptionist that 'every child has it, don't bother the doctor he is far too busy' will make the preventative role much less effective. It could also be that the mother needs such an excuse to discuss some more embarrassing symptom for herself or her husband. Or the mother may be under psychological stress and need more reassurance. The visit may count as therapy for the mother. The stress may well be caused by having a chronically sick or mentally disturbed grandmother living with the family. 'Community care' may well involve precisely this kind of additional and apparently irrelevant support work. It is even conceivable that the GP may be doing some epidemiological research. Yet general practice is not an odd exception, by far the greater part of the public's contact with the health service is with their GP. Precisely the same arguments apply to school teaching. We know from detailed studies something of what teachers do in the classroom.[5] We know a great deal of time is spent tying up shoelaces, shepherding children down corridors, taking dinner money and so on. It is by no means clear to which, if any, of the deeply controversial aims of education these activities contribute. Nor are the more obviously instructional activities much easier to classify. The 'seamless robe' of a university don's teaching and research is now a well-worn example.

To get round such difficulties General Practice expenditure can be allocated in a largely arbitrary way between the different headings, or it may be put into the one category called general medicine or primary care. Either way it is only a partial view of this central activity, which is both practically indivisible and contributes to other activities in an important way.

Allocations between budget categories will, or should, differ depending on what kind of question the policy maker needs answered. For example, if the question is 'how much will it cost to expand the teaching of chemistry in a university', the whole additional cost of employing new staff and extra laboratory space must be included. It is irrelevant that the staff may spend half their time doing research. If the teaching is to be done and good staff recruited, the research must needs be bought too. If the policy question relates to the funding of research then it is relevant to include an estimate of the cost of research undertaken by university teachers. Thus any single budget structure is likely to be inadequate to answer different policy issues.

Quite apart from these theoretical difficulties there is the sheer practical difficulty of collecting information of the kind required in most hierarchical programme structures. It is extremely difficult, at present impossible, to collect information regularly on the way professionals use their time, in allocating, say, a nurse's time between different types of patient in the same ward. Where attempts of this kind are made very little reliance can be placed on the results. At the periphery where the raw data are assembled it is either done by accounting officers who often aim to return figures which either look good for the institution or give answers they hope the civil service or senior management want. Alternatively, the allocations tend to be done in an arbitrary way by junior or clerical staff. Consistency and accuracy are of a low order. The UGC's surveys of universities asking for allocations of expenditure between research and teaching are one example. None of this argues against occasional and well-controlled surveys of how individuals in an organisation are using their time. What resources and skills are devoted to what kind of activity? Such work is difficult but not impossible. It involves the careful allocation of like activities to comparable accounting categories, the identification of the many organisational variables and regression analysis. Such serious work can be positively harmed by crude and arbitrary attempts to allocate expenditure on a regular basis to fit some apparently neat and 'logical' budget framework.

5 Hidden Objectives

It is not infrequently the case in social policy that the overt objective of a programme, which may even be enshrined in legislation, is very different from the real political objectives which produced it. Title 1 of the US 1965 Elementary and Secondary Education Act has been quoted as a case in point. The legislation is overtly designed to give special help to children from poor families, but the political motives were mixed and the dominant one may simply have been to tap federal funds to support local school districts.

The objectives were thus both mixed and hidden. One useful bye-product of seeking to design a programme structure may be to expose some of these implicit or hidden objectives. The solution is less obvious. It is one thing to clear the minds of senior officials or ministers with the aid of a paper on objectives, and quite another to produce a programme structure for everyday use. Conflict, carefully avoided before, will win no friends amongst those administering the programme or amongst the politicians who may prefer to drop the whole idea of changing the budget format.

6 Changing Objectives

Social policy is concerned with people not products or processes. The services are delivered by professionals working locally and with a very high degree of independence. They are trained to be responsive to the needs of their clients. Donnison[6] has argued that most changes in social policy at the local level originate with the 'providers', are transmitted to and adopted by the 'controllers of resources' and subsequently may become formalised in statute or regulation. In this way social policy can remain adaptive and responsive to changing human needs. Any attempt to impose a set of centrally determined objectives is likely to frustrate such a process or merely be ignored.

Reformers claimed that the budget structure could be continually adapted to meet such objectives but in practice this is unlikely, especially if the structure of the budget has been tied to the management structure.

7 Measurement

An important part of the logic behind the original concept of a programme or output budget was that measures of output could be attached to each objective and hence to each programme or part of a programme. One part of the impetus to the development of 'social indicators' lay in providing such measures of achievement. Certainly most text books assume that some kind of concrete measure can be provided for each programme element even if it is only a measure of 'intermediate' output, i.e. something which facilitates the achievement of the final output rather than being a direct measure of it. As late as 1972 the House of Commons Committee on Expenditure expressed the view that:

'The idea of a comprehensive set of statistics of outputs over the whole range of public expenditure is an ambitious one. But we believe that it ought to be regarded as a realistic and reasonable aim.'[7]

Is it? Two fundamental difficulties have been encountered. First, it is generally true that social conditions, of one kind or another, very largely determine the 'success' of social service programmes. Changes in staying on rates at school are probably as much the consequences of the changes in the labour market as of changes within schools. The same is undoubtedly true of delinquency rates or health indicators. There are, to use the economists' jargon, multiple inputs, of which schools, medical care and social workers are only part and in most cases rather insignificant participants. Now, it is possible to try to disentangle these complex relationships. It is possible to compare situations, sometimes experimentally, in which one or a few of these variables differ but the rest remain the same. We shall describe some studies of this kind in a later chapter. But merely to append such crude statistical indicators as staying on rates, infant mortality rates or delinquency rates to expenditure figures on schools or clinics or probation services, is not merely useless, it is positively misleading. What is more they may in themselves harm attempts to measure results. What usually happens is that so-called 'intermediate' indicators are used – numbers of hospital beds in use, or schools built. In short they are measures of inputs. Such measures are, to quote Schultze, 'quite literally meaningless'.[8] More than that they may mislead. More hospital beds for confinements may be counterproductive if mothers would rather have their babies at home. An increase in the number of tanks the army possess is no help if tanks are to be valueless to any defence strategy.

This raises the second difficulty. Even if such measures did only reflect the impact of the service they are still meaningless until a value has been placed upon them relative to the other consequences that service may have. The particular danger lies in using as an indicator just one possible outcome. Yet to use many measures for one activity would be highly confusing. The point may be illustrated with reading attainment.

Every four years or so since the war the DES has sponsored a survey of reading standards in schools. In each survey since the war the reading ability of children has risen. But in the last survey no statistically significant change took place.[9] This produced all kinds of explanations. Most had to do with *schools*. Yet, as we have seen, the most likely explanation in statistical terms is that non-school factors were responsible, just as they may have accounted for the improved reading scores up to 1964. Yet even if we assume that primary schools were partly responsible and even if reading scores had fallen substantially it would be difficult to know what to conclude. Let us suppose that in response to all kinds of 'signals' from parents – more or less subtle – teachers conclude that many parents are more interested than before in making sure that their children can swim, learn to read music, play football or enjoy school and that if reading comes a little bit later this does not matter too much. The relative 'value' placed on these outputs compared to the others has increased. If this hypothesis is correct then, if swimming has improved, the total product has increased. Indeed, if reading scores *had* improved and swimming had not in the light of changed tastes, it could be said that output had fallen.

Olsen has argued that precisely because social services are to a significant extent 'public goods' there is no way that we can gain any estimate of the value that individuals place upon the public good element.[10] If some measures are easily measured and others cannot be measured at all the former assume an undue importance. This general point is frequently made but equally frequently ignored in practice. It is particularly relevant to social service provision, where courtesy, sensitivity and the quality of human relationships are at the very heart of the services' purposes.

Careful research studies are one thing. Crude indicators of output attached to budget categories are quite another. The need for the first is elaborated in subsequent chapters. It should not be confused with the latter.

A Partial Resolution of the Difficulties

For all these and other reasons when the analysts and civil servants actually came to apply the original models to the real world of social policy they modified their approach and instead adopted a strategy which might be called the 'bottom to top' approach. It began with the existing framework of activities – legislation or institutions – and took these as the basis for the budget structure. Moreover, instead of conceiving the budget as a tool for detailed managerial control the programme budget came to be seen as a medium term planning tool. Programmes were not going to change overnight simply because someone in the budget office drew up a more 'rational' budget which began from highly generalised first principles. It made more sense to begin with the activities which existed and the way agencies made their plans for them. In more specific terms it meant constructing a budget structure by asking what is provided, for whom and how?[11] This approach avoids many of the difficulties outlined in the previous sections. By not beginning with objectives it avoids the difficulties raised by differences in objectives, by hidden and multiple objectives, but by the same token it misses the theoretical advantages advanced in favour of the 'top to bottom' approach – the questioning and regular re-examinations of objectives. While it is possible to distinguish certain difficulties that were inherent in the creation of programme budget structures the issues faced by the analysts in HEW were significantly different from those met in Whitehall.

The following section illustrates the way in which the HEW programme structure developed in response to both the practical and political constraints. The subsequent section discusses the problems the DES and the DHSS have faced in developing their programme budget structure.

The HEW Experience

We have already emphasised that federal social programmes are both extremely numerous, relatively narrow and specific, and scattered between several different agencies. It was this situation which gave particular force to the case made by the reformers that a more rational budget structure was of central importance. For example, in the original Novick volume Hirsch pointed out that at that time (1965) forty-two federal departments, agencies and bureaux were involved in the finance of education. They varied from the Veterans Administration and the National Aeronautics and Space Administration through the National Institutes of Health to the Office of Education.

It was crucial for the Bureau of the Budget and for the President to gain a clear picture of what impact the Federal Government was making upon the education system as a whole. Universities were receiving funds from the Federal Government under scores of separate programmes and from many different agencies of government. How important, in total, was Federal aid to higher education? It was clearly necessary to know this before discussing the merits of any system of general aid to universities or even more limited proposals.

A similar situation was to be found in the field of health care. In 1974 twenty-five different agencies contributed to health expenditure. Merely to consider all health expenditure together would be a considerable advance. From the analyst's point of view much could be gained in terms of rational discussion merely by a few elementary aggregations of existing programmes without even raising difficult questions about basic objectives. The Special Analyses Volume of the Federal Budget now contains overviews of Federal expenditure in six social programme areas: education, manpower, health, income security, civil rights and 'reduction of crime'. Although a beginning was made on these in the 1965 budget they have grown in coverage and detail since the formal inception of PPB. By 1974 they comprised just over 100 pages of descriptive analysis, and this is only a summary of the information collected.[12] There is no doubt that the analyses give a much clearer picture of Federal involvement by broad function, by the kind of activities, by economic category and by agency. As a very tiny example the accompanying table shows how many separate programmes are directed at undergraduates (see Table 8.1).

Such a breakdown shows the OMB, Congress and the public today much more about the Federal Government's role in higher education and how it is changing or is proposed to change. Thus the quality of information provided as part of the President's budget documents to Congress alone has improved substantially since 1964. Yet it essentially involves nothing more than a comprehensive and logical grouping of existing legislative programmes.

What applied to social programmes overall also applied within

Table 8.1   *Federal Outlays for Higher Education by Agency*

Sublevel, Agency and Programme Undergraduate level (3 year courses or more)	*Outlays 1974* (proposed) *$ millions*
Military service academies	208
Reserve Officers' Training Corps	159
Health Manpower (NIH)	65
Office of Education:	
Basic Opportunity Grants	485
Work Study and Supplementary Grants	199
Guaranteed Student Loans	320
Direct Student Loans	25
Construction Loans and Grants	93
Disadvantaged Students and Developing Institutions	120
Other	44
Student Grants (OASDI)	678
Special Institutions	19
Bureau of Indian Affairs	21
Community Development (HUD)	19
Veterans' Readjustment	896
National Foundation on the Arts and Humanities	25
Science Foundation	13
Other	39
Subtotal	3,428
Total Education	13,645

Source: 1974 Budget Special Analyses

HEW. Several constitutent agencies are concerned, for example, with health – the National Institutes of Health, the Social Security Administration, the Social and Rehabilitation Service, the Food and Drugs Administration as well as the Health Services and Mental Health Administration. No Secretary of HEW could hope to consider his budget intelligently unless all these agencies' activities were considered together. Moreover, ultimately the headings used had to be consistent with those describing the activities of health related activities in other Federal Departments. The initial problem was to devise a structure in which to submit the Programme and Financial Plan documents to the BOB. In the first instance fairly complex structures were devised but what emerged in the end were broad groupings of existing appropriations. The health programme produced in 1967 was as follows.[13]

Health purposes:
  Development of Health Resources
    Increasing Knowledge (research)
    Providing facilities and equipment
    Increasing the health manpower pool
    Improving the organisation and delivery of health services
  Prevention and Control of Health Problems
    Disease prevention and control
    Environmental control
    Controlling consumer products
  Provision of Health Services
    Direct Services to Individuals
    Financing Services
    Health service support for special groups (Indians, etc)
  General Support

By comparing this structure with the Novick proposals shown earlier it is clear that this is a 'bottom-upwards' approach. 'Health Resources' are not outputs but inputs. Research could logically be seen as contributory to both prevention and provision. Yet in political and administrative terms it would make no sense for the Programme and Financial Plans to be presented with the research budget chopped up into little pieces and distributed across other programmes. What the politicians, the Secretary of HEW, the OMB and congressmen would demand to know was: what is happening to the NIH budget? Unless the administration felt capable of dismembering the National Institutes of Health, there was little point dismembering their budget. This whole approach made a lot more sense, too, because the Congressional appropriation categories already reflected the multitude of fairly specific legislative enactments made in the health field in the past. Thus it made political sense for the Secretary of HEW to consider whether he gave more of his marginal resources next year to improving certain programmes for the direct health care of special categories of poor people or increased general financial support to poor people to pay for their own health care. The trade off between cash and kind is precisely the type of planning and budgeting decision that can be illuminated by clear presentation of the alternatives within one programme document. The relative simplicity of the task compared to the British situation can be appreciated by looking at the current disaggregation of the 'delivery of services to individuals' category. In Britain this heading would comprise virtually all the activities of the National Health Service and hence virtually all health care in Britain. In the HEW budget it comprises the following:

Comprehensive Health Services

Planning grants to States	(Public Health Act, section 314(*d*))
Grants to set up health centres	(PHS Act Section 314(*e*))
Care facilities for migrant workers	(PHS Act Section 370)
Professional and technical assistance	(Social Security Act, Title XVIII)

Maternal and Child Health

Grants to States	(Social Security Act, 1967, Amendments)
Project Grants	(Social Security Act, 1967, Amendments)
Research and Training	(Social Security Act, 1967, Amendments)

Family Planning

Project Grants	(Social Security and PHS Act)
Direct Operations	(PHS Act)

National Health Service Corp. PHS Act (Section 329)

   (for aid to areas with acute shortage of medical staff)

Special Health Services

   (e.g. health care of American seamen and coastguards and federal employees)

This gives some impression of the gains to be had from a relatively 'common sense' approach to the grouping of activities as an aid to planning. As a next step in 1972 HSMA reduced these multiple appropriation categories and asked Congress to approve one single appropriation for health delivery, which would give the administration more freedom to switch funds within that heading.

What we have illustrated in detail about health was also true of other areas of HEW's activities. Education was broadly divided by level, income maintenance according to the broad categories of social insurance and assistance. The broad programme areas developed for the 1970 budget are shown in Table 8.2. No major change has been made since in either health or education headings. The Social and Rehabilitation Service sub-categories which had the most abstract or a *a priori* labels were, by 1973, much more

Table 8.2   *Programme Distribution of Budget Authority – 1970*

	$ millions
Education	
Development of basic skills	2,179·0
Development of Vocational and Occupational skills	304·1
Development of Academic and Professional skills	1,020·7
Library and Community Development	96·0
General Research	31·1
General Support	45·3
Category Total	3,676·2
Health	
Development of Health Resources	2,395·6
Prevention and Control of Health Problems	480·5
Provision of Health Services (Finance and direct)	10,739·0
General Support	64·4
Category Total	13,679·4
Social and Rehabilitation Services	
Improving Individual Capacity for Self-support	853·6
Improving Social Functioning of Individuals and Families	399·2
General Development of SRS Resources	132·6
General Support	43·1
Category Total	1,428·5
Income Maintenance	
Aged Assistance	24,787·0
Disability Assistance	4,842·6
Other Individual and Family Support	10,769·6
General Support	327·3
Category Total	40,726·5
Management – Office of Secretary	35·2
Total	59,545·8

Source: 1970, Budget Special Analyses – Table R4

clearly related to kinds of activity: basic assistance programmes (subdivided by types of recipient) – old age assistance, assistance to the blind, disabled, single parent families emergency assistance, etc; medical assistance; personal social services; and training schemes.

However, from the beginning the HEW planners sought not merely to produce one basic structure within which to present the

Financial Plan to the BOB, they also produced different analyses to give the Secretary various perspectives. This was perhaps their most valuable elaboration of the original concept.

Some administrators felt the whole exercise went too far, and that the cross cutting breakdowns, e.g. by age of recipient, were little more than guesses, but it was an explicit recognition of the fact that there are a great many equally legitimate ways of viewing a budget and one by itself is not enough for planning purposes. The President's budget categorises Federal health expenditure by the age and income groups of recipients as well as by the kind of treatment received within broad programme groupings.

It should not be thought that the exercise was a purely logical deductive one. The idea that all education or health programmes should be considered as a whole implies a threat to the individual agencies and programme administrators.

Finally, as we saw earlier, the HEW planners gave up emphasising the central importance of the budget structure and instead concentrated on ensuring that more detailed analyses of issues were undertaken and fed into the budget timetable at the appropriate time and they gave up the attempt to put so-called output measures with each programme. It would be wrong to leave the impression that the debates about budget categories were purely technical, behind many lay ulterior motives and political strategies. For example in Table 8.1 there appears a category 'Student grants OASDI'. This figure relates to the benefits paid to dependent children whose parents are on social security. The SSA insist these are income maintenance payments. The Secretary's staff at one stage argued the money should be used for other more important educational purposes. Merely transferring an item from one category to another may hide, or be seen to hide, some sinister purpose.

In Brief

The grouping of expenditure for similar purposes in one programme even though it was undertaken by different agencies was, in effect, a weak substitute for administrative reform. Secondly the structure was concerned to illuminate annual budget decisions not to act as a long-term planning or management tool since in effect HEW had little power to do either.

The original conception of a detailed and logical programme structure derived from concepts of final outputs gave way in practice in HEW's experience, to a structure based upon grouping together similar activities authorised by many different acts of Congress and undertaken by different agencies. Emphasis shifted to multi-dimensional analyses of expenditure and deeper analytical studies.

British Experience
It should already be obvious from what has gone before that the difficulties of creating programme structures are very different in British central departments. First, there were nothing like the obvious or simple gains to be had from grouping existing programmes. Administrative unification had done that already. For example when the author, in conjunction with two colleagues, produced an analysis of UK education expenditure financed from all sources, private as well as public, only a tiny part of it could be seen to fall outside the jurisdiction of the Secretary of State for Education and Science even though the actual channels of finance were indirect.[14] Since 1974 the Secretary of State for Health and Social Security will have sole responsibility for the administration and finance of virtually all health care in England and Wales.

The creation of programme structures in the US have been a weak and largely ineffective way of dealing with a situation that has been avoided in Britain through administrative unification. Clearly then, PPB in the UK cannot perform the same function that it has in HEW.

The second difference lies in the fact that there had been, in Britain, a good deal of academic work applying social accounting conventions to social service expenditure. Titmuss and Abel-Smith in the mid 1950s had presented the Guillebaud Committee on the Cost of the National Health Service with an analysis of health service expenditure over time categorised by economic categories and by function with some estimates of the expenditure on different age groups.[15]

The same was true of education. Vaizey did for education what Titmuss and Abel-Smith had done for health.[16] Statistics on education expenditure by level (excluding the private sector) have been available since the early 1960s even though until the late sixties they contained certain discrepancies and misleading or mistaken accounting categories. As we have seen the sources of public funds were nothing like as complex or difficult to comprehend as the American. Social security, as in the United States, largely analysed itself, in the aggregate at least. It was already categorised by recipient or 'client group'. Thus the kind of broad functional aggregations the US planners were seeking already existed in outline in

M

Britain by the mid 1960s. They were being used in the public expenditure survey returns.

The third difference lay in the needs of decision-makers. We have seen that, in practice, long-term forward planning was not one of the major successes in HEW. In Britain it was the main driving motive. The emphasis as we said in an earlier chapter was on containing the growth of public expenditure. Departments' powers and functions differ. The DES actually spends a tiny part of the education budget but it has considerable powers to ration and allocate resources to other spending bodies – universities and local authorities. It is above all a planning department. On the other hand, the DHSS is directly responsible through its subordinate agencies for expenditure on health service provision in nearly all its aspects. It performs a planning and managerial function. Taken together all three factors meant that the basic theory would be more stringently tested than in HEW. There were no simple gains to be made merely by grouping like activities. There were no narrow legislative commitments to ease the conceptual task of determining objectives. The application of basic economic categories had already been done. There was nothing for it but to tackle the basic philosophical issues. Moreover, since the primary purpose was to facilitate forward planning and since capital planning formed a large part of that activity the programme budget had to extend over a period of up to ten years. In the case of the health service there was an opportunity to extend the budget downwards to include the lowest level decisions matching the management hierarchy.

How did the theory stand the test? We discuss first the work of the DES which was the first social service department to experiment with the tool.

The DES Programme Structure
The pilot study contained in the DES *Planning Paper No 1*[17] sets out the purpose of its endeavour in much the same way as the Treasury did in its evidence to the Select Committee on Procedure in 1968–9. It prefaced the elaboration of its actual programme structure with broad generalisations under the heading 'The Objectives of Education'. They included the acquisition of basic skills like numeracy, literacy and powers of communication, economic objectives like providing a more skilled and mobile labour force as well as social and cultural ones. It goes on to raise the possibility that these objectives could be used as the basis of a programme structure only to reject the idea immediately: 'But this is not possible. There is no unique identification between the various activities

which go on in, say, a secondary school and the achievements of these objectives.'

The DES, very early on therefore, avoided the problem of objectives. It considered the possibility of structuring the budget by subject or institution or the groups at which education is aimed. It rejected the first as irrelevant. It rejected the second because different kinds of institutions provided similar kinds of education, further education colleges and schools are the most obvious examples. Its planners in the end decided to allocate according to 'the groups at which education is directed'. This, in effect, meant categorising expenditure by level of education, as can be seen in Table 8.3 Two other major blocks of expenditure for which the Department was responsible were distinguished – Block B Research and Block C Cultural and Recreational Activities. It was decided to go ahead with the regular production of a programme budget for Block A, that is the education sector, which comprised by far the greater part of the expenditure for which the Department was responsible. Since then the broad programme categories have changed very little. In so far as they have developed they are even more closely categorised by level than before. The broad and very large expenditure category – compulsory education – has been divided into primary and secondary education and the latter now goes up to 16. The split of the old 'compulsory' sector into primary and secondary not only reflects the unwieldy nature of the previous programme but the Conservative Government decision to give greater weight to primary as opposed to secondary education.

From a purely 'objective centred' point of view these programme divisions make little sense. Education provided in many nursery classes is not very different from that provided in the reception class, certainly the objectives are likely to be similar and it is usually undertaken in the same school, with the same head. On the other hand the objectives of education for the 16–19 year old group are widely divergent. Some courses are purely vocational, some are largely academic. Viewed from a planning rationale, however, these divisions make much more sense. Local Education Authorities have to provide facilities for all children from 5–16. They have no such obligation up to 5 years, and until recently have been forbidden to expand such facilities. From 16–19 provision in school and college is broadly 'on demand' tempered by the institution's view about the young person's suitability for the course. Provision below degree level is broadly within a local authority's discretion with the Industrial Training Boards significantly affecting both the level and nature of demand. The demand for first degree courses is

Table 8.3 *The Programme Budget of the Department of Education and Science Major Categories*

The Proposed Scheme	The Present Scheme
A1 Compulsory Education (5–15)	Nursery (3–4)
A2 Nursery Education	Primary (5–10)
A3 Education for the 15-year-old	Secondary (11–16)
A4 Education for the 16–19-year-old	16–19-year-olds
A5 Higher Education below First Degree level	Non-advanced Higher Education
A6 Higher Education for First Degree level	First Degree level
A7 Postgraduate Education	Postgraduate

B Research
C Cultural and Recreational Activities.

determined very largely by the number of students gaining A levels, and post-graduate education by the number of studentships the central government is prepared to finance. The basis for making estimates of future costs is different for each of these groups. In short, the rationale behind the choice of these major programme categories lies in the planning system which the Department already operated. This point is even more clearly illustrated by the programme structure within each major programme area. Common to most of the major programmes are the following 'sub-headings' or sub-programmes: Maintenance of the existing pattern and scale of provision; reduction of the cost of provision at existing standards; changes in the proportion of the age group receiving education; changes in the proportion in different types of institution or taking different subjects; changes in the standards and quality of accommodation; other changes in the pattern of inputs (e.g. changes in the student/staff ratio) and in efforts to raise the quality of staff such as initial and in-service training; changes in the incidence of costs.

These categories, or most of them, are repeated under all the major programme headings – under pre-school, under Primary education, and so on. Each is then further sub-divided into 'elements'. These again are sub-divisions common to each programme so that under the 'existing pattern and scale of provision', we have expenditure required for existing numbers, to accommodate shifts of population, to accommodate changing total numbers. All the costs are expressed in constant prices and figures are presented for each of the subsequent ten years. This means that the budget has to use projections of student numbers fourteen years ahead in order to include capital expenditure figures which depend on estimates of student numbers four years ahead.

Neither major programmes B – research nor C – culture and

recreation, have been elaborated or used. The budget itself is not published and remains a 'classified' document.

Now this whole structure is no more and no less than a presentation of the process through which anyone would have to go in order to build up a forecast of future expenditure requirements needed to meet existing policy decisions using a logical set of assumptions. It is a useful way of clarifying the issues in the annual and continual discussions between the DES and the Treasury within the PESC framework. It will show a minister what rate of expansion in the PESC allocation is necessary to maintain existing 'standards' and meet the demands of a rising school population. The Department in its evidence to the expenditure committee of the House of Commons in 1971 explained:

'An essential function of the programme budget within the PPB structure is thus to show the extent to which educational expenditure is susceptible to policy choice.'[18]

Such a structure helps to clarify where, within a constrained growth path, there is room for expansion. These are clearly the resource questions which dominate the minds of senior people in DES and their political masters as well as the Treasury. Hence the structure which emerged. Talk of the 'objectives of education', and 'final outputs' is so much decoration on the cake. Indeed the DES has now dropped its original title of an 'output budget' and calls it a 'programme budget' instead.

Similarly the 'indicators of intermediate output' suggested in the original document were quite simply *input* planning targets – new places provided in schools, changes in the proportion of under-fives in school, changes in the proportion of young people in higher education. They do represent reasonable indicators of progress towards politically determined targets and, if such targets had been announced, their regular publication would illuminate public discussion of the contents of the public expenditure white paper and the issues it involved. But by 1974 they had not been included in the programme budget. Some thought has been given to measuring output but little has been done.

The reason for the structure and the activity are therefore reasonably clear. Unlike the American PPB system which attempted to force a degree of planning into the budget system this is an elaboration of an existing planning system. It has essentially been seen as an adjunct to the basic PESC procedure and will continue to be undertaken by a different section of the finance division of DES. It has served as a kind of check on the PESC figures. In the first place the planning time scale is longer. It covers a ten-year time span, not the five-year one used in PESC. In the second place the method of calculation is different and far more complex. For example, in calculating the future total cost of teachers' salaries a fairly crude assumption was made in PESC discussions that the average salary in real terms would stay the same. The programme budget introduced the consequences of a changed graduate/non-graduate mix, of the changing age structure of school population and other factors which produced a different overall answer. As a result PESC assumptions have been refined. It also aims to give officials and ministers a much more detailed appreciation of options open to them in PESC discussions. It throws up areas for special study – exploring options in more detail and it provides basic source material for the work of the policy groups undertaking PARs in the Department. It is a kind of back-up to the expenditure planning and policy review systems rather than the central tool that the original reformers envisaged.

The original difficulties we discussed at the beginning of the chapter have, in the words of the DES chief economist, been 'side-stepped' rather than solved.[19]

The difficulty presented by disputed final objectives has been overcome by concentrating on agreed planning targets. For the largest single blocks of expenditure from 5–16 these targets turn out to be targets for inputs – pupil/teacher ratios, school building targets, etc. For the non-compulsory sectors they turn out to be participation rates of the percentage of the age group enrolled. Whether these can be said to be nearer to an output concept is debatable, students could be viewed as an input. Yet such a discussion is purely academic. So long as political debate centres on numbers gaining entry, this will remain the way the planning targets are measured.

The difficulty presented by multiple objectives has been met in the same kind of way by taking educational level as the basic dimension. The problem of hidden objectives has simply not been faced, while the difficulty posed by changing objectives has turned out not to be particularly important since the programmes are not essentially about objectives. By the same token the programme *structure* does not appear to have been much positive help in illuminating policy discussions. During the preparation of the plans for the next ten years which culminated in the 1972 White Paper a great many policy options were considered. These had to be costed. Yet it was to the working sheets used in the production of the programme budget that the economists had to turn for their cost estimates rather than the final product. The budget structure had illuminated the constraints under which policy makers had to work. The policy options emerged from political debate rather than a consideration of the programme structure. Once new policies had been decided upon the programme structure was adapted to them.

None of this is meant as a criticism of the way the DES operated. It does illustrate the weakness in the original conception of a programme budget.

The political importance of the categories used should again be emphasised. One example is the concept of 'improvements'. The central logic of the budget and of the PESC negotiations is that money must be found first to ensure that 'existing standards' are maintained. This means keeping present staffing ratios and expenditures per pupil while increasing the building stock as larger numbers of pupils have to be catered for. Basic programme needs therefore consist of the resources required to maintain the same level of resources for present numbers, plus that required to do the same for increasing numbers due to national population increase and that required to cope with population *movement*. Anything else constitutes improvement. This includes extra resources needed to provide for a higher staying on rate – or participation ratio – even though the overall staffing standards applied are the same. This is a rather odd use of the word 'improvement'. From the budget it looks as if one fifth of all resources are devoted to improvement, but only a small part of this goes towards raising the level of resources per pupil. Whether that constitutes an 'improvement' also begs the basic question.

To label something improvement clearly makes it more vulnerable. It is in a sense up for debate, potentially at least, in every PESC round. The participation ratio used for planning need not be age-specific (a percentage of the potential age group) but could be qualification specific (a percentage of those with two A levels) or it could be a transition proportion (a percentage of qualified leavers from the previous level). If it is then accepted that the basic aim is to ensure a constant proportion of qualified people from the level below enter the next stage (the Robbins principle), then if the number of qualified persons in the age group rises it becomes possible to count the resources needed to house and teach them as a basic programme not as an improvement. This happens now at the post-graduate stage. Hence, apparently doctrinal disputes about how to calculate participation rates have a certain political rationale.

A Programme Structure for the Health and Personal Social Services
The DHSS began developing a programme budget later than DES, in 1971, and the basic structure is still evolving (1974). The work began in parallel with a review of the organisation of the whole Department which led to the setting up of client group divisions, with the introduction of a new planning system, and at the same point in time as the reorganisation of the Health Service and a review of the management arrangements for the reorganised service.[20] In these respects the timing was propitious. The NHS was to be wholly financed out of central Exchequer funds. The Secretary of State was directly accountable for all its activities and in particular for all resource allocation. The new administrative structure laid down in the Conservative White Paper was a classic bureaucratic hierarchy. There were no intervening independently elected local authorities as was the case in education. Moreover health at first sight is less subject to disputes over objectives. This makes it all the more interesting to examine why, in the event, the classic PPB formula was not applied. In the first place, as the Grey Book suggests and as is even more clear from the pilot planning studies, the budget is not going to be the central management tool. This reflects the nature of the central controls. The Department's control over capital expenditure extends farthest into the future. Perhaps next in long-term significance is its control or influence over manpower – the number of places in medical schools and hospital medical establishments. These powers are in the former case somewhat tenuous and weak, but once long-term decisions are taken about both sets of magnitudes and their distribution the medium term budgets are fairly constrained.

In the US the Federal Government's annual control of the budget is about the only weapon the centre has over the periphery. In the UK and especially in the NHS this is not the case. Hence the drawbacks of using the budget cycle for planning and management control carry greater weight. In consequence, the programme budget structure in DHSS has come to be seen as a formal planning tool primarily for use at central level. It will throw more light on the constraints and the options available within the PESC exercise. In this the parallels with the education budget are clear. So too are the ways in which the planning methodology has determined the programme structure.

The central notion is that of the client group – that is groups in the population who require a specialist or distinctive type of service. Medical care planning begins with demography. The age structure plays an important part in determining the kind and level of demands made upon the service. The next planning step has involved applying certain ratios of bed use or staff per 1,000 population. Ideally, it involves making assessments about changes in morbidity by age group and making some assessment of the number of doctors or beds required. Client group targets can then be fixed so that local areas are set to reach certain standards of service in terms of beds or manpower per head of the relevant population. Such progress can be monitored. The concept is similar to that of a participation rate which is applied by the DES.

Yet even this concept could not be applied systematically across all health activities. Planning has to be done on an institutional as well as a client basis. Hospital specialities and general practice are the basic operational units and capital and manpower planning reflect that fact. General practice presents particular difficulties that we have touched on already.

Finally, there was the need to include in one programme activities which were already clear candidates for 'trade-offs'. Domiciliary versus hospital maternity care is one example, community care versus institutional care for the aged is another. Policy has already developed to the stage where these are seen as alternatives and in which, in principle at least, there is agreement about the direction of change. Policies have played their part in another sense too. The stress laid upon the mentally ill, the mentally handicapped and the elderly as separate groups in the Grey Book and in the programme structure, would probably not have happened ten years ago. They reflect ministerial concern which in its turn reflects the public pressures of the late 1960s and early 1970s. Once again it can be seen how programme structures *follow* policy.

Early on, therefore, it was agreed that the basic programme structure had to represent something of a compromise between client groups and existing institutional categories. Several kinds of structures were considered for example: disease, diagnostic groups, specialities, age or degree of dependency. The disease approach had been the original suggestion in the Novick volume and logically provides the most obvious way to facilitate cost effectiveness studies between programmes. Yet it was rejected as impractical. Even if the thousands of diseases had been grouped in an acceptable way the financial information required was simply not obtainable. Diagnostic groupings made little sense either in practical terms for resources are devoted on a speciality basis. Hospital specialities, however, tend to cater for a whole range of diseases. They do have the advantage that hospital activity returns are available on a speciality basis and average costs by speciality can be derived, at least roughly. There is even some possibility of output data. Some specialities correspond to a client group classification, for example psychiatry – mental illness and mental handicap – and geriatrics. They also relate across to services in the community for the mentally ill and the elderly. However, the medical and surgical specialities are heterogeneous. Many elderly patients are in medical wards.

In the end the decision was to adopt hospital specialities as the basic unit for allocating hospital expenditure. Some of the specialities – like obstetrics, psychiatry, and geriatrics – were to be included in the programmes which spanned the hospital and community care sectors. General practice and the chemists were to go in together with community health care into the largest single programme – primary care. Personal social services followed a rather different logic based on the type of handicap – social, physical or mental, plus mental illness.

The outcome will probably be a programme structure of the following kind:

Services for the whole population:

Primary care and prevention	GPs, pharmaceutical, dental and ophthalmic services, community health.
General hospital services	

Services (including personal social services) specially for:

Elderly	
Mentally ill	
Mentally handicapped	
Reproduction	Gynaecology, obstetrics, domiciliary care, family planning.

Children and families with children

Unallocated

It will be a structure on one level, i.e. without a hierarchy of sub-objectives beneath. The aim is rather to produce different perspectives at this 'top' level, and more detailed analyses of the input structure. The elderly, for example, are cared for by a whole range of professionals and non-professionals in their own homes, from GPs to home helps. Many are cared for in hospitals. Merely to gain a systematic picture of how much was devoted under each heading in what kind of circumstances and at what ages would tell us a good deal about options and constraints. Age and degree of dependency are other ways of categorising receivers of resources. However, if emphases in policy were to change and prevention were to be given a higher priority the budget could be cut differently again.

In short this is a bottom to top approach. Just how different this outcome is to the original ideas in the Novick volume can be appreciated by looking back at the start of this chapter. The DHSS like the DES are 'side-stepping' the issue of final output. Like education they are concentrating on a structure which will illuminate forecasting, using existing planning techniques, but it will also enable politically determined trade-offs between similar activites to be more explicit and informed. In both cases work on 'output' indicators is put well into the distance.

Unlike education there is more concern in the DHSS work with seeking to explain and understand past trends in expenditure within programmes as a basis for forecasting and rather more recognition of the case for more dimensions to the budget as opposed to elaboration downwards in a more detailed sub-programme structure.

Doubts about Programme Budgets in British Social Service Departments

There are at least three points to be made about these first two attempts to develop programme budget structures for social service departments. The first is a doubt about tactical priority. The exercise of mounting the pilot study in DES and then refining it to make it operational has taken considerable time and effort from a tiny staff of economists. It could be argued that they could have been better employed on more substantive policy issues. For quite some time the PPB process ran in parallel with the PESC process, conducted by a different set of people. The same is happening in DHSS. In 1969, the first year after it was decided to go ahead with the DES scheme – on a regular basis – the programme budget took a year to complete, too long to figure in the PESC discussions. The 1970 version took eight months. The aim is to produce it by February when the PESC returns go into the Treasury. The eventual aim is to computerise the operation and fuse it with the PESC categories. Here too one can see the over-riding importance of the budget control function dominating the contribution economists might have made to other planning activities.

The second doubt concerns the confusion of aims which seem to exist. It was not clear at the outset for whom or why the budgets were being prepared. Some confusion has been caused by the continued use of PPB terminology for what is essentially a very different exercise from that originally envisaged. DES now talks of its programme budget rather than an output budget, the term with which it began. This reflects their view that the exercise has less to do with outputs than it was originally seen to have, and its purpose seems to be a more accurate forecasting of future costs for PESC. Laudable as this may be, it has not really helped with issues of choice or of monitoring effectiveness which were part of the original conception. Some of those in the DES still have these purposes in mind but the machinery by which they will be achieved is far from clear, and the need for them may be obscured by the fact that something called a 'programme budget' exists.

The third doubt is that even as an *analysis of expenditure* it is an inadequate planning tool. First, the DES budget is entirely concerned with projections and not with analysing past experience. Who benefited, where and why? Secondly it is a one-dimensional budget. Unlike the HEW planners' early conception it gives the minister one view of expenditure – dominated by planning norms. It is deficient in the *distributional* picture it gives of the impact of education spending. Nor is it concerned with the source of income – the finance of education. Just because the two British programme structures reflect on their departments' planning procedures it does not mean they are 'value free'. A budget which categorises expenditure by level and expresses increases in the participation ratio of higher education as an 'improvement factor' reflects one view of the world. An analysis of expenditure according to the social class of the recipients would give a very different picture. Over the sixties it shows, for example, that the 'higher' social classes benfited more from the increased public spending on education than the 'lower' classes. The higher income groups benefited more than the lower income groups. Those in the less prosperous regions benefited less than the more prosperous, suburban areas more than central urban areas, the urban child more than the rural child, men more than women, white more than black, adolescents more than pre-school children, academic children more than vocationally oriented children, children more than adults. The public sector grew, the private, overall, declined. Private sources of funds for the public sector declined but may have increased more recently. Less has been spent on science proportionately and more on recreation.

All of these perspectives throw a different light on the education budget and reflect different values. The present structure emphasises equity between this generation of qualified school leavers and the last generation. Another budget structure might emphasise equity between social classes or sexes, or ethnic groups.

The final doubt has to do with the link between the programme budget ideal and evaluation. The application of final output indicators has never been seriously pursued, but both departments express their intention of doing so. We have argued that such indicators are unhelpful and can be misleading. Work on them could detract from the longer term and very difficult aim of trying to study in detail and in narrowly defined areas how, to whom and with what effect social services are delivered.

In Brief

When analysts came to construct programme budgets for the social services they ran into at least seven major difficulties: their objectives were disputed; they were provided by independent professionals with their own responsibilities for determining priorities and objectives; there was little or no information on the objectives consumers looked for; the objectives whether viewed by controllers of resources, or providers or recipients were in any case multiple; the 'real' political objectives were frequently different from the stated formal objectives; they changed and because they were in large part collective or public goods their outputs were difficult if not impossible to measure.

In trying to resolve these issues programme planners 'side-stepped' them and relied instead on structures which were client-based or institution-based or were groupings of similar activities. They did so in the UK because such structures fitted in well with existing or emerging planning assumptions and practices. In America the budget reforms were really a poor substitute for administrative reforms which would have put like functions under a single unit of government. The reforms have had their uses, but also bring their dangers. The control and management function linked to a budget may lead to excessive reliance on a single budget format for planning purposes whereas what is in fact needed is a multiple set of expenditure analyses giving different perspectives embodying different sets of values.

REFERENCES

1 Novick, op. cit., p. 229.
2 Rein, M., *Social Policy*, Random House, New York, 1970.
3 Byrne, D. S. and Williamson, W., *Sociology*, 1972, Vol. 6, No. 1, pp. 71–87.
4 House of Commons Expenditure Committee, Session 1971–2, *Relationship of Expenditure to Needs*, HC 515.
5 The National Foundation for Educational Research, *The Teachers' Day*, Slough 1972, Scottish Education Department, *Primary School Survey: A Study of the Teacher's Day*.
6 Donnison, D. V. *et al.*, *Social Policy and Administration*. op. cit.
7 HC 515 report, para. 19.
8 Comments on a paper by Olsen in M. Moss (Ed.), *The Measurement of Economic and Social Performance*, Columbia University Press, New York, 1973.
9 Start, K. B., and Wells, B. K., NFER, Slough, Bucks., 1972.
10 Moss, M., op. cit.
11 Brown, P. L., 'Establishing a Programme Structure' in *Planning, Programming, Budgeting*, Eds. Lyden, F L., and Miller, E. G., Markham Publishing Company, Chicago, 1972.
12 *The Budget of the United States Government, 1974, Special Analyses*, Government Printing Office, Washington, DC 1973.
13 Levin, A., 'Multi-Secting the Nation's Non-Defense Programs', *Public Administration Review*, March/April, 1971.
14 Peacock, A., Glennerster, H., and Lavers, R., *Educational Finance: its Sources and Uses in the United Kingdom*, Oliver and Boyd, London, 1968.
15 Titmuss, R. M., and Abel-Smith, B., *The Cost of the National Health Service*, Cambridge University Press, 1956.
16 Vaizey, J., *The Costs of Education*, George Allen & Unwin, London, 1958.
17 *Output budgeting for the DES* (*Education Planning Paper No. 1*), HMSO, London, 1970; Also see: *O and M Bulletin*, Volume 24, No. 4, November, 1969, and Vol. 25, No. 1, February, 1970, articles by J. M. Bridgeman.
18 Second Report of the Expenditure Committee, Session 1970–1, HC545, p. 92.
19 Rodmell, B. E., 'Output Budgeting and the DES', Paper given to the IMTA, September, 1973.
20 HMSO, London, 1972.

Further Reading

Department of Education and Science, *Output Budgeting for the DES: Education Planning Paper No. 1*, HMSO, 1970.
(The pilot study made by the DES.)
Reekie, W. D., and Hunt, N. C. (Eds), *Management in the Social and Safety Services*, Tavistock, London, 1974. See article by G. J. Wasserman, 'Applying PPB to police expenditure'.

Chapter 9

Evaluation — US Style

At the very heart of the original budget reforms was the belief that it would be possible to build into the budget process a systematic comparison of alternative courses of action. It was only after a series of such comparisons had been made that a 'forward plan' would emerge. The very purpose of disaggregating the budget structure into a logical hierarchy of means and ends categories was to enable 'cost utility' comparisons to be made between each category of expenditure. Yet, as we found in Chapter 2, what precisely 'cost utility' or systems analysis meant was somewhat unclear. Different proponents adopted rather different versions but the critical element in 'evaluating' the alternatives clearly lay with cost benefit or cost effectiveness studies. McKean who originally argued for the extension of systems analysis to the whole of the Federal Budget claimed that if activities of agencies were broken down into discrete activities 20 per cent of the non-defence budget could be assessed in cost benefit terms.[1] Or, to express it another way, present values could be assigned to the outputs from 20 per cent of the non-defence programmes and in consequence cost benefit calculations could be used to assist in choosing priorities between them. Moreover he claimed that in 40 per cent more cases it was possible to assign quantitative indicators of output to programmes or parts of programmes. Examples quoted included the number of crimes committed or the number of man hours lost due to hospitalisation. In these cases it would be possible to make cost effectiveness studies that would show the different costs of achieving a given result in different ways. The Novick[2] volume was not as specific and it hedged its definitions of 'cost utility', but again it is quite clear that cost benefit or cost effectiveness was to be the essential tool. As one advocate rather inelegantly, but characteristically, put it 'A capsule definition would be: Systems analysis is the application of "benefit-cost" analytical techniques to several areas of the PPBS anatomy.'[3]

The HEW work certainly began with a heavy emphasis on cost effectiveness. As we saw in an earlier chapter the group of analysts in the Secretary's Office began comparing a number of existing programmes that were directed at clearly definable client groups and with similar objectives – disease control and education and training programmes. They were chosen as examples that would illustrate the contribution that a cost effectiveness approach could make. In none of the published examples was any very elaborate methodology used. The disease control analyses relied on existing medical literature to arrive at rough indicators of the 'cost per death averted' associated with alternative ways of controlling tuberculosis or syphilis, or different forms of cancer. Child health strategies were compared in terms of the results which might be expected from spending a given sum of money on each option. 'Outcomes' included the avoidance of so many maternal deaths, infant deaths and premature births.[4]

Right at the beginning this group of economists had abandoned the notion that they could systematically compare the results of health, education or social work services in terms of financial returns though it was hoped that some at least of the education and training programmes might be compared in this way and that in time such comparisons could be extended.[5] As time went on even the enthusiasm for the more limited cost effectiveness approach waned. It was never entirely dispensed with, but its use became limited. Since so much had been expected from both these approaches it is important to see why neither was developed further.

The human capital approach had, at the outset, seemed to offer a reasonable chance of comparing the benefits of individual education and health programme. Higher education or vocational training schemes could be seen to raise the earnings of those who passed through them. It was widely accepted that these higher earnings reflected, at least in part, the improved productive potential of the individual concerned and that in consequence society gained from his superior skills. Hence a 'social rate of return' could be calculated from the 'investment' of social capital in his education or training.[6] Similar arguments applied in the case of health services.[7] Why was this approach never extended in a systematic way? There were, of course, serious theoretical objections to assuming that earnings were a true or close reflection of productive worth and these objections have gained greater force more recently but in the end this was not the real stumbling block. What carried most weight was the fact that politicians, regardless of any niceties of economic theory, simply did not regard income effects as particularly important when it came to making decisions about health or even education. The first occasional paper produced by the Office of Program Coordination[8] began with a lively statement of the need to compare the effectiveness of different programmes but then went on to discuss all the limitations of using income as a measure of benefit. It undervalued illnesses which, though painful or restrictive, did not limit an individual's productivity. It valued whites more than blacks, men more than women, the young more than the old. These were valuations politicians could not be expected to accept very readily. It was possible to attach weights to benefits received by different groups, to make the poor count for more, but in practice it was probably better to say who would benefit in what ways and leave the individual politician or voter to make his or her own judgements. Alice Rivlin, who had been the Assistant Commissioner for Planning and Evaluation during this period concluded:

'It is my hunch that analysts would be wasting time and effort if they gave high priority to making dollar estimates of the benefits of social action programs, for politicians and decision makers are unlikely to pay much attention to them. They and their constituents have strong, intuitive ideas about the relative importance of health, education, and social well-being that are not likely to be shaken by benefit-cost estimates. The ratios are unlikely to sway the choice of a congressman between a reading program and a cancer cure programme. He is more apt to be influenced by clear statements of the benefits in physical terms, such as the number of children who will read with specified proficiency or the chances of curing certain types of cancer, and by identification of the probable beneficiaries'.[9]

On the other hand, it could be argued that there were occasions when politicians or pressure groups actually made what were essentially cost-benefit statements. They may make claims, for example, about the impact day care provision will make on wives or single parents' incomes. 'The provision of nursery schooling will pay for itself.' Now this is an explicit proposition that can be tested. The Plowden Committee, in Britain, actually tried to do this and showed that on their assumptions the economic return was likely to be very small and certainly well below the overall cost of providing universal pre-school facilities.[10] In similar cases cost-benefit calcu-

N

lations might be needed but they are limited in their political value.

As time went on another fundamental objection emerged. It was possible to measure or estimate the higher incomes which recipients of Federal loans received or the higher earnings which vocational training, sometimes, brought to the recipients in a particular programme. But, critics asked, was this not merely because those who had not been in such programmes were now in worse jobs or unemployed altogether? On a more theoretical level there was the problem posed by the impact that a significant increase in educated or trained workers would have on the general level of earnings. Without assuming that such programmes had only a tiny or marginal effect it was difficult to justify the use of existing earnings differentials as a basis for calculating rates of return. Yet the 'Great Society' programmes were intended to 'eliminate poverty', which implied anything but a marginal shift in wage relationships.[11] Rate of return analysis was never to play a significant role and without it there was very little basis on which to conduct cost-benefit analyses between social programmes.

What of the more limited cost-effectiveness comparisons with which the Office began? They made no assumptions about the value of human life, for example, they merely suggested how much it would cost to save a life or reduce impairment. All the difficulties we discussed in the previous chapter associated with defining the goals of social programmes, applied *a fortiori* to such analysis. Yet the real difficulties turned out to be practical rather than political. Even when there was general agreement about what programmes were seeking to achieve, and how to measure the results, there was very rarely any information about *what* they achieved. For the most part such questions had not been asked and where they had been asked there were still no answers.

Typical instructions for the new systems analysts had been: select alternatives, collect data, build explanatory models, weigh cost against effectiveness. It soon became clear that to build models in the field of social policy was far more complicated than had originally been supposed. Education is a good example. The early attempts to examine the impact of compensatory education programmes on children from deprived and minority groups produced virtually no positive results. Meanwhile, Congress had ordered a vast national survey of schools, their resources, the opportunities available to children from different racial and social groups and their attainments. The resulting Coleman report which was published in 1966 provided raw material for a whole series of studies which re-analysed his data in an attempt to show the impact of school resources on pupil achievement.[12] Despite the fact that the variations in per pupil expenditures were considerably greater in America than they were in Britain, very few positive correlations were found. The societal, class and family background variables overwhelmed all the rest. There have been complex disputes about whether schools with more resources can be said to have produced better results, other things being equal or not. The debate hinged upon which variables were entered into the model first. So far the most that the more positive interpreters can say is that more experienced teachers and teachers with greater verbal skills may be slightly more effective in educating children. Politicians may be forgiven some degree of irritation at this outcome of so much academic dispute. As much of the variance between pupils' achievements remains unaccounted for and since the measurement of the school variables is so crude, it is still legitimate to argue that the results show more about the inadequacy of social scientists than they do about the inadequacies of schools. It is possible that there are different production functions for different kinds of children in different circumstances and that in these 'macro' studies the effects cancel out. Or in non-economic language, more teachers may produce better results with some kinds of children and not with others. Some children may do better with less teaching and more books. So long as both types of children are educated in the same way there is no way of knowing whether, or how far, this is the case. Moreover, in the studies that have been undertaken only one of the many 'outputs' of schooling has been investigated – scholastic achievement. Others such as socialisation, or later job mobility, or innovativeness, or being good citizens or just sheer consumption benefits, like enjoying school – remain largely unexplored. Nor did the research even seek to tackle the crucial theoretical problem of how to assess the changing values placed upon the different objectives of education by parents, which we discussed in the last chapter.

We simply do not yet have any satisfactory production function model of schools or indeed much understanding of possible relationships. Yet this kind of input/output analysis has been taken much further in the case of schools than it has with other social services. Social work and even health is less well explored. In principle one would expect that the 'output' of social workers relative to social variables would be even less significant than is the case with teachers. Health raises exactly the same difficulties. Not the least important is the problem of the possible long term impact of social service provision, and the impossibility of putting a value on their collective good element.

None of these considerations should be taken as arguments against studying in depth, for example, what impact social workers or teachers make in particular situations. Yet experience of research into teacher effectiveness suggests that results will be sparse. However, if we now know so little about the relationship between inputs and outputs it makes little sense to invest great effort in valuing the outputs. It is the *processes* which need to be studied. It can only be done by fairly elaborate research design and in small scale experiments. That, at least, is what some of those in HEW concluded.

If the cost-effectiveness approach had proved difficult to apply to programmes with agreed objectives it proved even less useful where the objectives turned out to be many and confused. It also proved unhelpful when it came to making decisions about significant new departures in social policy. It tended to favour a conservative response to innovation or departures from existing policies.[13]

Formal Evaluation – A Duty

The evaluators therefore switched their attention to initiating more fundamental research.

The child health study concluded:

1 The inter-relationships among the effects of environment, education and medical care make it extremely difficult to predict either the improvements in health which would result from improvements in the delivery of services or to predict the human or economic benefits that would result from improvements in health. Data are lacking moreover, on the effectiveness of past programs in reducing mortality or preventing disability.

2 Future maternal and child health care programs ought to include funds for evaluation of program effectiveness in delivering health services and in improving the health of the target population. Such evaluation would typically be conducted by an organisation different from the organisation administering a given program.[14]

This was echoed in other areas of policy and the planning and evaluation staff pressed hard for legislation to specify that a given proportion of the total expenditure should be devoted to evaluating the programmes's outcomes. They managed to convince the Secretary and Congressional Committees. In 1967 and 1968 Congress enacted amendments that provided HEW with evaluation funds under eleven separate pieces of legislation. The percentage most commonly prescribed was up to 1 per cent of total programme appropriations. These funds have gradually come to be taken up more fully. It was not until mid-1970, for example, that the new funds were used on any scale for education. The number of staff employed to initiate and monitor these studies also grew.

So it is fair to say that when PPB passed away in a formal sense one of the most important survivals was the *concept* of evaluating programmes, the *creation* of a legislative duty to evaluate specific programmes and the *allocation* of major funds to achieve it.

These were also the early days of the 'Great Society' programmes. They had a number of characteristics which lead naturally to studies of their effectiveness. First, they broke new ground as far as the Federal Government was concerned. As we saw earlier, Federal involvement in education at all was a highly contentious issue up to the mid 1960s. Secondly, most of the programmes were narrow, at least by British standards, and the funding was specific. The objectives of those who framed the legislation may have been mixed but the target groups and the scope of the activity funded were clearly defined. Thirdly, many had been strongly influenced by social scientists who made explicit and indeed exaggerated claims for what they would fulfil.

It was therefore quite natural that on all three grounds these particular programmes were the first to which formal evaluation were applied on any major scale. Congress attached a requirement to evaluate the compensatory education programmes under Title 1 of the 1965 Education Act. These evaluations were to be undertaken at the local level and proved of little value. In 1967 new provisions covering all the Office of Education programmes were introduced. These evaluations were to be undertaken at Federal level and the results were to be reported to Congress.

There was at this time too a ready supply of expertise. Research institutes existed or were created who could undertake the work. The Defense Department had already helped to create a network of institutes and private companies to undertake its research contracts. RAND was only the best known. Many of these institutions moved over to the social policy field with great ease and aplomb – 'almost without changing gear' as one of those involved put it. While this may be seen as a *response* to a growing and changing pattern of demand their influence on the demand side of the process was not negligible as our previous references to RAND indicate.

Another major factor at work was the demand for more and more *critical* information. The 'new breed' of departmental heads were, as one person put it, 'cast in the modern management role'. Of

Richardson one said 'he places a high value on analysis. Indeed he is scarcely a politician, he is perhaps a prototype social programme manager.' His successor – Weinberger, ex-head of the OMB – is by reputation the same kind of person. Again the parallels with the Heath government and its emphasis on 'management' are clear. In short, the political climate in the Nixon period, associated with a commitment to economy in social spending, favoured asking difficult questions about social programmes – do they work, what results do they bring? Congress too was asking increasingly awkward questions. It had been promised a great deal in the days of the 'Great Society' programmes and since. It had become clear that America was no nearer the solution of its major social problems. The scale of expenditure on many of the projects had increased vastly and both radicals and conservatives were questioning their appropriateness. This helps to explain why the word 'evaluation' tends to be applied to the work done on this particular group of social programmes – and tends to imply that the question being asked is, does it work?

Such an approach has not been without its critics especially amongst those responsible for administering the programmes. Attempts to measure the total impact of a policy like Head Start for disadvantaged pre-school children showed only limited or almost non-existent results. The early evaluations of Title 1 of the 1965 Elementary and Secondary Education Act produced the same kind of conclusions. The administrators argued that this overall approach was unhelpful. It did not tell you whether some approaches were more successful than others. Since the programme as a whole was popular no administration was going to cut off Head Start funds and to be told that it made no difference in those circumstances was just not very helpful. Other critics argued that so little was known about what actually happened to the Federal funds that it was far from clear whether the negative results of an overall impact study told you anything. Did it mean the funds were not spent on poor children (as indeed was very largely the case at the beginning), or that they were, but it made no difference? The Urban Institute in reviewing the large number of rather unhelpful evaluations undertaken on Title 1 projects came to the conclusion that the first priority should be to see what was actually happening – *monitoring*. Who was receiving the funds, what kind of projects were undertaken, how many of the target population were 'benefiting'?

Another approach, increasingly favoured, was to try and assess the *relative* effectiveness of different approaches, e.g. in teaching 'disadvantaged' children to read. This might be related to the effectiveness of broad strategies or individual projects – an example of the former might be the conclusion drawn from the Head Start evaluation that the year long projects did produce some results whereas the summer six-week projects did not.

As a direct result of the criticisms levelled at Head Start another project – Follow Through – employed a different approach. It had originally been intended as a follow-up to Head Start giving special help to deprived children in the first grades of elementary schools. The money was not voted in sufficient quantity to make this possible. Consequently it was decided to use the money to undertake what was called 'planned variation'. This was really a cross between provision and experiment. The Office of Education produced a selection of projects involving different teaching strategies and approaches. It then asked local areas to bid for money to run such schemes. To each would be attached a common evaluation scheme. The hope was that it would demonstrate which approach was proving most effective. As it has turned out the plan fell completely between the two stools of experiment and provision. The localities looked upon it as extra provision with little regard for the scientific niceties of evaluation while the Federal Government could not exercise enough control to make it scientific. A very similar outcome befell the bilingual programme, which catered for children for whom English was a second language.

From the high point of optimism in 1965 the social scientists fell to a much more humble attitude in the late sixties and early seventies. They emphasised their ignorance about the way these social programmes worked or might work. They recognised much more clearly the *political* nature of the evaluation process. Once a new programme was in operation it collected its own interests around it and no matter what the results of evaluation studies it would tend to have a momentum of its own. Hence the planners in the Office of Economic Opportunity and HEW argued that it was necessary to experiment on a small scale at first, to try in a 'controlled' environment, to test and understand the impact a potential programme might make. This had to be done on a small scale which could be modified or dropped altogether if it did not work. Another rather different rationale for such experiments was that if an innovation could not carry the political pressure necessary to carry it through the idea could be kept alive and some of the criticisms met in advance. This idea in particular lay behind the experiments with negative income tax, first begun with a grant from the Office of Economic Opportunity (see below).

In short, the concept of evaluation had broadened substantially since the mid-sixties. It had been viewed at the outset as the systematic application of cost benefit analysis. It then took on a more basic research role but still sought to answer the question: how far is a given programme producing results? As time went on the sheer complexity not only of the effects of social intervention but of the processes themselves led evaluators to ask more and more fundamental questions. The research became even more basic 'What impact do cash supplements have on work incentives?' 'What affects people's attitudes to work?', 'How do various kinds of teaching resources and methods affect different kinds of children's learning?'

In following this course the evaluation of these new programmes was beginning to converge with a much older tradition.

An Older Tradition
Although some accounts of the development of Federal evaluation policy would lead one to believe that it began with the poverty programmes of the mid 1960s there are really two quite distinct strands to the history. The other is the long established research role of the Social Security Administration and its work on income maintenance programmes.

The 1935 Social Security Act laid a duty on the Social Security Board to study and make recommendations 'as to the most effective methods of providing economic security through social insurance.' (Section 702.) The research functions laid down by the Board for the Research Bureau included: evaluating the relative adequacy of these (social insurance and social welfare) programmes and their combined effectiveness.[15]

It does indeed have a very modern ring about it. In its early years the research activity not only included the creation of the basic programme statistics but work on the effectiveness of the existing programmes in meeting 'financial insecurity'. The outcome of this early work was a set of proposals for a complete system of social security and health insurance, modelled on the Beveridge plan for Britain in 1942.[16] We have described the planning work undertaken for the Advisory Councils in an earlier chapter. Nevertheless in the late 1950s and early 1960s senior staff came to the view that the research effort was too fragmented.

In 1963 when the agency lost its oversight of welfare and assistance programmes research and evaluation activities were re-organised. The Division of Programme research, then in the Commissioner's office, and the Division of Programme Analysis, then in the Bureau of Old Age and Survivors Insurance, as well as some other statistical services were amalgamated. The result was the Division (Office as it is now called) of Research and Statistics. In charge was an Assistant Commissioner. At that stage the combined staff totalled just over 250. From the beginning this Division produced regular work plans and from them it is possible to get a fairly clear picture of the way research policy developed over the next decade.

The 1965–6 work plan said:

'The research programme of the SSA is designed to provide new knowledge and analytical tools for continuous and forward looking evaluation of the social security system and its effectiveness in providing for economic security and its relative contribution to overall economic and social policy.'

It went on to summarise its broad strategy:

'i. Studies which investigated at a micro and a macro level the inter-relationships of different income maintenance programmes.
'ii. Studies which brought to light "threats to economic independence" which were not adequately met by existing programmes.
'iii. The relative advantages and costs of different approaches to the "basic objective of income security".'

Though general in tone these are revealing statements because they indicate a much broader conception of evaluation than was often employed in the new tradition. It is an attitude consistent with and crucial to what we earlier called 'promotional planning.' The Division was not satisfied with research aimed at finding out how long new applicants had to wait to receive benefit or how many who were entitled to benefit, failed to claim. They did this but in addition, and indeed very largely, they were concerned to show which groups fell outside their programmes altogether. Their criterion was not a narrow set of programme objectives but the broader ideological objective of income security for all, explicit as they saw it in the 1935 Act. The work was, in short, directed to long term policy development as well as immediate administrative efficiency.

The Division continued the work already in progress, notably the regular studies of the financial and social circumstances of the aged and the disabled as well as a longitudinal survey of the aged. These gave 'bedrock' data about the groups the programmes were then serving and pinpointed their changing circumstances and financial needs. In addition, a survey was undertaken of public assistance applicants and recipients in an attempt to illuminate the relationship between the public assistance and social insurance programmes. Who were receiving both, who was not, how many were refused assistance and why? But there was also a considerable emphasis on carrying forward and elaborating earlier studies on private and voluntary health insurance coverage and employers sickness benefit plans, individuals' expenditure on health, especially by the elderly and the overall extent of private insurance cover. This was all directed to the then current political discussion of health insurance (see p. 111).

A particularly interesting feature of the Division's work at this period in the early 1960s was that of the long range research branch – including in it such individuals as Mollie Orshanski and Alvin Schorr whose work has become well known since in its own right. They were concerned with long term trends in the distribution of income in the US. How could one define poverty and who were the poor? At this time very few academics outside government were doing work in this field.

Then there was the development of indices which might be used for adjusting benefits in line with living standards. The next major addition which came in 1965–6 was more 'managerial' in concept. A section was set up called the 'evaluation and measurement branch' responsible for designing a statistical quality control system. A small sample of recipients was drawn to ascertain how many and what kind of applicants failed to obtain benefit, how many errors occurred in assessment of entitlement to whom and where. In subsequent years the sample and elaborateness of the procedure have been extended. Since 1966, when Medicare began, work has developed in the health field – on costs, on the use of hospital facilities, and physicians' services. A monthly sample of those on medicare was instituted to see how far they claimed, why they did not, when they ran out of benefit and what happened when they did. From 1968–9 more research was undertaken on the finance of social security, its economic role, its distributive effects and its impact on retirement. By 1973 the special research projects conducted by the office numbered about 130, and this was in addition to regular on-going work on basic statistics. The staff employed numbers about 450 and this excludes those doing basic data analysis most of which is contracted out.

The research strategy relies heavily on ensuring that there is sound and detailed basic programme data on which more elaborate analyses can be undertaken.

Perhaps the best way of illustrating the kind of approach which this organisation has adopted is to relate in a little more detail how it responded to the new programme of adult assistance for which the Social Security Administration assumed responsibility in January, 1974 (see page 59). The programme is now known by the title 'Supplementary Security Income' and bears a close resemblance to the British Supplementary Benefit scheme. By the summer of 1972 ORS had set up a separate, though as yet skeleton, division of Adult Assistance Studies. It was aiming to set up an information base that would show:

1 Who the recipients of the new federal means tested benefits were, how much they were receiving, how much more or less this was than the benefits they obtained under the state run systems where they had been members and whether their states were supplementing these basic benefits and by how much?
2 How large the total population 'at risk' was, i.e. who in theory was eligible for benefit and what were their characteristics. From this some estimate of those not claiming should be possible.

This would mean putting all the applicants' records, including details of his social circumstances, on tape but this was needed for administrative purposes too, drawing a sample and not merely analysing it in the first year but using it as a basis for a cohort study in later years. In November, 1973, a survey was launched of those expected to be eligible, those already on adult assistance and the population 'at risk'. This would then be repeated a year later to see what the effects of the new programme had had, as well as to describe the populations served.

The current population survey with its income questions would, it was hoped, provide a continuing basis for determining total eligibility and hence lack of take-up as well as the extent to which other groups in financial need lay outside the programme.

Over and above these basic surveys a number of people were set to identify areas in which they felt new issues would arise and to design studies that would give some basic information 'when the bells started ringing'. The kind of work already clearly needed included criteria for fixing levels of benefit, on the various exclusions built into the legislation, on the extent and nature of discretionary additions, on the rationale for reductions given to those in institutional care, on the definition of disability for this programme.

Altogether it was hoped that some 30–40 people would work in this division. Up to 1974 when this was written this plan had been carried through broadly as envisaged and was running on schedule.

This illustrates the concern with the impact of programmes on recipients, with policy gaps and with possible future developments, that seems to characterise this Office's work. This approach, typified by the research on the supplementary security income programme, compares strikingly with the comparable British experience when the National Assistance Board became the Supplementary Benefits Commission. This was a relatively minor change compared to the American. Yet the public and the Department know very little indeed about the consequences of that change – how it affected those on National Assistance, whether the new procedures, designed to encourage new applicants, did in fact do so; whether the new procedures which were designed to be less stigmatic were perceived as such by the applicants and so on. We shall return to this in the next chapter.

Converging Traditions

In short it was possible to see the 'new' and the 'old' traditions of evaluation converging by the 1970s. The social security research effort had always been strongly concerned with programme developments, with gaps in provision and future needs. More recently it had begun to devote more effort to evaluation in the 'does it work' sense – how quickly and how accurately are benefit claims processed, what are the consequences of different financial formulae, what are the trade-offs between assistance and insurance benefits. At the same time agencies in the newer tradition were finding that the simplistic 'does the programme meet its objectives' formula was none too easy to apply and more attention was being focused on planning studies and surveys of demand and need. What was emerging was an eclectic research tradition very familiar to a social administrator from Britain. Even so, the conceptualisation of concepts like social demand and need had not been elaborated to anything like the same degree as they have within the social administration tradition. Does this mean the British have nothing to learn from the American tradition? The answer we believe is that it does, in three particular respects – organisation, scale and approach.

In 1974 the SSA was spending over 20 million dollars on research. A sum that was equivalent, even so, to only 0·03 per cent of the agency's total outlays or 1 per cent of its administrative costs. The 1967 (General Provisions) Education Act gave the Secretary of HEW power to spend up to a given sum on studies which were either concerned with 'planning for the succeeding year' or with 'the evaluation' of programmes. (Section 402a.) Another section,

404a, laid a duty on the Secretary to report the results to Congress by 31 January each year. In particular he had a duty to produce a comprehensive evaluation of any programme which was entering the last year for which funds were authorised. As we saw earlier, it was common for Congress to put a time limit on many of the new social programmes. In these cases evaluations had to include a detailed review 'for its entire first life, based to the maximum extent practicable on objective measurements'. Moreover, the Commissioner had to publish an annual report indicating the 'impact' of agencies' programmes and the results of any investigations by the Office of Education. (Section 412.) The formal Congressional role in promoting evaluation and funding is clear, but it should be added that the last section calling for an annual report went by default until recently and it was the OE evaluators that drew this to Congress's attention.

We saw that Congress had typically authorised spending of up to 1 per cent of programme funds on evaluation studies. These were not necessarily spent. The Office of Education spending had only begun building up in 1970. The evaluation expenditure reached $9·5 million in 1970. It rose to $12·5 million in 1971 and then dropped back to about $10 million in 1973. On top of this must be added the cost of the 'Follow Through' experiment, a special enquiry on school finance and other extras. Thus in 1973 evaluation expenditure had reached 0·4 per cent of total Office of Education funds.[17]

Just as there have been rather different traditions of Federal evaluation and research in the US so the organisational structure has differed. Once again this reflects the very different nature of the programmes. The Social Security Administration has been directly responsible for delivery or payment – other agencies for the most part give grants. The SSA has been able to rely on its own basic statistics generated within its own organisation. Other agencies have either had to rely on returns of information from states and localities or undertake sample social surveys. While SSA is highly centralised, and had been operating for nearly four decades, the Federal – State – local cash relationship in education is less than one decade old, and has to contend with a basic outlook of suspicion if not distrust between these levels of government. Nor is the Federal Government the dominant partner. For all these reasons it is natural that the research undertaken by SSA should have been done largely 'in-house', i.e. by research workers actually employed by that organisation. Those involved see other virtues than the sheer technical ones. They argue that full time research staff who can be in close contact with administrators gain a much better appreciation of the realities of day-to-day administration and the problems as these staff perceive them. Their research is more likely to be used if these perceptions are shared. Outside academics do not have an interest in acquiring a detailed knowledge of the programmes and their reports reflect that. Moreover if most of the work is done by outside research agencies the task of administering the research grants is nothing like as attractive and the quality of staff is lower, and turnover tends to be high. A large research staff with job security running their own research projects, with opportunity for publication and technical and professional assistance, produce work of a consistently *high* standard as well as *relevant* in content.

In contrast agencies like the Office of Economic Opportunity and the Office of Education have had to rely largely on contract work on the insistence of Congress. Contract work is similar to the concept employed in the Rothschild Report in Britain which talked of the need for Departments to develop a 'consumer contractor relationship' with those undertaking research. In short, buying a piece of work. The US agencies, as we shall see, exercise strict regulation over the research in progress. The Social Security Administration could in more recent years make *grants* to outside bodies like universities which did not involve close supervision and were given for proposals made by the researcher, but they were very small in amount.

Broadly speaking contracts usually went to profit making or non-university research bodies, grants went to universities or non-profit making academic research institutes. The Nixon administration strategy favoured contract research.

Despite these differences evaluation in both the Social Security Administration and the Office of Education shared basic characteristics which have been largely absent in Great Britain, at least until very recently.

First, it is undertaken systematically as a significant part of the agencies' work. The SSA, as we saw, had a separate section conducting studies on each group of programmes. So did the Office of Education. The latter was gradually initiating research studies on each of its 100 separate legislative programmes. When the studies initiated in fiscal year 1972 were completed roughly 40 per cent of the major programmes would have had formal evaluations. Each year an evaluation plan had to be drawn up. Ideas were collected from programme managers, from recommendations by or sometimes legislative instructions from Congress, the White House staff, etc. Then the draft plan was submitted to the Office of the Secretary where the education section of the central evaluation office would go through it and react to it. This section of the Secretary's office had 25 per cent of the total evaluation funds at its disposal. It also drew up a separate evaluation plan.

Both were seen as part of the whole forward planning system (see p. 102) and the OE plan was drawn up with policy priorities clearly to the forefront. It contained a summary of the results of the past year's evaluations and a detailed rationale for the future year's projects. These were divided into two groups: those which were mainly concerned with evaluating the impact or effectiveness of particular programmes, and those which were concerned with identifying new areas of need and unmet need, e.g. in the case of handicapped children, and adult illiterates. The fact that a quarter of the funds were in the hands of the Secretary's Office ensured that another perspective on research needs was included. It was notice-able that their projects were distinctively different. They were pitched at a higher level of generality, and were more concerned with potential trade-offs between programmes than the OE evalua-tions. They were much nearer the basic or academic research end of the spectrum. One study was concerned with the imperfections in the labour market for teachers, the reasons for shortages in particu-lar areas, the tenure system and its effects on hiring well-qualified younger staff. Then there was a study of the extent of overlap between certain categoric programmes, of certain aspects of the transition from school to work, aimed at developing the career guidance programme. Another study was concerned with tracing the impact of revenue sharing (a new general grant to local authorities) on education expenditure in different districts. Yet another con-cerned identifying the impact of higher family incomes (e.g. through NIT) on the demand for education.

In the Office of Research and Statistics in SSA the same kind of role was filled by the 'long range studies' section. But here again the Secretary's Office had funds which it was investing in three highly expensive experiments in income maintenance (see below) testing the impact of negative income tax type schemes on families, especially their work experience, but in many other ways too. This was an approach of which the SSA had been very sceptical. There was, in short, a clear appreciation that different parts of the organi-sation would have different perceptions of the issues facing it and that in consequence research funds should be spread, while at the same time trying to ensure that each programme was systematically reviewed.

This leads on to a second organisational point – the deliberate separation of the evaluators from the administrators who actually ran the programmes. This procedure has its critics but it also has its logic.

John Evans (head of evaluation at the Office of Education) described how, when he went to the OEO, there was only a very small central unit. Every programme had its own evaluator and a bit of money to spend on evaluation. He decided to amalgamate all the evaluation and planning activity into one Office. Otherwise, he argued, evaluators become the tools of those running the programmes, their rationalisers. Since, in that situation, evaluation became evaluation of self, it was almost certain to become justification of self and this had to be avoided at all costs. The whole point of evaluation was to create a body of information that enabled the planners to make decisions about priorities. To work effectively those who did the planning had also to initiate the evaluation plans, and oversee their operations. They also had to be quite separate from the programme staff, devoid of loyalties to any one programme. This logic he had carried over to the Office of Education and taken further by the inclusion of the budget staff in the same office. The planning staff said that they spent about half their time on planning activities and half their time overseeing and following up evaluation. We asked earlier just how critical any organisation could be of itself, but there was certainly a clear recognition of the problem and an attempt to provide an organisational solution.

A third organisational characteristic is the very tight control exercised by the agency over the research programme. Where this is not done 'in house' the control exercised over individual 'contracts' is tight. Agencies wanting research done issue requests for proposals (RPFs) which ask for bids by research agencies which are then treated on a competitive basis. Only in special circumstances is an agency meant to approach a particular research organisation rather than submitting it to open tender. Evans again made the point that initially RPFs had been rather general in nature. The replies had been very different and difficult to compare and the results often too late, too voluminous and too technical. Now one man who had general responsibility for a group of programmes, e.g. higher education, would be given the responsibility of drawing up a highly specific RPF, giving the outline the eventual report should take, the output or effectiveness measures, the kind of sample to be drawn, the control groups and the analyses to be undertaken. If the firms or institutions take issue with any of these guide lines they are free to do so but this must be discussed and settled prior to any contract. This is then very tightly drawn so that there is little chance of the researchers producing something different to what was originally

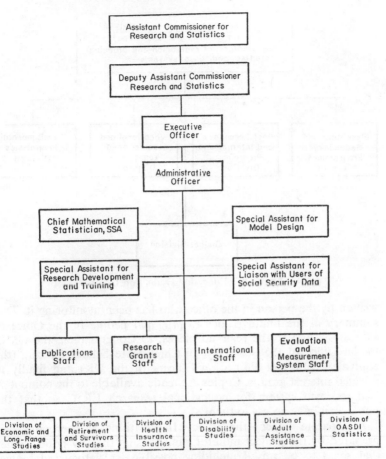

Figure 9.1 Social Security Research Office

laid down. Thereafter the man in the office chairs regular meetings with the contractors to make sure the research work does not stray either in terms of method or policy relevance. When the full contractor's report is received he is then responsible for summarising it and drawing out the policy implications.

The fourth distinctive organisational characteristic was the dissemination process. The SSA has had a regular vehicle for publicising its research findings – the *Social Security Bulletin*, as well as separate research monographs. The Office of Education again has an elaborate procedure.

Once an evaluation report is produced an 'executive summary' is

o

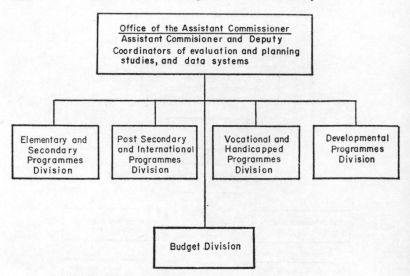

Figure 9.2 Education Evaluation Office

written by the person in the office who has been monitoring it. This summary of the findings goes to principal people in the Office of Education, and to the regional offices, to Congressmen, the OMB, to the Office of the Secretary, to Chief State School Officers (the equivalent of Chief Education Officers in the UK) and finally to selected interest groups. Copies are made available to the computerised retrieval system for educational research ERIC so that the public can have access to them.

A separate paper – the Policy Implications Memorandum – is prepared by the project monitor summarising the key policy issues that seem to be raised including possible legislative and budget consequences as well as ideas for further research. This goes to programme managers and relevant people throughout OE. The aim is to get agreement on a decision document and eventually to keep a running tally of these to see how far action follows. This last stage is more problematic (see below), but the first stages of dissemination have certainly been working since 1971–2.

One does not have to believe that all this worked like clockwork to conclude that here was a carefully organised attempt to get the education and social security programmes systematically reviewed using appropriate social scientific research methods, and to disseminate the results. The systematic nature of the activity, the social science training and quality of those who conducted it and the sheer scale of the operations are examples we can begin to learn from in Britain. But perhaps most relevant of all is the assumption that evaluation is for *public* consumption. Its purpose is to educate administrators, Congressmen, interest groups, and as much effort must be put into dissemination as into initiation.

The Approach to Evaluation
It is helpful to consider, if only briefly, the many different kinds of study that were supported with evaluation funds.

In 1970 the Urban Institute distinguished four major types of evaluation,[18] themselves mainly based on the categories originally employed by the OEO.

1 The first is 'programme impact', or the assessment of the overall effect of a programme. The aim is to give policy makers information that may help them decide between the merits of funding different programmes. The Head Start study by the Westinghouse Corporation was a classic example. (See p. 63). Impact studies include not merely attempts to measure effectiveness but increasingly are concerned to define the population in need and estimate how far the particular service is reaching those in need.

2 Programme strategy evaluations are designed to show the relative success of different ways of achieving the basic objectives of the programme. The Follow Through research was intended to be just such a study. It aimed to test what kinds of teaching and curriculum approaches were most successful with disadvantaged children.

3 Project evaluation is concerned to test the success of particular projects at a local level. The aim is to compare the effectiveness of particular projects, e.g. in several schools with a control group. Title One evaluations funded under the original legislation were of this kind, or were at least meant to be.

4 Project rating is concerned with the relative success of local projects in particular areas. Both of these last two types are primarily relevant to local administrators. But the recent evaluation of the experience of neighbourhood health centres by the OEO could be said to fall into this category. In a more recent review of federal evaluations Gross added two more categories embodying two kinds of 'experimentation'. This is somewhat confusing insofar as experiments can and do form a part of the research approach adopted under some of the above headings, at any rate 3 and 4. Nevertheless there is a point of substance here. As we have seen part of the logic behind social experimentation was that government should try out the effects of a *potential* programme before legislating it. This kind of research should not be put on a par with

research into the effects of existing legislation. Gross[19] distinguished between experiments designed to test what actually happened and demonstration projects which were merely designed to show if a particular approach *could* work in practical terms. We therefore have:

5 Field experimentation which is concerned to reproduce on a small scale the actual effects of a nationwide programme and test the results. The first experiment of this kind was the New Jersey Income maintenance project funded by OEO. This was designed to show the effect of introducing a Negative Income Tax scheme. It involved giving an income supplement to low income families in several towns for a period of three years. Since then similar experiments have been initiated by HEW, at Gary, Seattle and Denver and there are others in Iowa, North Carolina.

6 Experimental demonstrations. Many of the original community action projects under the poverty programme fell into this category. Gross puts the Office of Education funded experiment on performance contracting in this category. This was an attempt to see whether the principle of payments by results could be applied to education (See p. 246, note 29.).

So far all these categories are concerned with studies of outcomes. Yet as we argued earlier there has been a growing concern to study *how* things work. Very often these are studies designed to help central administrators understand what is actually going on in the field. A task which the Inspectorate try to fill in Britain. There are also studies of the administrative set up or the managerial system. One study of the Work Incentive Programme fell into that category as did another which was an attempt to examine the possibilities of measuring the performance of social work services. We can therefore add:

7 Process studies, designed to show how the system is operating either in the administrative or field context.

Finally as we have seen that the Office of Education distinguished between evaluation and planning studies, and the same could be seen in the subject matter of the Social Security work, this broad category could perhaps be divided between short-term or operational planning studies and long term planning. Examples of the first would be concerned with medium term projections of student numbers, or the costs of different benefit formulae or eligibility criteria. Examples of the second might be to investigate the long term or generational effects of poverty on the process of retirement. We can therefore add:

8 Short-term operational planning studies.

9 Long range planning studies. Distinctions like those above help to clarify the varied functions evaluation performs, though when one looks at the actual studies they frequently comprise several of these headings. Most of the impact studies also aim to throw light on the relative effectiveness of different categories, for example. Yet the list does illustrate the diversity of the work undertaken under the one general heading – evaluation. Most striking by its absence is any formal category of research that attempts to assess consumer satisfaction or reaction. Some studies did this in passing. A study was being mounted on the public's perception of social security. A tenth category could be:

10 Studies of consumer satisfaction.

Quality of Work
There has been a good deal of criticism of the variable and poor quality of many of the evaluation studies carried out for Federal agencies and its lack of relevance or use to policy-makers and administrators at different levels. Congress has come increasingly to share this view to judge from some of the recommendations included in committee reports. The OMB is also sceptical. Certainly much of the original work, especially that at local level, was scarcely worth the paper it was written on. Some of the later work, too, is more impressive in its packaging than its contents. Some of the units give the apperance of considerable shoddiness, of young men drifting through and hoping for a university job to turn up, scarcely interested in real policy issues. Nevertheless, the situation has been changing. It has become increasingly difficult to maintain a 'sloppy shop' and the best work produced is now very good indeed. The Head Start survey, precisely because it produced such depressing and controversial conclusions aroused enormous debate and was scoured for methodological faults – far more than any normal piece of academic research. By and large it emerged unscathed. A more typical example was a report on the Educational Opportunity Grants Programme that had been established under the Higher Education Act of 1965. Under it grants were given to institutions who in their turn were to distribute money to assist 'high school graduates in exceptional financial need'. The normal administrative data did not enable anyone to know who was getting the money or the extent to which they benefited from it. The legislation was specific. The money was intended to go to well-qualified but poor high school graduates who would not otherwise have gone to college. Nevertheless the study recognised that students, institutions, the Federal Government and Congress might view the policy

differently. It sought to identify these perceptions and include them. The results showed quite clearly that the programme was reaching poor and black or minority group students, that on many counts they could be classed as disadvantaged, that once in college they received more advice and teaching support than other students. There was an attempt to provide more residential accommodation, but this, as well as extra support, was difficult because of limited funds. Despite the lower qualifications and other disadvantages students stayed at college as long as other students though there were differences between types of institution and student. Institutions' views as to the success of the programme and its side effects on the institutions were investigated. Many difficulties in administration and funding came to light. Students were surveyed on their reactions to the programme and to alternative forms of financial support.

Certainly the study could have been improved upon. It could have had a longitudinal element and a control group, but it had to be done quickly to be relevant. The limitations were clearly stated.

Another evaluation covered the workings of the Emergency School Assistance Programme which gave special assistance to schools undergoing integration.[20] Again as a pure academic study one might have hoped for a longer-term survey but as a short-term picture of how the programme was developing in its first year it had a lot to give. It took just over a year to complete. Twelve measures of racial climate were produced and tested in 200 schools. Five measures were found to have high inter-correlations and hence some claim to constitute real measures. They were:

1 Inter-racial friendship patterns.
2 The extent to which students of different races worked together.
3 The extent of co-operation between staff of different races.
4 The extent of integration between groups on campus and in cafeteria.
5 The attendance rates of black students.

The study tested changes in these measures over the year, in schools where integration was recent and where it occurred some time before. In both it was improving. It distinguished between seventeen different activities that were designed to assist integration. Only five seemed to be correlated with improvements. More money was spent on ineffective activities than effective ones and in particular special teacher training programmes produced no measurable change at all. Finally, the money was actually reaching desegregating schools. Again perceptions of different groups within the school system, of teachers with different racial groups and administrators, as well as students' perception were tested.

A further point is illustrated by this study. Clearly to be able to mount a major study like this involving the creation and application of measuring instruments to 250 schools in districts throughout America as well as interviews with 9,000 individuals and 20 case studies all within a year involves not only a large budget but a large research organisation by British standards. Both studies had clear relevance to administrators, both showing clearly not only the extent to which programmes were reaching the target groups but especially in the latter case they had an indication of which strategies were working compared with those which were not. This presumably reflected the degree of control the central staff in OE had exerted.

In short if evaluation studies were properly conducted they could give timely, relevant results which did show appreciation for some of the inherent difficulties of assessing how far a programme was 'succeeding'.

The Impact of Evaluation

Did any of this work make any difference? A frequent criticism of Federal evaluation studies is that they simply get shelved, and succeed in doing no more than line the pockets of the companies employed to do the work. Once more there is a good deal of truth in the assertion overall, but it is difficult to place all the blame on the evaluators. Even if research is good and relevant politicians may choose to take no notice. That scarcely invalidates the attempt to see what is happening to a programme. It is also argued that agencies misrepresent or put a favourable gloss on critical evaluations and publicise only the favourable ones. Again there is truth in this. This happens with all research findings, but, at least, much of the critical work in the US is open to public access.

The more substantial criticisms relate to quality and relevance and these we now discuss more fully. We have argued already that the research work of the SSA has been of crucial importance in what we called programme development or promotional planning. We gave a number of examples.

The impact of education evaluations are more difficult to trace for they only began to be funded in a serious way more recently and completed work was limited. However the Head Start evaluation almost certainly contributed first to halting the growth of Head Start funds and to switching the effort from short summer projects to longer term projects lasting one year, which proved slightly more effective. The stabilisation of Title One funds for compensatory education may reflect the impact of early studies which showed such disappointing results. Indeed the very negative results of many studies have led critics to suggest that evaluation is merely used as an excuse to cut social service expenditure. The supposition is that the results are always negative, or alternatively that notice is only taken of the critical ones. Yet this view is unfair and can be balanced against the opposite criticism that such studies are never critical of the bodies who fund research. Many believed that the real reason so many of the poverty programme studies revealed poor results was the basic weakness in the original conception of the poverty programme – namely the belief that poverty could be eliminated by attacking its symptoms, not the more basic causes of economic inequality. It may seem a long learning process but there is no cause to shoot the teacher. In the period 1971–2 several studies by the Office of Education had helped produce legislative response. The student aid programme had been more directly focused on disadvantaged students, support formulae in some of the compensatory programmes had been altered and equipment grants which seemed to be unproductive had been scaled down. The studies on the impact of student grants had arguably helped create a climate more favourable to extension of grants to poor students.

In short, there has been a lot to be critical of from a purist academic point of view but good research is now being done and the fact is that, compared to the lack of such research in Britain, one can only be impressed by what *has* been produced. The amount that is now being found out about the working of Federal social welfare programmes in the fields of education, social security and health is impressive.

Some criticis have argued that it is not the quality but the relevance of the studies that is in doubt. In particular it has been argued that national impact studies do not really help those administering individual programmes. They fail to help them decide which kinds of approach work and which do not. Decisions about whether to continue a programme at all are political, the critics argue, and will be taken almost regardless of research evidence.

Again these criticisms are much less valid than they were. Moreover, it is worth remembering that an agency like the Office of Education was administering nearly 100 programmes. Each year decisions had to be taken in the budget process about marginal adjustments and priorities between these programmes. Every so often the whole programme came up for Congressional review. If approval is not forthcoming the programme lapses. It is difficult to see how, as a first priority, the Office could avoid trying to get some picture of how each of these relatively specific programmes is working.

Social Experimentation

As we indicated earlier, a rather different approach has been advocated by some of those involved in evaluation work. They recognised that great political difficulties arose if an evaluation study turned out to be severely critical of the underlying rationale beyond the programme. By the time the evaluation is undertaken the programme will have generated its own 'constituency', parents of pre-school children, teachers, employers, negro organisations, etc. So, argues this school of thought, experiment first. Have a trial run and test to see whether a pilot scheme produces the kind of results its proponents and critics suggest are likely. Yet, the political analysis must be pushed rather further than this. Where there is substantial political support for a new initiative no one is likely to be ready to pause and wait for a large-scale experiment. If the problem area is politically unpopular no action *or* research is likely.[21] It is only if a proposed reform with some chance of success runs into a great deal of opposition that an experiment may come to be seen as an acceptable compromise. An experiment may be launched to refute its critics or keep an idea alive. The income maintenance experiments in New Jersey were of this kind. Allowances not unlike the British Family Income Supplement were given to a sample of poor families. Income guarantees of different levels with different marginal 'tax' rates were used in an effort to test their impact on the families concerned, their spending patterns and above all the effect they had on work patterns. The first results were published in 1974.[22] They show that despite the predictions based on economic theory fairly high marginal 'tax rates' experienced by those receiving the means tested income supplements, apparently had hardly any effect on work participation or effort. There were certain limitations to this experiment and HEW was supporting experiments of a similar kind in other parts of the United States.

The Office of Education Follow Through Project – essentially testing planned variations in teaching strategies – has already been referred to briefly. A project to test the effects of educational vouchers was undertaken. One on performance contracting had also been completed.

The Department of Housing and Urban Development proposed some elaborate experiments with housing allowances.[23] The aim was to test a scheme for giving allowances to private tenants in the same way that the 1971 Housing Act did in Britain. Three separate studies were proposed. One was designed to investigate the impact of such a scheme on the *supply* of private housing in a town. The second was to study the impact on the households affected, i.e. the *demand* side and a third was to ensure that the administrative complications had been assessed. To make this possible, all the poorer households in several communities had to be given housing allowances for a specified period. Clearly the technical difficulties are enormous and the size and cost of the projects far outweigh the normal run of social science research. It may help to outline what the 'supply' study alone would involve.

The Housing Allowance Experiment

Stage 1: Before the actual intervention began three studies should be mounted in specially selected 'modular' neighbourhoods: to appraise the state of property; to survey the financial circumstances of landlords in the area; a tenant survey to ascertain incomes and social variables. A smaller scale study of tenant property and landlords outside these sample neighbourhoods would be conducted to determine how far they were untypical.

Stage 2: This involved the mounting of the scheme itself. All those who applied to the project team who were within the income limits would receive a certificate – tenants and owner occupiers. Anyone who moved into the area after the scheme began would not qualify and anyone who moved out would lose their allowance. Families could use these certificates in lieu of rent or mortgage payment and the landlord would cash them from the project offices. The 'face' value increased with the size of the family. The certificate was only issued when the property had been approved as of an adequate standard. Those who lived in substandard housing would not gain unless they sought better accommodation or unless their landlord improved it to gain a higher rent.

Stage 3 concerned the monitoring of results. There was to be some 'informal' monitoring: 'community reactions' and residents surveys on an annual basis. Then there were to be regular surveys of the property – all of it in the sample neighbourhoods and samples outside as well as all the property in the tenants' survey. Altogether the surveys would have to last for ten years both to show the longer term effects and to limit possible Hawthorne effects. Above all it was felt that if the allowances were given for a shorter period people would not be prepared to invest in the costs of moving or purchasing a house. The aim was to measure the supply response in terms of repairs and improvements, the output of housing and tenant satisfaction and take-up.

Such experiments on the poor raise all kinds of ethical, political and practical questions. Would the articulate middle class ever lend themselves to such a process? Are the results going to be much help in ten years time? Can the results be said to hold on a national scale? Is it possibly easier for the building industry to respond readily to increased demand in one experimental area than to expand its capacity in response to a national scheme?

Whatever their limitations and the problems such experiments raise, they do illustrate very well the difference in attitude in the two countries. The British observer cannot but be struck by the paradox when he considers the introduction of housing allowances and income supplements in Britain. In a few years time the Americans are likely to know far more about their economic and social impact than we do in this country. Britain has implemented both schemes on a national scale. America will in all probability have the knowledge and no programmes.

In Brief

We have seen that despite the importance originally attached to them cost benefit and cost effectiveness studies soon proved to be of only very limited value in assessing priorities between existing social programmes or in introducing new ones. Instead the planners turned more and more to fundamental research in applied social science. It is in the systematic pursuit of relevant applied research that we have most to learn in Britain. There is also a toughness and a vigour about the kind of questions that are asked and the methods that are used to find the answers which is challenging. Above all it is the vastly greater scale on which applied research is undertaken that is impressive. That becomes clear when we compare the American efforts with comparable ones in Britain.

REFERENCES

1 McKean, R. W., *Efficiency in Government and the Use of Systems Analysis*, op. cit. Chapter 14 and appendices.
2 Novick, D. (Ed.), *Program Budgeting*, op. cit. Chapter 3.
3 Greenhouse, S. M., 'PPBS Rationale, Language and Idea Relationships', *Public Administration Review*, December, 1966.
4 HEW Office for Program Coordination, Disease Control Programs, Human Investment Programs, Child Health Programs, Program Analyses 1965–6. HEW Office of Assistant Secretary (Planning and Evaluation) Program Analyses, 1967.

5 See W. Gorham's testimony to the subcommittee of the Joint Economic Committee, September 14, 1967.
6 For the classic argument see Schultze, T. W., 'Investment in Human Capital', *American Economic Review*, March, 1961. For a favourable assessment of the approach see Blaug, M., 'The Rate of Return on Investment in Education in Great Britain'. *The Manchester School*, September, 1965. For a critical assessment see Vaizey, J., *et al.*, *The Political Economy of Education*, Duckworth, London, 1972. Arrow, K. J., 'Higher Education as a filter', *Journal of Public Economics*, Vol. 2, No. 3, 1973; Wiles, P. J., 'The Correlation between Education and Earnings', *Higher Education*, January–February, 1974.
7 For example Mushkin, S. J., 'Health as an Investment', *Journal of Political Economy*, Vol. 70, 1962.
8 HEW Office of Program Coordination, Occasional Paper No. 1, *Problems of Assessing the Effectiveness of Child Health Services*. May, 1967.
9 Rivlin, Alice M., *Systematic Thinking for Social Action*, Brookings Institution, Washington, 1971, pp. 59–60. The whole of this book and especially Chapters 3 and 4 are a lucid account of the practical limitations of cost benefit and cost effectiveness analysis in the social policy field, as well as suggestions about what research might produce results. In particular Chapter 5 makes the case for 'social experimentation' which is discussed below.
10 *Children and their Primary Schools*, op. cit., see annex B to Chapter 31.
11 For discussion of the issue see Ribich, T., *Education and Poverty*, Brookings Institution, Washington, 1968.
12 Coleman, J. S., *et al.*, *Equality of Educational Opportunity*, Government Printing Office, Washington, 1966. For a review of the subsequent American research see Averch, H. A., *et al.*, *How Effective is Schooling*, Rand Corporation, Santa Monica, 1972.
13 Fein, R., 'On measuring the economic benefits of health programmes' in *Medical History and Medical Care*, Ed. G. McLachlan, Oxford University Press, 1970.
14 HEW Office of Program Coordination, *Maternal and Child Care Programs: Program Analysis*, October, 1966.
15 Quoted in I. Merriam, 'Social Security Research in a Government Agency', *Journal of Social Policy*, Vol. 1, Part 4, 1972.
16 Social Insurance and Allied Services, Cmd 6404 (1942); Social Security Board Annual Report, *Facing Forward to Peace*, 1945.
17 Office of Education, *Evaluation Plan 1973*.
18 Wholey, J., *Federal Evaluation Policy*, Urban Institute, Washington, DC, 1970.
19 Gross, P. F., 'A critical Review of some of the considerations in Post-Secondary Evaluation', *Policy Sciences*, 4 (1973), pp. 171–95.
20 Office of Education, 1971, Final Report Grant No. OEG 0–9–099013–46 43.
21 For this and other points see Timpane, M., 'Educational Experimen-

tation in National Social Policy', *Harvard Educational Review*, Vol. 40, No. 4, 1970.

22 The original New Jersey experiments were described in *American Economic Association Papers and Proceedings*, December 1970, published May, 1971. The first published results are contained in a series of articles in the Spring, 1974, issue of the *Journal of Human Resources*, Vol. IX, No. 2 and No. 4.

23 Research Proposals for the experiments had been prepared by Rand and the Urban Institute, Washington.

Further Reading

Caro, F. G., (Ed) *Readings in Evaluation Research*, Russell Sage, New York, 1971.

Rivlin, A., *Systematic Thinking for Social Action*, op. cit.

(A readable overview of what social research has and has not said about the effectiveness of social policies and the case for experiments.)

Williams, W., *Social Policy Research and Analysis*, Elsevier, New York, 1971.

(An account of the role of research in the Federal bureaucracy especially the old Office of Economic Opportunity.)

Wildavsky, A., 'The Self Evaluating Organisation', *Public Administration Review*, September/October, 1972.

(Raises the question can any organisation evaluate itself?)

Chapter 10

Evaluation —
UK Style

Formal evaluations of the kind we described in the previous chapter
scarcely exist in Britain. The main elements of evaluation – British
style – are the political process, the press, the other media, academic
research, the work of research units and institutions, committees of
enquiry and, moving nearer to the formal process – the inspectorate,
government departments' research work and the new Programme
Analysis and Review procedure.

The Political Process
Social policy has come to fill a larger place in political discussion
since the Second World War and social service ministries and
Departments of State have taken an increasing share of the lime-
light. To head such a department carries greater status now than
used to be the case. Bentley Gilbert commented that the British welfare state was founded 'in a fit of absence of mind'.[1] Social policies
were not something to which senior politicians devoted much of
their attention. Whatever the truth of that proposition in the 1920s
and 1930s it does not hold today. Social policies had, by the mid-
1960s, become the very stuff of political debate. Since British
politics are so much more centralised than American with the
national parties the really important organs, since Britain is a much
smaller and more homogeneous society, since the mass media
largely operate at a national level, so it is at least arguable that the
political system is far more effective a vehicle for ventilating
grievances and bringing pressure to bear upon central departments
than is the case in America.[2] Television interest in social welfare is
now substantial. The same is true of the national press and its
coverage has increased. In order to test out what was no more than

a personal feeling on this matter the author analysed past issues of *The Times* for the first three months of 1959 and the first three months of 1969. All the news items that referred to housing and town planning, education, health, social security or personal social services were measured in column inches and expressed as a percentage of a full news page for the two periods. The results were striking. In 1959 there were approximately $3\frac{1}{2}$ pages of home news and of that one-fifth of one page was devoted to social policy items. In 1969 with slightly more total coverage of home news – 4 pages – the social policy coverage had increased to two-thirds of a page a day. The share of the total home news devoted to social policy had tripled in that decade. *The Guardian* has an even higher social policy emphasis and has increased its coverage as well. Not only has the quantity increased, so has the quality. The serious papers now have specialist correspondents for education, social services and housing matters.

The national newspapers are only one guide to the impact of journalism. The 1960s and 1970s have seen the launching of several new specialist journals devoted to the social services and the expansion of others. The magazine *Where* began in 1961 as the journal of the Advisory Centre for Education. It is written for parents and includes popular articles by those who teach and administer education, by academics and by other parents. *The Times Educational Supplement* has prospered and brought forth a separate journal *The Times Higher Education Supplement. New Society* was launched in 1963 as a specialist social science weekly and many of its articles focus on the social services. What is more, it has prospered while its more ancient political and literary competitors, the *New Statesman* and the *Spectator,* have struggled to maintain their existence. The financial success of these specialist journals depends, of course, on the advertising revenue they gain from job advertisements in their particular field, for school teachers, college lecturers and social workers. The consequence is also that much more is published about social policy than ever used to be the case even ten years ago and the political importance of this should not be overlooked.

Pressure groups representing *clients* or users of the social services are a relatively new phenomenon in Britain, but they are beginning to appear. Local Committees for the Advancement of State Education grew in number in the early and mid-sixties. In the late 1960s Claimant Unions began to organise recipients of Supplementary Benefits. In the housing sphere Council Tenants' Associations have existed for a long time, but here too action groups concerned about general housing conditions or redevelopment schemes became increasingly common. Nevertheless, the most political influence is probably still exercised by the interest groups representing the social service professions: teachers unions, the BMA, the social work profession or the local authority associations. The professionals also provide the most important internal source of feedback on the way services are operating at a local level. It is they who play such an important part in promoting new developments. Their perspectives are inevitably affected by the interests of the profession concerned. It is not to the advantage of hard pressed supplementary benefit officers to seek to quantify or draw attention to low take up. Teachers are unlikely to draw attention to their lack of success in helping certain kinds of children and they may actively oppose research which they fear will produce results contrary to their sectional interest. But most of the professional organisations have also played a constructive role by promoting a critical examination of the services they work in, which should not be forgotten in the fashionable denigration of professions.[3] The NUT organised a national survey of school building standards. They have campaigned for smaller classes and for the extension of nursery schooling, producing both propaganda and new information in the process. The Schoolmasters' Association has financed several independent surveys of the teachers' salary structure by the Economist Intelligence Unit. Indeed to date (1974) they remain the only published studies of the labour market for school teachers, deficient though they are in many respects.[4] The BMA and the Royal Colleges study group (the Porritt Committee) produced the first constructive proposals for a reformed administrative structure for the Health Service.[5] It formed the basis of most discussion about reform until the first 'Green Paper' was produced.[6] The new structure owes a good deal to the proposals in that report. The social work profession played a significant role in the Seebohm reorganisation[7] and Professor Donnison's studies[8] have shown what an important part professionals at a local level have played in policy developments within local authorities and voluntary organisations. They do so not only as employees but as co-opted members of local authority committees. Teachers' organisations can act as important pressure groups on local authorities.[9]

These institutional feedback mechanisms are the ones which political scientists have studied most. Almost ignored is the pressure which users of services exert simply by exercising their freedom of choice to opt for particular types of service like schools or to move out of particular areas. The opportunities for 'exit' may not be great but they exist and have some impact on planners and members of local authorities.[10]

In London recently while local organisations and teachers unions were campaigning to maintain many older smaller schools, parents themselves were opting for the larger newer schools. In the end, the march of parents' feet will prove the more effective. The more informed the users of services the more such 'market' pressures will have their impact. The end result then is that politicians, senior civil servants and local administrators now have a far more elaborate and a more effective feedback system than they used to from local and national pressure groups, the professions, the press and users acting individually, or in organised groups. Even so it is a process in which the values and interests of the providers still tend to dominate.

Academic Research

Academic research by social scientists has formed one of the most important sources of critical evaluation. Education has been the most researched of all the social services. It has increasingly attracted the interest of psychiatrists, sociologists and economists.[11] It has become almost habitual for radicals to decry the work of educational psychologists in the inter-war period because they are seen as the villains who created the eleven-plus. In fact Burt and others used their new measuring rods to show up the weaknesses, as they saw it, of the *old* system of secondary selection – the purse. Burt also indicated the importance of social conditions in affecting children's progress at school.[12] In the 1950s psychologists studied the system of selection that had followed the 1944 Act and showed its limitations.[13] These were classic pieces of evaluation. So, too, in the sociological tradition was the work of Floud and Halsey on the same issue.[14]

The economists have shown less interest in education in Britain compared to either their American colleagues or to the sociologists, but a small body of work exists which is of direct policy relevance on costs, finance and rates of return from different kinds of courses.[15]

Apart from education, health and psychiatry, where some of the best work has been done,[16] virtually all the academics who have attempted to evaluate social programmes have been social administrators. This tradition dates back further than the usually ascribed founding fathers – Rowntree, Booth and the Webbs – at least to Chadwick and the Benthamites who, in their approach, if not in their philosophy, laid the foundations of administrative empiricism in

Britain. This is not the place to begin a history of social administration except to remark that until very recently a similar tradition has been noticeably lacking in the United States. Academic social administration derives its continued impetus from the fact that the courses it runs are designed for those who will go to work in the social services or who have returned from doing so for a period of post experience study. Its 'vocational' links are important to its research interests.

In general the pressures of academic life, neither in Britain nor America, are conducive to evaluative research, which is specifically directed to analysing how social services work. The pure snobbery of academic life militates against such a mundane and inevitably semi-political activity. The academic is the most likely source of work which challenges the basic assumptions on which a programme works or which makes criticisms that are politically embarrassing. But that is only one part of the total flow of information that is needed. Services are not dismantled and rebuilt every other year, though currently workers in the field may be forgiven if they have that impression. Programme managers also need detailed and highly specific studies by people thoroughly conversant with the statutory framework, regulations and political problems that officials face. These are approaches that the pressures of academic life do not normally encourage.

Research Institutes

The sheer wealth of America and the supply of trained social scientists available are reflected in the number of independent research institutes which exist on that side of the Atlantic. There are very few in Britain though some have been founded in the last ten years. The National Institute for Social and Economic Research is primarily concerned with economic research. The newer Centre for Environmental Studies has a town planning and housing focus. The Centre for Studies in Social Policy is still very small. Yet the evaluation of social policies entails both inter-disciplinary and relatively long-term research with the administrative and technical support that ordinary university departments cannot usually provide. One of the most powerful tools for examining the impact of social services is the longitudinal or cohort study. There are two outstanding examples in Britain – the Douglas Survey of children born in one week in 1946 and the National Child Development Study which has followed children born in one week in 1958. They have both produced some of the best work we have on what health services reach what families, what effect this has in the long run, the long term impact of nursery schools on primary and secondary schooling and the selection process.[17] Then there has been the National Children's Bureau work on the effectiveness of different adoption practices, on the care of illegitimate children and a good deal more. The impact of the social services can only be fully measured over the long term with individualised data on social background, family situation and all the other variables which so complicate the picture. More specialised studies can be 'hooked' on to the basic survey material. More regular and comparable longitudinal studies are needed. Yet they can best be mounted by units or institutes funded on a long term basis.

Committees of Enquiry
We have already seen that these bodies have fulfilled an important planning function. They have also initiated important research on the way social services are currently operating. Royal Commissions such as those on Medical Education and Doctors and Dentists Remuneration[18] have occasionally been used to examine some aspect of administration involving a particularly high status group like the medical profession. But it is the standing Advisory Committees to Ministers who have undertaken the most extensive work. Departmental committees have examined what are usually narrower and more technical issues. Then there are *ad hoc* committees or commissions like the Robbins Committee on Higher Education[19] or the Public Schools Commission.[20] The terms of reference these committees are given are often wide. Partly as a result they may end by doing little more than expressing or encapsulating the current orthodoxy amongst 'informed opinion' in their field. Yet at the same time they have initiated a great deal of research which has a longer term pay off and probably would not have been undertaken otherwise. The Robbins survey of 21-year-olds[21] was the first official attempt to analyse social class access to higher education. The sheer magnitude of the task and the amount of co-operation that was required from many schools and other institutions throughout the country, both public and private, shows how difficult it is for any private individual or institute to repeat it. An official commission or committee can get co-operation from groups and institutions who would not otherwise give it. The author's survey of the finances of independent schools for the Public Schools Commission illustrates the same point.

We know more about how the education service works than we do about any other social service and one of the main reasons is the contribution the advisory and other committees played both in initiating research themselves and in stimulating academics to follow it up or criticise it.

Yet these committees also have their deficiencies as users and initiators of research. Often when a major research programme is initiated, its results come too late to be incorporated in the main proposals or the conceptual framework used by the committees. Second, the research once completed is often never repeated. The planning methodology may be adopted by government, but the actual detailed surveys are not repeated. For example, there was no follow up to Crowther's survey of students in further education on day release or evening classes, no follow up of Newsom's sample of schools working under stress, no follow up of Robbins' survey of social class access to higher education. Plowden's national survey of primary school children was followed up as a sample three years later, but there has been no follow up of a similar sample of primary school children. The value of many of these original surveys would have been substantially enhanced by repetition. Indeed one may go so far as to suggest that their main value for policy lay in establishing regular studies on the basis of which the outcome of the policy prescription could be tested. It is fair to say that none of the surveys attempted to *evaluate* the services or any part of them in the way we described in the previous chapter. Such surveys have been predominantly descriptive in nature or concerned to estimate demand or need. Most of the Robbins' surveys, apart from Appendix One, were descriptive. So were most of the studies in Plowden, Newsom and Crowther.

Despite Plowden's support for the 'new' philosophy and practice in English primary schools nothing in the way of explicit research was undertaken to evaluate it.

The Inspectorate

The inspectorate form an important independent check on the professionals in both the education service and in the personal social services. Indeed, it is possible to see the various inspectorates as the original evaluators. Their origins date back to the nineteenth century when central government needed to find some way of ensuring that the local authorities were complying with the statutes and were worthy to receive continued financial assistance. The story begins, as most things do in British social administration, with the Poor Law. The Poor Law Commissioners had the power to appoint assistant commissioners whose task it was to visit the local Boards of Guardians and report on the ways in which they were implementing the 1834 Act as well as to undertake any other duties placed on them.[22] Their first task was to create the new administrative units – the unions. Each Assistant Commissioner was assigned to a separate geographical area and once this original task was complete his instructions were:

1 To examine into, and report upon, the state of the workhouses, and of the indoor and outdoor relief in the several unions in your district;
2 To attend the meetings of Boards of Guardians;
3 To take the averages of unions;
4 To make special inquiries into cases of alleged hardship sustained by paupers, and into areas of alleged malversion or misconduct of union officers;
5 To collect and diffuse information relating to the administration of relief, and the state of pauperism, and the conditions of the industrious classes.[23]

Each workhouse had to be visited once in six months. The inspector was officially told:

'You will find no part of your duties productive of results so obviously and immediately benefitial as your transplanting into a union the arrangements and modes of management which, either of your own personal knowledge, or by means of information communicated to you from the Poor Law Commissioners you know to have been introduced into other unions with successful results.'[24]

So by 1841 we see established the basic characteristics of the inspectorates which remain today. The recruitment of a relatively small group of able people, as these evidently were, assigned to a particular area, with a responsibility to report back to the central department on the effectiveness of the local services, with power to make special enquiries and above all an instruction that they should seek to spread 'good practice' by timely advice.

When the Poor Law Commission was finally dissolved in 1847 in response to continued agitation it was replaced by the Poor Law Board directly responsible to Parliament and its Assistant Commissioners became Inspectors. Their task was essentially to seek to ensure that the deterrent nature of the new system of poor relief was maintained. But as the functions of the unions changed and they came to undertake more specialist activities, hospitals and schools and the boarding out of children, the duties of the General Inspector became more difficult to perform and the Webbs were rather hard on him. The minority report recommended that with the break up of the Poor Law separate specialist inspectors should be appointed for each of the new services. In practice this was already beginning to happen. As the number of children who were boarded out increased so the first woman Inspector was appointed in 1885 as Inspector of Boarding Out, and the number of such appointments increased.[25] Their modern equivalent were the Inspectors appointed by the Home Office to oversee local authorities' duties in the care of children, and the welfare Inspectors. Responsibility for both now lies with the Department of Health and Social Security, but their functions are still broadly the same. A good deal of tact and persistence is required not only with officials but also with elected committees, but their influence can be considerable.[26]

The education Inspectorate, too, dates from the 1830s. Immediately the Privy Council Committee on Education was created in 1839 it appointed two Inspectors to visit schools that received grants of public money and to convey to them 'a knowledge of all improvements in the arts of teaching, and likewise to report to this Committee the progress made in education from year to year'.[27] No school which refused to be inspected could receive a grant of public money, though the denominations were given a say in choosing inspectors for their own schools. The Inspectors' reports make fascinating reading today. They were a body of able men, Matthew Arnold was perhaps the most famous, but at first their duties were strictly regulated. They had to make returns on the nature of the school buildings, the size of the classrooms, the number and qualifications of the staff, attendance, places available in the school, its income and expenditure, indeed the returns they asked heads to make will be familiar to the headmasters and headmistresses of today who have to fill in similar, though more elaborate returns, for the Department of Education and Science. In addition the inspectors were concerned with more professional tasks – commenting on teaching methods, the relationship between parents and teachers and the adequacy of the school library. Beyond that their task was to give advice on methods and good practice. Kay-Shuttleworth, who, as secretary to the Committee introduced this system, had himself been an Assistant Commissioner for the Poor Law Commissioners. The Inspectorate's advisory role developed until, in the 1850s, occurred one of those spasms of concern about the burden of educational spending that have recurred at intervals ever since. The enquiry which resulted – the Newcastle Commission[28] presented a cogently argued case against further state involvement in education and it sought to increase the efficiency of the schools by offering a financial incentive. Grants should be tied, in part, to examination performance. So the British government responded to the call for economy in the 1860s, as some local boards of education in the US did in the 1960s, by introducing a system of 'payment by results'.[29] Her Majesty's Inspectors, much to their fury, if Matthew Arnold is any guide, had to set examinations in the three Rs. If a pupil failed the examination, part of the government's capitation grant was removed. It was not until after 1895 that this system began to be phased out.

Even though the payments by results system had ended the Inspectors' task was very clearly to judge and evaluate a teacher's competence, not merely to give advice. This was nowhere more threatening than in the secondary schools all of which depended in the early part of the century on per capita grants from the central government. In the schools that were not run by local authorities this continued to be so. For secondary schools the Board of Education therefore developed the practice of full inspections. A team of Inspectors would descend on the school and stay for perhaps a week or more and examine every part of the school's activities. Inspectors entered classrooms, observed all the teachers at work, questioned the children, looked at their books and acquired as much data as possible on the school. Then the Inspectorate would withdraw, discuss their overall impressions and report to the Head and the Governors, making such criticisms and proposals for improvement as they thought appropriate. A full account of the inspection would be written and made available to those concerned. Their guides to action evidently included asking such questions of the school as what were its aims, what resources and opportunities did it have? What success did it achieve?[30] The basis of their work was to assess the quality of teaching as they saw it as experienced ex-teachers themselves. When the 1944 Act abolished the distinction between secondary schools and senior elementary schools full inspections were undertaken in all the secondary schools on a regular basis. But as time went on the practice of full inspections began to give way to more frequent and less formal visits. Increased emphasis was laid on giving professional advice, the spreading of new ideas and on running in-service training courses. The rise of 'new maths' in British primary schools in the 1950s and 1960s, for example, owes a great deal to the inspiration of an almost legendary inspector, Miss Biggs.[31] Since the Second World War there have been a team of rather more than 500 inspectors. They combine three functions. They inspect a group of institutions, they are responsible for maintaining links with the local education authorities in their area on matters of policy and as subject inspectors they are responsible for inspecting and giving advice on their subject over a wide geographical area. All inspectors cover at least two of these functions.

Three hundred inspectors cover schools, about ninety further education colleges, and fifty colleges of education.

In 1968 a House of Commons Select Committee recommended that the practice of full inspections should be explicitly terminated.[32] Very few were then being undertaken, and the practice has now been stopped altogether.

The history of these nineteenth-century evaluators and their modern equivalents had some current lessons. When the Poor Law Inspectors merely had to ensure that the local guardians were applying the deterrent principle rigorously their task was relatively straight forward. One fairly clear measure of success were the numbers on the Poor Law. A fall indicated success. When guardians began to develop more varied – more humane – approaches, when opinions began to differ on what constituted an appropriate response to different categories of pauper, then their measuring rods and the basis for their judgements became more disputable and their role changed to a more tentative and advisory one. In the same way the early Inspectors of schools had to worry mainly about the three Rs. As schools' functions became at once less basic and more disputable the Inspector's role changed. The simple evaluation of success and failure became impossible. The more varied the objectives the less readily they could be judged.

Despite this it is difficult to exaggerate the importance of the modern Inspectorate. Their advice is constantly available, and relied upon heavily in policy discussions at the highest level. They give departments direct access to the real world. They bring a sense of realism and a feel for what will go and what will not which is much needed in an office bound career civil service, where life revolves around files and briefs, where you may have come from administering subsidies on beef cattle one day to allocating teachers to local authorities the next. Moreover, the functions of the Inspectorates have developed in important ways in recent years. In addition to their normal advisory role the education Inspectorate mounts regular surveys on issues of immediate concern to the Department where fast and reliable information is needed, that is not of a purely statistical kind. It might concern the extent and nature of difficulties faced by schools in teaching immigrant children, or the extent and nature of violence in schools. These surveys lie somewhere midway between a social survey and the informal tendering of personal views by the Senior Inspectorate. A systematic attempt is made to get local Inspectors to collect information and views about specific issues, but there are no rigorous questionnaires or interviewing schedules. So in six months or less the senior officials and the Secretary of State may have a considered report from the field, a compilation of some statistics, reported views and personal judgements.

Although the Supplementary Benefits Commission are administering their own local offices, not overseeing the work of elected local authorities, they too have developed a similar system. A group of the most able and on the whole fairly young officials with experience of the system at various levels, have the task of monitoring the effective operation of the service, pin-pointing emerging problem areas, and making more extensive reports on areas of concern.[33] They have a schedule of such surveys to undertake planned six to twelve months ahead. One of their first tasks was to investigate the wage stop. They undertook a review of about 50 representative cases of the way the rule had been operated, going into each case in some detail and drawing from all the cases some general propositions and recommendations. The Commission's recommendations for changing wage stop rules were published along with a summary account of the inspector's findings.[34] The same was done with the co-habitation rule. A recent paper by the DHSS describes their present role.[35]

Some Inspectorate inquiries may be quite brief, 'finger-dipping' exercises, such as an examination of a comparatively small number of case papers to see if any pointers can be found to suggest whether a matter is being administered well or ill. Mostly, however, they are inquiries of considerable length, devised and interpreted with the aid of the Department's statistical service and their conclusions resting on a solid statistical base. The inquiry involves examination of case papers, detailed discussions with staff at all levels, accompanying staff at work, carrying out a job themselves, interviewing clients. It can take twelve months or more to complete and the resultant report will be a substantial volume.

Both inspectorates have therefore been moving towards a more elaborate feedback and appraisal process which is much nearer to a firm social science base. Indeed the mixture of hard statistical analysis, survey method and participant research outlined above could well be emulated by more social scientists. The topics chosen for study remain fairly narrow. What the Inspectorates could learn from the academic is the case for the publication of their results.

The Department of Health and Social Security argue that it is crucial to the validity of the whole of the Inspectorate's function that these reports remain confidential. They have to have the complete confidence of the staff and the value of the research lies in the fact that everyone from junior staff upwards speak frankly about their difficulties and express serious criticisms of the way the system is working from their point of view. The reports themselves may be highly critical and no one would talk if they thought these criticisms would be published. The inspectorate would not draft such critical reports.

While accepting that these arguments do carry weight especially on certain more embarrassing issues, they do seem on balance mistaken. It may be important for *individuals'* comments to be kept confidential, but this is a basic rule of social science research too. If the service showed that it favoured the publication of constructive self-criticism individual officers should not feel ashamed from voicing it so long as their remarks are not personally attributable. The second proposition, that the inspectorate would themselves be inhibited in their comments could be met by leaving out their judgements and specific proposals and publishing merely the basic analysis. To do so would have positive advantages. It would make public and academic discussions more informed. It would enable outsiders to gain a much more realistic picture of the dilemmas and constraints within which departments must work. It would be invaluable as teaching material and in consequence it might even attract better recruits to the service.

Research of Government Departments

Considering the enormous economic and social importance of health, housing, social security and education the departments concerned have, until recently, devoted negligible resources to research, let alone any specific evaluation of the delivery of these services. Until the early 1960s virtually nothing was spent by these departments on 'in house' research and very little on grants to outsiders. The total research budget of the DES at that time amounted to no more than about £20,000, and this was then probably the most research-minded of the social service ministries. It was a situation that the Heyworth Committee criticised in 1965.[36] The most important outcome of that committee's report was the creation of the Social Science Research Council. As a result more funds have become available for academic research in the social sciences, including social administration, and education. The report also stimulated some departments like the Ministry of Social Security to begin a research programme. In general it would be true to say that in Britain the tradition of departmentally sponsored research programmes is relatively recent. Secondly, British departments have concentrated almost exclusively on giving grants to outside bodies or individuals to do research. Thirdly, they have relied for the most part on outside initiatives to determine the scope and emphasis of the research programme. When a good idea comes up they will support it. They have had nothing akin to the Request for Proposals procedure we described in the last chapter. There were some signs of a shift of emphasis towards departmental initiation of projects before the Rothschild Report (see below) and rather more since, but this is an even newer tradition.

The Rothschild report by the head of the new Central Policy Review Staff was mainly concerned with the organisation of scientific research but it had implications for most governmental departments.[37] He was critical of the procedure by which much government sponsored research was financed out of DES funds and distributed through research councils like the Science Research Council, the Medical Research Council and the Social Science Research Council. Making explicit views that some officials had pressed for some time, he argued that where applied research was undertaken it should be funded by the appropriate specialist department – DHSS in the case of health research for example. Government departments were urged to control the allocation of such funds more closely applying what was called a customer/contractor principle, with one person responsible for coordinating the department's research policy. His recommendations were accepted in principle by the Government.[38] The Department of the Environment appointed a Director General of Research and the DHSS a Chief Scientist (see below), but the growth of policy oriented research in the social service departments has been slow.

Education

Although the 1944 Education Act had given the Ministry of Education the power to support research it initially used this power merely to grant aid the National Foundation for Educational Research which was founded in 1947.[39] Yet that body decided its own research strategy and was largely concerned with the devising of tests which local authorities used as part of their eleven-plus selection procedures. It was only in 1961 that the Ministry's research policy began to develop. First came the creation of a Research and Intelligence Branch. This was fairly short-lived and never very important. It was transformed into the Planning Branch in 1966 whose fate we have described earlier. Second and more important was the growth of a research programme that was designed to fund outside research. The budget at first grew rapidly, from £20,000 in

1962–3 to £500,000 in 1968–9. For most part the Department responded to proposals put up to it, mainly from academics in universities. The rest of the money went to the NFER or to the two semi independent bodies – the Schools Council for the Curriculum and Examinations and the National Council for Educational Technology (NCET).

Table 10.1 *Educational Research Expenditure commissioned by DES 1962–73*

Receivers of Funds	No. of Projects	£	Percentage
Universities	167	2,972,000	59·4
Polytechnics and Colleges of Education	15	158,000	3·1
NFER	36	931,000	18·6
NCET	59	285,000	5·7
Schools Council	4	9,000	0·2
Others, including individuals	81	649,000	13·0

Source: *Times Educational Supplement*, 24 May, 1974

After 1968 two new trends became apparent. First, in the wake of the general economy drive, research funds were cut, both in real and monetary terms. In 1971–2 the budget fell well below £400,000 and while the present budget (1974–5) has reached £600,000 it has still not caught up the 1968 figure in real terms. Second, the Department also tried to adopt a more active role. It sought to commission new work. After 1970 block allocations were made to some branches to enable them to pursue their own research needs with greater independence and an official in each branch was designated branch research officer. The total research budget expended over the ten year period 1962–73 amounted to only £5 million. Even the 1973 figure of £600,000 amounted to only 0·016 per cent of education expenditure (England and Wales). Or more fairly it is 0·03 per cent of the central government's contribution. Compare this to the 0·5 per cent of the US Office of Education's budget that was devoted to specific evaluation research. (The DES is not the only source of educational research money of course, but even when funds from all sources are combined education research and development costs in the UK amounted to no more than 0·12 per cent of the UK education budget current and capital in 1968–9.)[40] Comparable American expenditure *per head* is about five times as great.

The policy planning committees described in an earlier chapter were given the task of determining a broad research strategy along with their other tasks. There was a plan to introduce a series of research advisory committees for each of the policy branches on which outsiders would sit. It was a proposal similar to that adopted in the DHSS and the Department of the Environment. But the idea was evidently dropped, the assistant secretary responsible for research at the time, John Banks, was said to have been moved 'precipitately'.[41] The Department was left with no very clear structure to enable it to initiate research, especially evaluative research designed to assist its planning function.

The studies that have been undertaken with DES money have been extraordinarily diverse, mostly tiny and hardly at all concerned with the delivery of education. Even these have been mainly planning studies.

It is, in fact, possible to point to fewer than a dozen studies initiated or funded by the DES in the period between 1963 and 1973 which could be said to be concerned with evaluation in the American sense. These include the comprehensive schools project conducted by NFER,[42] its survey on Streaming in primary schools,[43] the Educational Priority area projects,[44] the cost/benefit study of higher education undertaken by the DES itself with outside assistance,[45] and the regular surveys of reading attainment we have mentioned before. Taken on their own as policy indicators they are really not too helpful, for, as US experience shows, it is the gradual accumulation of evidence with one study pointing on to others, that begins to pay dividends. The British work which has been done therefore loses much of its usefulness. For example, local authorities all over the country have been taking decisions about the size of comprehensive schools they will adopt in their reorganised system. The DES have to approve these schemes and have had fairly firm views on minimum and maximum sizes of schools. These have very largely been based on time-tabling constraints and an 'appropriate' range of courses in sixth forms. Educational opinion more generally has been sharply divided but has also swung about from favouring large schools to small schools and back – largely on the basis of 'hunch'. The NFER study showed there was no clear relationship between size and achievement or other indicators but it did raise questions, was it rurality or smallness which led to the greater participation of children in school activities in the smaller schools which were also rural, or the size? Did size matter more in schools in deprived urban areas as teachers often claim? The sample was too small to answer these questions and the study was not designed to test size as a major variable. Nevertheless there were sufficient indicators for future research to make the results worth while as a beginning.

The other study which dates from this period was the education priority area project, though this must essentially count as a series of demonstration projects. More recent initiatives do suggest that a different trend may be beginning. One was the statement in the White Paper – *Framework for Expansion* – that the expansion of nursery provision would be accompanied by on-going research.

Health The over-emphasis in medical research on pure research and the neglect of applied research on health care have been eloquently argued by Archie Cochrane in his book *Effectiveness and Efficiency*. He argues that no treatment should be introduced without randomised control trials first to test its effectiveness. It was not until 1963–4, in fact, that the Ministry of Health began to support any research work beyond that in the public health field. Grants were made after 1958–9 to minor projects in hospitals but for the rest research had been concentrated in the Public Health Laboratory Service. There was a tiny research fund distributing £2,500 a year, a relic of Sir John Simon's time a hundred years previously, which enabled the Chief Medical Officer to initiate research. In 1962 a small research section was created to explore the possibilities of 'service oriented' research and a small fund was set up to finance such work in 1963–4.[46]

In 1968 the Ministry of Health was combined with the Ministry of Social Security to form the Department of Health and Social Security and a joint research department was created. In 1970 the DHSS took over responsibility for the personal social services and the scope of the research department was extended similarly. A small 'in-house' group of social scientists was set up in 1967 which has studied the results of some small scale experiments, e.g. the multiple screening clinic at Rotherham. For the most part, however, health and personal social service related research has been undertaken extra-murally, but DHSS did help create a number of social medicine and epidemiological research units. By 1970–1 the total Research and Development expenditure on health and personal social services (current only) accounted for £5 millions, broken down as below. Only in the category 'medical social scientific etc' is our concern here relevant. Moreover, of that only a relatively small part could strictly be said to be concerned with determining needs of particular groups or assessing the impact or effectiveness of services. However, even if we were to broadly categorise *all* this work as evaluation or planning in the American sense it would still be true that only 0·08 per cent of programme funds in 1970–1 were being devoted to this purpose. Following the Rothschild proposals and the White Paper health research has been further reorganised. Twenty-five per cent of the MRC funds were transferred to the DHSS to control. A Chief Scientist was appointed for DHSS as a whole. The Departmental Planning Committee responsible for policy planning in the DHSS will determine broad policies on research in the light of advice from the chief scientist. He in turn has a Research Committee with outsiders on it. Its task will be:

'to give strategic advice to the Planning Committee on research and development in the field of Health Care, Personal Social Services and Social Security.'

A Health Service Research Board will be specifically charged with health *service* related research and a separate panel will be concerned with biomedical research. Another group again is concerned with research on the personal social services.

Table 10.2   *Health and Personal Social Service Research Expenditure*

	(£000s) Revenue 1970/71
Medical, social scientific, operational and public health	1,450
Equipment, supplies and appliances	1,400
Building and engineering	680
Locally organised clinical research	940
Total Research	4,470
Development	550
Research and Development	5,020

On the health side of DHSS which is organised on the basis of policy divisions that are broadly responsible for separate client groups, the aim is to create a research liaison group for each division. In mid-1974 two had been created, one for mental health and another for nursing. These will have on them not only administrators from within that division but outsiders with research experience. A great deal depends on how these bodies see their work and whether they have enough resources – money *and* interested research workers – but they do provide an encouraging basis for better policy oriented and evaluative work.

Social Security: Until the mid-sixties the Ministry of Pensions and National Insurance had really done nothing in the way of research apart from collating and publishing statistics which were a by-product of its administrative operations. Then in the mid-1960s, following the publication of the poverty studies by Abel-Smith, Townsend and Wedderburn, and the new Labour Government, two major national surveys were undertaken to test the results of these studies. The results were published as the *Financial and Other Circumstances of Retirement Pensioners* and *Circumstances of Families*.[47] A small in-house research group was created. Then a Chief Economic Adviser – J. L. Nicholson – was appointed and a small team of economists was built up. Two of the three sections in that office are concerned with social security. Basic 'programme statistics' in the American terminology have been extended very substantially, by taking regular samples of all the main groups of beneficiary. A small programme of research grants to outside bodies has been built up, it currently amounts to about £100,000 (1973-4). Surveys have been undertaken with the co-operation of the Office of Population and Censuses and Surveys. Finally, since the Department is directly responsible for a large network of local offices it has a significant programme of management research which clearly overlaps into the evaluation field. In short in the space of ten years a significant, if modest, research effort has been built up.[48] The small research group in DHSS have been pursuing a programme of small scale surveys on particular groups of recipients. In 1974 there were five such groups being surveyed: separated wives receiving supplementary benefit, sick and disabled men on SB, families on Family Income Supplement, unemployed men on SB and fatherless families on SB. The object of the research was to find out more about their financial and social circumstances and their knowledge of the existence of other benefits. They could be termed need surveys. So too could a number of the surveys commissioned from the government's social survey, for example, on the financial, social and employment needs of the long term sick and disabled.[49] Research that comes nearest to the American notion of experimentation is the Swansea experiment where a new local office organisation is being monitored internally from a management point of view but is also being subjected to a survey of consumer reactions.

The economists' studies are partly concerned with the relationship between social security and the economy, with pressing further the concepts of financial need and poverty and with the impact of benefits on the distribution of income. A computable model is being constructed designed to measure the combined impact of changes in taxes and means tested benefits on typical families. Organisation and management work with an experimental and evaluation function includes testing a procedure by which Supplementary Benefit recipients can be given an explanation of how their payment is calculated, and the development of a multi-purpose means test application which would include all the possible benefits to which a claimant might be entitled whether given by a local authority or central departments. It is an idea that has been discussed for a long time but it has now reached the 'development' stage.

Compared to the American research programme we described in the last chapter the British equivalent is therefore both recent and very modest. There are no more than a dozen separate 'in-house' projects compared with 130 in Washington and no more than a score of people involved compared with 450. But the quality of what little has been published is good. One can only hope that the scale of work is allowed to increase steadily in the next few years despite economic restrictions. It makes little sense that the largest spending social service department spent the least on research and evaluation especially when it has the most direct control over the delivery of services and cash.

Programme Analysis and Review
This approach conforms most closely to the original concept of formal programme evaluation. A broad organisational and conceptual description of PAR has already been given. What actually happens can only be surmised, for there has been a blanket of secrecy drawn over the whole process from the outset. But it must already be clear that the practice must be very different from the theory in the case of many social service programmes. We have seen what a limited amount of basic research exists on the effectiveness of social programmes. To work on past trends in the size and scope of a programme and cost various alternative options at the margin are feasible in a nine-month study but very little else. So much can be deduced from the outside merely by surveying what material there is to work with. A second indication is to be found in the evidence the DHSS, the DES and the Home Office gave to the House of Commons General Subcommittee on Expenditure in 1972.[50] Each gave illustrative material of three programmes that had presumably been the subject of PAR type analysis – the elderly, nursery education, and prison expenditure. In commenting on needs for the elderly the DHSS stated:

Q

'It may, for instance, be possible in time to devise means of measuring the condition of individuals against agreed scales of, for example, mobility or social participation and correlating changes in different areas over time with the pattern of services provided; or to establish indicators of the health and social well-being of the elderly in particular communities or areas and to undertake similar correlations. An increasing amount of work is being done in the field of health and social indicators and a number of attempts are being made to establish measures of the kind described. But it will take many years to develop and test agreed measures, to establish a methodology for applying and interpreting them and to collect the necessary information.'[51]

The paper on the elderly went on to elaborate resource targets – the development of geriatric services in district hospitals, day hospitals, psycho-geriatric services and so on. The paper from the DES on nursery education was almost entirely about the costs of expanding pre-school provision, and the paper on prisons was mainly about prison expenditure not penal policy and its effectiveness.

A third indication of what goes into the process is what comes out. Two examples are the 1972 White Paper on Education[52] and the 1971 White Paper on Services for the Mentally Handicapped.[53] (This was the outcome of a PAR *type* exercise.)

The education White Paper is, in content and style, very like most of the other education white papers in the last two decades. The section on the under fives contains three brief paragraphs on objectives of the most generalised kind, and what follows is not noticeably affected by them. The exception is the paragraph on research which states that:

'The government propose to set up a research programme to monitor the development of the new provision. This will include studies of the results and effectiveness of nursery education in reaching its several goals.' (Para. 34.)

What *is* new about that white paper and that on the mentally handicapped which is also mainly concerned with resource targets, is their comprehensiveness. They set out to consider and set priorities over the whole field of education and over the whole complex network of services directed to the mentally handicapped. This appears to be their one really important achievement.

Their major weakness lies in the absurd amount of secrecy that surrounds them, not merely while they are being undertaken but subsequently. Since the process of identifying social service objectives and judging between options is so value laden and essentially political, the task can only be effectively undertaken, in the fullest sense, if it is open to public scrutiny or at least if the results are.

In Brief
The virtue of the British style evaluation is its diversity – the varied sources of support for research, the role of advisory committees and independent academic research. It means that much open and informed questioning of social legislation has taken place – albeit in a very haphazard and disjointed fashion. The departments themselves possess an important source of feedback in the work of their Inspectorates. They have come to be used to collect information in a rather more 'scientific' way about particular areas of concern. The Health Service lacks such an institution though it has taken a hesitant step in that direction by the creation of the Hospital Advisory Committee and its new information system should provide greater knowledge about needs and resources at the centre. Yet no department has developed any systematic way of evaluating the impact or consequences of social service expenditure. In the wake of Rothschild and PAR there are some signs that this is happening in DHSS and the Department of the Environment, but it is too early to see any results. In other departments too there are straws in the wind. The programme of research on the new nursery programme announced in the 1972 education white paper is one example. The research projects initiated by the Department of the Environment on the impact of the 1971 Housing Act, the 1968 Planning Acts and the Community Development Projects are others. The Supplementary Benefit Commission's 'experiment' with a new model office is yet another.

Departments' reticence and reluctance to go any faster is commonly justified on at least four grounds: there are not enough good people in the field to do the research; there is no methodology – 'we don't know *how* to evaluate'; it is not our business, it is the job of local authorities or area health authorities; good researchers will not interest themselves in work which is going to be closely controlled by a government department and tailored to its immediate needs. All of these arguments have considerable practical weight in the present situation. Britain does not possess a superabundance of qualified social science Ph.Ds and research institutes as America does. The theoretical issues raised by the research task are very considerable as American experience also shows. There is a strong case for local authorities, who actually have to administer the services, undertaking such work. There have been some good examples – the ILEA literacy surveys have been an excellent and courageous example of this activity,[54] so has much of the work of the GLC Research and Intelligence Unit. It is true that academics given the choice will opt for freedom to do their research their own way and we have argued that that is the only way fundamental criticisms of social legislation get aired.

Yet these arguments keep us following a vicious circle. American experience suggests that you cannot build up good inter-disciplinary research teams unless there is a fairly continuous supply of work and grant aid to support the administrative infra-structure. It is no use expecting methodologies to appear except as a result of a lot of trial, error and failure. Moreover, like any market situation if there is a sufficient demand for the product the supply will in the end be forthcoming. It needs discriminating purchasers and most departments have lacked just that. Central departments have to see their primary task as one of fostering the capacity to undertake such work either internally or externally and preferably both.

We need not only diversity and independence in policy research, for that curbs the limitations of 'suboptimising', but also more specific and narrower evaluation of the way social services are operating and especially from the consumer's point of view.

REFERENCES

1 Gilbert, B. B., *British Social Policy 1914–39*. Batsford, London, 1970, p. 308. He concludes 'While the nation's greatest concerns were social and economic, most politicians, always excepting Chamberlain, while admitting the gravity of these problems, were willing to leave them to experts while devoting themselves to traditional questions'.
2 See Sharpe, L. J., 'America's Democracy Reconsidered', *British Journal of Political Science*, Vol. 3, Nos. 1 and 2, 1973.
3 Manzer, R., *Teachers and Politics*, Manchester University, 1970, and Coates, R. D., *Teachers Unions and Interest Group Politics*, Cambridge University Press, 1972.
4 The Economist Intelligence Unit, *The Economic Status of the School-master*, London, 1967, and subsequent reports. A study is now in progress at the LSE.
5 Porritt, Sir Arthur, *A Review of Medical Services in Great Britain*, Social Assay, London, 1962.
6 Ministry of Health, *The Administrative Structure of the Medical and*

Related Services, 1968; and *The Future Structure of the National Health Service*, HMSO, 1970.

7 *Committee on Local Authority and Allied Personal Social Services*, Cmnd 3703, 1968.

8 Donnison, D. V. *et al.*, *Social Policy and Administration*, George Allen & Unwin, London, 1965.

9 Donnison, D. V., *et al.*, op. cit., Chapter 12, also see Saron, R., *Policy Making in Secondary Education*, Oxford University Press, 1973; and Coates, op. cit.

10 The phrase and the point are made by Hirschman, A. O., *Exit, Voice and Loyalty*, Harvard University Press, 1970. He also shows how the consumers' sanction is limited by loyalty whether to a brand, an institution or one might add an individual – doctor or headmaster.

11 See Glennerster, H. and Hoyle, E., 'Educational Research and Education Policy', *Journal of Social Policy*, Vol. 1, No. 3, reprinted in *Research Perspectives in Education*, Ed. W. Taylor, Routledge, 1973.

12 Burt, C., *The Backward Child*, University of London Press, 1937.

13 Vernon, P. E., *Secondary School Selection*, Methuen, London, 1957; Yates, A. and Pidgeon, D. A., *Admission to Grammar School*, Newnes, London, 1957.

14 Floud, J., Halsey, A. H. and Martin, F. M., *Social Class and Educational Opportunity*, Heinemann, London, 1956.

15 For a review of the British contribution to the literature see Woodhall, M., *Economic Aspects of Education*, National Foundation for Educational Research, Slough, 1972.

16 For surveys of work in these two fields see Morris, J. N., *The Uses of Epidemiology*, Livingstone, London, 1970. Symposium on Psychiatric Epidemiology (Eds) Wing, J. K. and Hafner, H.; *Roots of Evaluation*, Oxford University Press, 1973.

17 Douglas, J. W. B. and Rowntree, G., *Maternity in Great Britain*, Oxford University Press, 1948; Douglas, J. W. B. and Blomfield, J. M., *Children under Five*, George Allen & Unwin, London, 1958; Douglas, J. W. B., *The Home and the School*, MacGibbon and Kee, London, 1964; Douglas, J. W. B., Ross, J. M., and Simpson, H. R., *All Our Future*, Peter Davies, London, 1968; Davie, R., Butler, N., *et al.*, *From Birth to Seven*, Longmans, 1972.

18 Royal Commission on Medical Education 1965–8, Cmnd 3569 (1968); Royal Commission on Doctors' and Dentists' Remuneration, Cmnd 939 (1960).

19 Cmnd 2154 (1963) see especially Appendices 2–5.

20 Department of Education and Science, *The First Report of the Public Schools Commission, Volume 2*. This volume contains the only comprehensive source of information about pupil numbers, resources, finance, an assessment of boarding need, the leaving qualifications and social class origins of pupils, etc., for both boys' and girls' schools. *The Second Report, Volume 2* does the same thing for the direct grant and day Public Schools as well as summarising all the then

available research on selection, comprehensive education, and the education of highly able children.

21 Op. cit., Appendix 1.

22 Poor Law Amendment Act, 1834, Section 7.

23 Seventh Annual Report of the Poor Law Commissioners, 1841, quoted in Harris, J. S., *British Government Inspection*, Stevens, London, 1955.

24 Ibid.

25 Harris, p. 29.

26 For the present situation see Klein, R. and Hall, P., *Caring for Quality in the Caring Services*, Centre for Studies in Social Policy, London, 1974.

27 Harris, p. 79.

28 *Royal Commission to enquire into the state of Popular Education in England*, 1861.

29 The Americans in fact called it 'performance contracting' but the principles are not really different. Private companies were permitted to run school systems on condition that they would be paid according to the academic results they achieved. Both the Office of Economic Opportunity and the Office of Education mounted several experiments to test the results and found they were not a success.

30 Harris, p. 102.

31 See *Mathematics in Primary Schools*, Schools Council Curriculum Bulletin No. 1, HMSO, 1965. Also her contribution to *British Primary Schools Today*, Vol. 1, Macmillan, London, 1972.

32 House of Commons Select Committee on Education and Science, 1967/8, *Report on Her Majesty's Inspectorate*, HC 400 (1967–8).

33 See the account by Titmuss, R. M., in 'The New Guardians of the Poor' in S. Jenkins *Social Security in International Perspective*, Columbia University Press, New York, 1969.

34 Ministry of Social Security, *Administration of the Wage Stop*, HMSO, 1967.

35 *Social Security: Research Activities of the DHSS*, a paper given to the Social Administration Conference at Edinburgh, 1974. Recent inquiries have covered the following: Coloured claimants, treatment of last earnings from work, liable relative cases, the blind scale rate, expenses of single householders in hospital, living on the wage stop and the administration of the wage stop.

36 Committee on Social Studies, Cmnd 2660 (1965).

37 *A Framework for Government Research and Development*, Cmnd 4814, 1971 (a discussion document – a green paper – including a very different set of proposals from the Council for Scientific Policy).

38 *Framework for Government Research and Development*, Cmnd 5046, 1972.

39 See Taylor, W., 'The Organisation of Educational Research in the United Kingdom' in *Research Perspectives in Education*, Ed. W. Taylor, Routledge and Kegan Paul, London, 1973.

40 Ward, A. V., *Resources for Educational Research and Development*, NFER, Slough, 1973.
41 Times Educational Supplement, 25 May, 1974.
42 Ross, J. M., *A Critical Appraisal of Comprehensive Education*, NFER, Slough, 1972.
43 Lunn, J. Barker, *Streaming in the Primary School*, NFER, Slough, 1969.
44 Department of Education and Science, *Educational Priority*, HMSO, 1972.
45 Morris, V. and Zidermann, A., 'The Economic Return on Investment in Higher Education', *Economic Trends*, May, 1971 (HMSO).
46 McLachlan (Ed.), *Portfolio for Health*, Oxford University Press, 1971, see pp. 1–22.
47 Ministry of Pensions and National Insurance, *Financial and other Circumstances of Retirement Pensioners*, HMSO 1966 – Ministry of Social Security, *Circumstances of Families*, HMSO, 1967.
48 The description which follows summarises the account given in the DHSS paper referred to earlier.
49 Survey conducted by the Office of Population Censuses and Surveys.
50 Eighth Report of the House of Commons Expenditure Committee, 1971–2. HC 515 (1971–2).
51 Para. 16, p. 4.
52 *Education: A Framework for Expansion*, Cmnd 5174 (1972).
53 *Better Services for the Mentally Handicapped*, Cmnd 4683 (1971).
54 The Inner London Education Authority Research and Statistics Group undertook a survey in 1968/9 of children born between 2 September, 1959, and 1 September, 1960, The original aim was to discover the extent of reading difficulties in this group of 30,000 children at transfer to secondary schools. A report was made of the findings in 1969 and the group have been followed through secondary school.

Further Reading

Cochrane, A. L., *Effectiveness and Efficiency; Random Reflections on Health Services*, Nuffield Provincial Hospitals Trust, London, 1972.
(A vigorous and extended argument for the use of randomised contro trials in the planning of health care.)
Keeling, D., *Management in Government*, George Allen & Unwin, London, 1972.
Goldberg, E. M., *Helping the Aged*, George Allen & Unwin, London, 1970.
(An experiment to assess the impact of professional social workers on the needs of the aged. The only major study of its kind in Britain.)

Chapter 11

Retrospect

It is now possible to draw together some of the threads from the preceding chapters. At the outset we contrasted the managerial model of resource allocation with the incrementalist view. We distinguished a third approach – pluralist social planning. This stressed the virtues of open, political and explicit decisions about resource allocation at all levels in the social services. Explicitness in this context was taken to lie in a combination of forward planning, a clear knowledge of who were the net beneficiaries from existing programmes, and an evaluation of their past results. Because of the contentious nature of social service goals such information and analysis must derive from as many different sources as possible, and be subject to political debate.

None of these models entirely fits the picture we have painted in previous chapters, but it is the last which approximates most closely.

Although many of the criticisms advanced by the incrementalist school have proven only too well founded, economic and social pressures have forced the adoption of longer term perspectives in policy making and the increasing use of quantitative techniques of appraisal, primarily in assessing alternative cost consequences rather than in cost *benefit* calculations. The scale of political demands have called for increasingly complex sets of policy proposals. Social legislation has wide ramifications over long-term periods. Nor is it possible to rely on a gradual evolutionary process, especially when there is fundamental disagreement between the two major political parties on what is needed. Both points are well illustrated in the rival proposals on pensions produced by the last Conservative and Labour governments. They exemplified almost opposite political philosophies on the role of the State in provision for retirement. Their impact and cost accrued over a time span of twenty or more years. They demanded universal application and set highly complex administrative and planning problems. The same can be said of the Conservative Government's Tax Credit proposals or the Labour Government's Land Commission. Each involved major recasting of existing legislation and institutions. Even in non-controversial areas long-term planning became necessary.

In Britain in the mid 1950s social service departments at central government level began to develop capital and manpower planning as well as less formal approaches, but during the 1960s tax control planning, in the form of the public expenditure survey system, came to dominate all these other activities.

As part of this process central departments had to assess long-term priorities and the scope for new developments in a systematic and regular fashion. Rather more information is available now about who benefits from existing policies but the development of output budgets has been largely dominated by the need to produce expenditure projections for forward planning purposes. Finally, although the informal evaluation of social services through academic research and press coverage has improved, systematic formal procedures within government have scarcely begun.

In contrast forward planning by United States Federal agencies has been something of a failure, yet a much more elaborate system of evaluation has been developed in Washington than anything that is even envisaged in Britain. Such differences may be explained by the different contexts within which the planning process takes place.

Contexts for Planning

Political: Of the basic constitutional differences between the UK and the USA, the separation of powers is the most obvious and it turned out to be one of the most significant. The independent power of Congress to initiate and amend social legislation of all kinds made forward planning difficult. Congress has powers to initiate financial legislation and uses its powers to scrutinise and amend the budget with real independence. We saw that attempts to implement five-year rolling budgets failed, but informal planning by individual agencies to promote their own programmes was the hallmark of a successful agency. It was, in fact, the only kind of forward planning well suited to the American political system at Federal level.

It is when we reach evaluation that we see the particular virtues of an independent legislature. While the original idea to devote a regular percentage of programme money to evaluation did not originate with Congress the idea was more easily sold to those in Congress than it was to traditional programme administrators. Once launched Congress expects to see the results and has increasingly asked informed questions about impact, effectiveness and who is using the funds for what purposes? Congressmen's staffs and Committee staffs provide an important audience for such research which does not exist in Britain. While we argued that many of the formal evaluations left a great deal to be desired and few of them had a direct and identifiable impact on policy, they have been important in a number of instances and seem likely to become more so.

Thus we see that an independent legislature makes budget control and operational planning difficult but is more favourable to evaluation than the relatively supine British legislature.

Obversely a strong executive with a weak legislature in Britain has provided conditions more favourable to forward planning. Evaluations are never popular with those who administer or staff services. A powerful central ministry is surrounded by pressure groups of various kinds. The most influential are those representing the providers – teachers, doctors, local chief officers and increasingly the social work profession. They reinforce the general reluctance of administrators to test the effectiveness or impact of their activities and often actively oppose such studies. Where power is highly centralised such opposition has a greater chance to succeed. Such, at least, is our contention.

The Federal-local division of responsibility in America compared to the much stronger control which central departments exert in Britain has also had an important impact on the development of social planning in the two countries. The relatively close control which central departments can exercise over local authorities' use of resources has enabled the British system of public expenditure control to cover all forms of public spending – local and national – and to achieve a fair measure of success. In America the relatively recent introduction of Federal aid to local school districts meant that initially very little control could be exercised on the way funds were used. Matching grant formulas for social services made planning impossible. On the other hand the very uncontrollability of the programmes and the remoteness of Washington from the states made both Congress and the government agencies want to know in more detail what was actually happening. Just the same kind of suspicions led the British Parliament in the nineteenth century to appoint Inspectors as well as district auditors to ensure that local authorities were providing services of an appropriate standard and not misusing public money. In mid-twentieth-century America, Washington turned to the social scientist to perform part of the same function.

Where the US Federal Government had direct responsibility for a social programme, as with social insurance or grants and loans to students, all forms of planning are more in evidence. Computable planning models were being used by both the Social Security Administration and the Office of Education. The macro forecasting model used by the Social Security Administration was being developed so that it could test the long-term implications of current social security policies on the distribution of income. It was used to investigate the inter-relation of social security with other forms of transfer – private and public. The SSA was also experimenting with simulation models on a micro level to test the impact of changes in benefit rates, taxes, and new schemes of family assistance just as the DHSS is doing in Britain. Here Federal responsibility has been conducive to more sophisticated planning. It is also noticeable that the one area where similar planning techniques were in use in the Office of Education related to the programme over which the agency had direct control – namely the federal loans programme.

Both organisations were responsible for considerable evaluation activity by British standards. It was noticeable that the most critical studies tended to be those concerned with programmes administered by the states. A central department or agency is less likely to encourage a sceptical approach to a programme it is itself running than it is to a programme it is supervising through a local authority or state agency.

American political parties are far less cohesive both in organisational and ideological terms than their British counterparts. Heads of Departments are less likely to be career politicians in the British sense. A British minister will not find it easy to be sceptical about the success or failure of grammar or comprehensive schools or the impact of housing allowances or public housing subsidies. There are too many long-standing party positions and carefully worked out compromises in existence. This is not to say that a financial crisis or other disaster may not force him to alter his position. The more pervasive air of scepticism about social policy in the United States is encouraging for the researcher and professional evaluator, but it is less conducive to action. In Britain politicians are given to strongly held party views about social policy which encourage action but not reflection.

Economic: We saw that tight fiscal constraints, which were partly economic and partly political in origin, were a major reason for the British government's attempt to design a much stricter system of long term budget planning. The different fiscal position of the United States went a long way to explain why such planning had failed in the 1960s and suggested that it might begin to develop in the mid 1970s as the budget constraints tightened. What was true of tax control planning was also true of other planning. Tight budget constraints in Britain forced forward planning to become more sophisticated and accurate. Projections and forecasts of expenditure had to be more detailed and there was value for a spending department in a programme budget which clearly distinguished the cost of current policies, suggested possible fields for economy and indicated scope for improved or expanded programmes.

Such a situation was also conducive to more powerful pressure from the Treasury to evaluate critically the contribution of whole programmes and to stress the question can it really be justified? Hence, the introduction of the PAR system in Britain and the assumptions built into it.

Yet until recently both countries had enjoyed a fair measure of economic stability and growth. We saw that the recent more violent fluctuations in the economy in Britain and the longer term uncertainty were making forward planning far more difficult. They could also increase the natural resistance of the professions to programme evaluation.

Types of Social Legislation: Highly specific programmes are relatively easier to evaluate. A piece of legislation which states that its aim is to devote funds to increasing the access of negro students to higher education has a clear immediate purpose and its impact can be measured fairly readily. Have negroes received the grants – have their numbers in higher education increased relative to the size of the age group? In contrast an act which gives the Secretary of State general powers to ensure that children are given an education 'appropriate' to their 'age, ability and aptitude' is difficult, if not impossible to evaluate as it stands. To translate such a general objective into specific goals capable of monitoring or evaluation is to raise the most fundamental political and philosophical disputes.

The nature of the basic legislation has other results. If the legislation sets a framework for expansion – to borrow a phrase – it is likely to encourage promotional and other kinds of planning. Both the 1944 Education Act in Britain and the 1935 Social Security legislation in the United States did this. Both presented a kind of agenda for the future development of the service beyond what was politically or financially feasible at the time.

Britain is more given to less frequent but more decisive legislation which is subsequently unmonitored. The first signs of change were to be found in the work sponsored on the 1968 Town Planning Act, the 1971 Housing Finance Act and the new nursery programme.

Trained manpower: Not the least important factor in Britain's relatively poor showing on the evaluation side lies in the enormous relative advantage America has in the sheer volume of trained social scientists. In neither country have the traditional academic disciplines shown much interest in studies of social programmes, partly no doubt because of the high status given to 'theoretical' work and partly because most social policy research requires inter-disciplinary enquiry. When Federal funds began to flow into such work there was a larger supply of trained people who could be more readily diverted.

A conclusion

In brief then we have set out to show that any generalised or ideal model of social planning is bound to flounder on the reality of the political and economic world. This is not to say that no kind of social planning is feasible, merely that different kinds of political system, and economic climate, encourage different kinds of planning and evaluation. More than that we would claim that there is a pronounced tendency for political and programme variables that are favourable to most kinds of forward planning to be unfavourable to most kinds of evaluation. Hence it is most unlikely that any ideal combination of the two will ever be achieved. Further, there is no point in social scientists in Britain lamenting the fact that few policies are effectively evaluated by government. That will occur only when political pressures demand it. Those who administer at the centre or who provide services at the periphery are not attracted to the idea of evaluation. Faced with angry objections from professional pressure groups ministers see no compelling reason to attract unpopularity. However, if ministers begin to feel that such studies may enable them to squeeze more out of their tight budgets, they may begin to gain an appeal. The Treasury clearly hope evaluation will produce reasons for economising.

The House of Commons expenditure committees could well see that more fundamental work on programmes, their impact and outcomes, might give them more material to work with and increase their influence. One leaf they could take out of Congress's book would be to insist that a given percentage of programme funds is devoted to research and evaluation. Thus, even in Britain, all is not necessarily set against much greater research and evaluation of social service programmes but it is important that this be seen as a learning process designed to illuminate political and administrative debate, not as some 'managerial' technique.

With this approach in mind what practical conclusions can be drawn about the system of public expenditure control in Britain?

The PESC System and Open Planning

This is now the single most important element in the social planning process. Although it has forced a more explicit debate about priorities within government neither public nor even Parliamentary debate have matched this development. There is a serious danger that the consequent increased centralisation and the secrecy which surrounds the process will make social planning less responsive to changing needs, as they are perceived by those delivering the services and by the consumer. The political process has not developed to match the control process. This is first and foremost a matter of public access to information. Information about the outcome of decisions *is* now available in more detail in the annual White Papers on public expenditure, but the bases on which these decisions were taken are not, nor are a range of possible options systematically presented. The House of Commons Sub-Committees on Expenditure could provide a forum for such discussion if they wished and if they were properly staffed, but ministers and senior civil servants would have to drop their suspicion and their reluctance to see greater public scrutiny. Ministers are unlikely to do this unless they see a political gain. Yet surely potential political gains exist. Much of the frustration with government may well arise from the failure of interest groups, of political parties, especially in opposition, and press commentators and hence consumers, to appreciate the realities of the resource constraints. This leads ministers to lecture their relevant interest groups on their irresponsibility. Yet in part it is the ministers' own fault. Realism requires open public debate on alternatives. The tendency to see information 'systems' as private internal management mechanisms only adds to the difficulties.

Instead, each autumn, each social service department might publish a detailed account of its section in the Public Expenditure White Paper, using figures consistent with their respective chapters, describing the forecasting assumptions used and presenting some of the consequences of alternative courses of action advanced by different 'constituencies'. Advisory committees still have an important role to play here.

Despite the tighter control of public expenditure, and the more explicit discussion of priorities within central government departments, the effective consideration of priorities between social service departments is still lacking. This is even more true of the *social* implications of other spending priorities. The Central Policy Review staff and the inter-departmental PARs have presumably begun to provide some basis on which ministers can face such issues but they require a much more powerful analytical input. This means a larger staff with experience of policy analysis whose role is to present the Prime Minister and the home policy members of the Cabinet with a non departmental perspective on social policy. This does not mean producing a 'comprehensive plan' but it does mean monitoring and highlighting key social policy objectives to which different departments contribute – urban poverty or general income redistribution are examples.

A non-departmental view of social service expenditure priorities, distinct from the Treasury view, could be available to the relevant Cabinet Sub-Committee – a kind of chairman's brief, just as the planning staff in the Secretary's Office in HEW present a non-agency view of priorities to the head of that Department at the critical time in the budget cycle. This will not change the essential departmental power relationships but could help ministers to see the impact of social policies in the way that they actually affect individuals and families – that is to say in combination.

This leads us on to expenditure or budget analysis.

Budget Analysis

We have argued that the original conception of an output or programme budget which envisaged a discrete hierarchy of objectives is unsuited to the character of social service activities. We have argued that the outcome of experience in both the US and the UK illustrates this. We have suggested that in both countries the programme structures that have emerged reflect the political requirements of the departments involved. In the US the main concern has been to group existing legislative appropriations together to give a clearer picture of their combined effects. In Britain departments have begun with existing policy commitments and techniques of planning and have built their budget structures around them. Since existing policies tend to be concerned with standards of provision in existing institutions or for particular client groups, so do the budget structures. It is not until policies are output oriented that budgets will be. Yet, for the reasons discussed earlier, this is unlikely.

We have also argued that the concentration on one programme structure is unnecessarily confining and indeed harmful to policy formation. Despite intentions to the contrary it tends to sanctify one particular view of the world – either the existing legislative framework in the US or the 'constraints' view of the world in the UK.

There is a case for developing instead a system that gives ministers varied perspectives – a multi-dimensional budget. Even accepting the present concept of public expenditure it should be possible to present a picture, for example, of the different distributional consequences of alternative policies and of trends over time. Clearly geographical distribution is one perspective, which regions have gained most or stand to gain most from current policies? Is it urban or rural areas, suburban or inner city areas, conurbation or non-conurbation areas? Social class or income groups or types of household are another distributional perspective. None of these could be undertaken in minute detail but the broad trends which were occurring could be illustrated as could the possible impact of alternative options.

Expenditure analysis on its own is only one side of the budget picture. The impact of systems of finance is the other side of the coin. Take, for example, the expansion of the local authority sector of higher education. The alternative is the faster expansion of a sector financed almost wholly from the central exchequer. Since rates are still the most regressive form of tax the first alternative has different distributive consequences to the second. One will have a harsher impact on the low income groups than the other.

To move one stage further would mean developing the concept of public expenditure to include those other dimensions of the welfare transfer system – fiscal welfare and occupational welfare. The closely inter-related effects of the tax threshold and the various social security taxes and mean tested benefits are now more widely appreciated. It is to be hoped that decisions about one are now taken with information to hand about the others.

At the outset only fairly crude measure of the distributional, finance and tax allowance effects could be expected. But if the objectives of social services are multiple and in doubt, multi-dimensional analyses of expenditure are necessary. 'Who benefits?' is not a question that can be answered one way in one dimension. Similarly the concept of public expenditure implicit in PESC or in the US budget is so limited and in some instances misleading that it should be supplemented by information based on rather broader concepts of transfer.

Finally, it is not the final structure that is ultimately important but the building blocks from which it is constructed. What all participants in the bargaining process require is a box of 'Lego' building blocks with which they can either build their own models of the future or analyse the cost effectiveness of current procedures on a micro level. For example, in the newly reorganised National Health Service in Britain it should prove possible eventually to produce a system of costed activity units.[1] (An activity unit may be a consultation with a GP, a home confinement or a hospital discharge.) They could be classified by medical condition and on a doctor-in-charge basis within each organisational grouping. They would have to include basic data on the individual patient concerned. At each stage appropriate resource costs could be allocated. It would not be necessary to do this for every activity in the country. Samples would be sufficient. As a result it would be possible to take any medical episode and cost it (ignoring for the moment the problems about deciding what constitutes the end of an episode). A patient might go to see his GP, be given a prescription, have an X-ray then a short stay in hospital followed by a period of home care with regular visits by a home nurse. Each phase in his treatment would have a resource cost attached so that at the end, the whole episode, together with its outcome, could be costed. Such information could be used for a whole range of purposes:

(a) Comparing the costs of undertaking similar activities in different institutions or areas and over time;
(b) Comparing the costs of different methods of medical treatment for a given condition;
(c) Providing a much more detailed basis for making projections and costing long term planning exercises.

Both (a) and (c) should be fairly obvious, (b) needs some elaboration. Clearly the degree of detail and accuracy that could be achieved in regular returns of this nature would be limited. In some cases the evidence may be considered conclusive by the management team. In others it might be argued that an apparently cheaper form of treatment in one institution was putting greater strain on the families of the patients with detrimental side effects, but the issue would at least have been raised. It might be concluded that it would be worth pursuing perhaps by commissioning one or more randomised control trials and publishing the results. In the ensuing debate different perspectives on the 'output' issue might emerge.

R

Whether action followed would depend on the extent of consensus about the findings and the 'politics' of the situation. We would merely argue that an 'economising' outcome is more likely with such information available than without it.

Evaluation

It is now thirty years since Simon suggested that public administrators should devote a major part of their activities to investigating the relationship between service inputs and outputs. Since then remarkably little effort has been expended in doing so. The fact that there is less general agreement on what constitute the objectives of social policy does not absolve the administrator or the professional from seeking to measure the effectiveness of their activities according to their own values, nor recipients and tax payers from doing so either. Indeed lack of a value consensus requires more evaluation from more sources of enquiry not less.

It is essential to the notion of pluralist planning that research on the impact of policies be undertaken by as many different participants in the bargaining process as possible. There can only be free competition for public resources if there is the maximum feasible diffusion of knowledge about the impact and consequence of social policies viewed from different perspectives. Hence the importance of diverse sources of research funding and the role of the Research Councils. Yet academics left to themselves will never be sufficiently motivated to undertake the detailed systematic and technical work which ought to be a regular part of social service administration. It is in this respect that the agencies in Washington have most to teach us in their different ways. The regular allocation of a proportion of programme funds to this work in the end brings results. Above all they show the virtue of linking the strategic planning, budget control and evaluation activities closely together. These are still excessively fragmented in Britain. As a minimum each social service department could produce an evaluation plan each year, perhaps as part of the PAR process and publish it.

The studies would have to be commissioned and overseen in a rigorous way or undertaken 'in house'. The results should be disseminated as widely as possible and could form the basis of discussion by the appropriate House of Commons Expenditure subcommittee.

The pressures of academic life do not encourage applied work. Even where there is a tradition of such work, as in social administration departments, current fashion seems to be leading in the direction of macro-theorising. Much of this reflects the influence of sociology on the subject, which has its value but may have led to less interest in answering the traditional questions with which social administrators have been concerned: how is the service working, who is it reaching, who is it not reaching, what are the consequences of delivering the service in one way compared to another, what difference do alternative administrative structures make, what is it like to receive the service, or be denied it, how do different participants perceive 'need', and what are the different dimensions of need, how is need translated into demand, what are the obstacles to access, what are the resource constraints and what criteria can be used to debate priorities? For both the academic and the practical social administrator work of this kind at the local or micro level is an essential prerequisite to building up a coherent theory of the rationing or allocation process in non-market systems.

REFERENCE

1 This proposal is elaborated in *Accounting for Health*, King Edward Hospital Fund, London, 1973.

Bibliography

OFFICIAL REPORTS

Control of Public Expenditure (Plowden), Cmnd 1432 (1961).

Department of Education and Science, *Output Budgeting for the DES*, HMSO, London, 1970.

Education: a Framework for Expansion, Cmnd 5174 (1972).

Framework for Government Research and Development, Cmnd 4814 (1971), Cmnd 5046 (1972).

House of Commons Expenditure Committee

Seventh Report (Session 1971–2), *Public Expenditure and Economic Management*, H.C.450 (1971–2).

Eighth Report (Session 1971–2), *Relationship of Expenditure to Needs*, H.C.515 (1971–2).

Eleventh Report (Session 1972–3), *The May 21st Expenditure Cuts*, H.C.398 (1972–3).

House of Commons Select Committee on Procedure, 1968/9, *Scrutiny of Public Expenditure and Administration*, H.C.410 (1968-9).

Ministry of Housing and Local Government, *Council Housing, Purposes, Procedures and Priorities*, Central Housing Advisory Committee – 9th report of the Housing Management sub-committee.

New Policies for Public Spending, Cmnd 4515 (1970).

Public Expenditure 1968–9 to 1973–4, Cmnd 4234 (1969).

Public Expenditure 1969–70 to 1974–5, Cmnd 4578 (1971).

Public Expenditure to 1975–6, Cmnd 4829 (1971).

Public Expenditure to 1976–7, Cmnd 5178 (1972).

Public Expenditure to 1977–8, Cmnd 5519 (1973).

Public Expenditure to 1978–9, Cmnd 5879 (1975).

Public Expenditure: A New Presentation, Cmnd 4017 (1969).

Public Expenditure: Planning and Control, Cmnd 2915 (1966).

The Reorganisation of Central Government, Cmnd 4506 (1970).

Treasury, *Public Expenditure White Papers: Handbook on Methodology*, HMSO, 1972.

Committee of Enquiry into the Cost of the National Health Service (Guillebaud) Report, Cmd 9663 (1956).

BOOKS AND ARTICLES

Aaron, H. J., *Why is Welfare so hard to Reform?*, Brookings Institution, Washington, 1973.

Abel-Smith, B., 'Public Expenditure on the Social Services', *Social Trends, 1970*, HMSO, 1970.

Averch, H. A., *How Effective is Schooling*, RAND, Santa Monica, 1972.

Bauer, R. A., *Social Indicators*, MIT Press, Cambridge, Mass, 1966.

Blaug, M., *Introduction to the Economics of Education*, Penguin Books, Harmondsworth, 1972.

Blechman, B. M. *et al.*, *Setting National Priorities: the 1975 Budget*, Brookings Institution, Washington DC, 1974.

Boyle, E. and Crosland, C. A. R., *The Politics of Education*, Penguin Books, Harmondsworth, 1971.

Bradshaw, J., 'A Taxonomy of Need' in Maclaghlan, G. *Problems and Progress in Medical Care*, Oxford University Press, 1972.

Braybrooke, D. and Lindblom, C., *A Strategy for Decision*, Free Press, New York, 1963.

Bridges, Lord, *The Treasury*, George Allen & Unwin, London, 1966.

British Medical Association, *Health Services Financing*, London, 1970.

Brittan, S., *Steering the Economy*, Secker and Warburg, 1969.

Brundage, P. F., *The Bureau of the Budget*, Praeger, New York, 1970.

Buchanan, J. M., *The Inconsistencies of the National Health Service*, Institute of Economic Affairs, Occasional Paper No. 7, London, 1965.

Burkhead, J., *Government Budgeting*, Wiley, New York, 1956.

Burkhead, J. and Miner, J., *Public Expenditure*, Macmillan, 1971.

Burkhead, J., *et al.*, *Input and Output in Large American High Schools*, Syracuse University Press, 1967.

Caro, F. G. (ed.), *Readings in Evaluation Research*, Russell Sage, New York, 1971.

Chapman, R. A. (ed.), *The Role of Commissions in Policy Making*, George Allen & Unwin, London, 1973.

Clarke, Sir Richard, *New Trends in Government*, Civil Service College Studies No. 1, HMSO, 1971.

Coleman, J. S., *et al.*, *Equality of Educational Opportunity*, Government Printing Office, Washington, DC, 1966.

Crossman, R. H. S., *Paying for the Social Services*, Fabian Society, London, 1969.

Culyer, A. J., *The Economics of Social Policy*, Martin Robertson, London, 1973.

Dahl, R. A., and Lindblom, C., *Politics Economics and Welfare*, Harper New York, 1953.

Davis, O. A., Dempster, M. A. H., and Wildavsky, A., 'On the Process of Budgeting: an empirical study of Congressional Appropriations', *Papers on Non-Market Decision Making*, Vol. 1, 1966.

Department of Health, Education and Welfare, *Do Teachers make any Difference?*, Government Printing Office, Washington, DC, 1970.

Department of Health, Education and Welfare, *Toward a Social Report*, Government Printing Office, Washington, DC, 1969.

Donnison, D. V., *The Government of Housing*, Penguin Books, Harmondsworth, 1967.

Donnison, D. V., *et al.*, *Social Policy and Administration*, George Allen & Unwin, 1965.

Downs, A., *Inside Bureaucracy*, Little, Brown & Co., Boston, 1967.

Dunsire, A., *Administration: the Word and the Science*, Martin Robertson, London, 1973.

Etzioni, A. (ed.), *Reading on Modern Organisations*, Prentice Hall, Englewood Cliffs, NJ, 1969.

Feingold, E., *Medicare Policy and Politics*, Chandler Publishing Co., San Francisco, 1966.

Fenno, R. F., *The Power of the Purse*, Little, Brown, Boston, 196.

Ferris, J., *Participation in Planning: the Barnsbury Case*, Occasional Papers on Social Administration, Bell, London, 1972.

Galbraith, J. K., *The New Industrial State*, Penguin Books, 1969.

Glennerster, H., 'The Plowden Research', *Journal of the Royal Statistical Society*, Series A, Vol. 132, Part 2, 1969.

Goldberg, E. M., *Helping the Aged*, George Allen & Unwin, London, 1970.

Goldman, Sir Samuel, *The Developing System of Public Expenditure Management and Control*, Civil Service College Studies No. 2, HMSO, London, 1973.

Griffith, J. A. G., *Central Departments and Local Authorities*, George Allen & Unwin, London, 1966.

Gross, B. M., *The Managing of Organisations*, Free Press, New York, 1964.

Gross, B. M., *The State of the Nation: Social System Accounting*, Tavistock, London, 1966.

Hall, A. S., *The Point of Entry*, George Allen & Unwin, London, 1974.

Harris, J. S., *British Government Inspection*, Stevens, London, 1955.

Haveman, B. H. and Margolis, J., *Public Expenditure and Policy Analysis*, Markham, Chicago, 1970.

Heclo, H. and Wilensky, A., *The Private Government of Public Money*, Macmillan, London, 1974.

Hitch, C. J., *Decision-Making for Defense*, University of California Press, Berkeley, 1965.

Hitch, C. J. and McKean, R. M., *The Economics of Defense in the Nuclear Age*, Harvard University Press, Cambridge, Mass, 1960.

Journal of Human Resources, Vol. IX, No. 2 and No. 4, 1974. (Accounts of the results of the Income Maintenance Experiment in New Jersey).

Kahn, A. J., *Theory and Practice of Social Planning*, Russell Sage Foundation, New York, 1969.

Keeling, D., *Management in Government*, George Allen & Unwin, London, 1972.

King Edward Hospital Fund, *Accounting for Health*, London, 1973.

Klein, R., 'The Politics of P.P.B.', *The Political Quarterly*, Vol. 43, No. 3, 1972.

Klein, R. *et al.*, *Social Policy and Public Expenditure*, 1974. Centre for Studies in Social Policy, London, 1974.

Klein R., and Hall, P., *Caring for Quality in the Caring Services*, Centre for Studies in Social Policy, London, 1974.

Kogan, M., 'Social Services: their Whitehall Status', *New Society*, 21 August, 1969.

Layard, R. (ed.), *Cost-benefit Analysis*, Penguin, Harmondsworth, 1972.

Layard, R. *et al.*, *The Impact of Robbins*, Penguin Books, Harmondsworth, 1969.

Levin, A., 'Multi-secting the Nation's Non-Defense Programs', *Public Administration Review*, March/April, 1971.

Lindblom, C., 'The Science of Muddling Through', *Public Administration Review*, Spring, 1959.

Lindblom, C., *The Intelligence of Democracy*, Free Press, New York, 1965.
with Braybrooke : *A Strategy for Decision* q.v.
with Dahl : *Politics, Economics and Welfare*, q.v.

Lyden, F. J. and Miller, E. G. (eds), *Planning, Programming, Budgeting: a systems approach to management*, Markham, Chicago, 1972.

McKean, R. M., *Public Spending*, McGraw Hill, New York, 1968.

McKean, R. M., *Efficiency in Government and the Use of Systems Analysis*, John Wiley, New York, 1958.

McLachlan, G. (ed.), *Portfolio for Health* 1 and 2, Oxford University Press, 1971 and 1973.

MacLeod, R. M., *Treasury Control and Social Administration*, Occasional Papers in Social Administration, No. 23, Bell, London, 1968.

March, J. G. and Simon, H. A., *Organisations*, Wiley, New York, 1958.

Mayer, J. E. and Timms, N., *The Client Speaks*, Routledge, London, 1970.

Mencher, S., *Poor Law to Poverty Program*, University of Pittsburg Press, 1967.

Miller, S. M. and Stein, B. (eds), *Incentives and Planning in Social Policy*, Aldine, New York, 1973.

Mishan, E. J., *Cost Benefit Analysis*, George Allen & Unwin, London, 1972,

Mosher, F. C., *Program Budgeting*, Public Administration Service, Chicago, 1954.

Moynihan, D. P., *The Politics of a Guaranteed Income*, Vintage Books, New York, 1973.

Moynihan, D. P. and Mosteller, F., *On Equality of Educational Opportunity*, Vintage Books, New York, 1972.

Musgrove, R. A., *Fiscal Systems*, Yale University Press, 1969.

National Plan, The, Cmnd 2764 (1965).

Novick, D., *Program Budgeting*, Harvard University Press, Cambridge, Mass, 1965.

Oakshott, M., *Rationalism in Politics*, Methuen, London, 1962.
Olsen, M., *The Logic of Collective Action*, Harvard University Press, Cambridge, Mass, 1965.
Ott, D. J. and A. F., *Federal Budget Policy*, Brookings Institution, Washington DC, 1969
Parker, R. A., 'Social Administration and Scarcity: the Problem of Rationing', *Social Work*, April, 1967.
Peacock, A. and Wiseman, J., *The Growth of Public Expenditure in the United Kingdom*, George Allen & Unwin, London, 1961.
Peacock, A. *et al.*, *Educational Finance: its sources and uses in the United Kingdom*, Oliver and Boyd, London, 1968.
Pechman, J. A., Aaron, H. J. and Taussig, M. K., *Social Security: Perspectives for Reform*, Brookings Institution, Washington, 1968.
Powell, J. E., *A New Look at Medicine and Politics*, Pitmans, London, 1966.
Prest, A. R. and Turvey, R., 'Cost Benefit Analysis: a Survey', *The Economic Journal*, December, 1965.
Public Administration Review, Vol. 26, No. 4, December, 1966. Articles by Schick, Wildavsky and others.
Public Administration Review, Vol. 29, No. 2, March, 1969. Another collection of articles.
Public Administration, Vol. 52, Spring, 1974. Articles on Corporate Planning (see especially on DES).
Reekie, W. D. and Hunt, N. C. (eds), *Management in the Social and Safety Services*, Tavistock, London, 1974.
Rein, M., *Social Policy*, Random House, New York, 1970.
Rivlin, A., *Systematic Thinking for Social Action*, Brookings Institution, Washington, 1971.
Rossi, P. H. and Williams, W. (eds), *Evaluating Social Programmes*, Seminar Press, New York, 1972.
Rothenberg, J., *The Measurement of Social Welfare*, Prentice Hall, Englewood Cliffs, 1961.
Schick, A., *Innovation in the States*, Brookings Institution, Washington DC, 1971.
Schultze, C. L., *The Politics and Economics of Public Spending*, Brookings Institution, Washington, 1968.
Schultze, C. L. *et al.*, *Setting National Priorities: the 1973 Budget*, Brookings Institution, Washington, 1972. (See also volumes on 1971, 1972, and 1974 Budgets.)
Self, P., 'Nonsense on Stilts: Cost Benefit Analysis and the Roskill Commission', *The Political Quarterly*, Vol. 41, No. 3, 1970.
Self, P., *Administrative Theories and Politics*, George Allen & Unwin, London, 1972.
Self, P., 'Is Comprehensive Planning Possible and Rational?', *Policy and Politics*, Vol. 2, No. 3, 1974.
Sharkansky, I. (ed.), *Policy Analysis in Political Science*, Markham, Chicago, 1970.

Shonfield, A. and Shaw, S. (eds), *Social Indicators and Social Policy*, Heinemann, London, 1972.

Simon, H. A., *Administrative Behaviour* (1st Ed. 1945, 2nd Ed. 1957) Collier Macmillan, Toronto.

Titmuss, R. M. and Abel-Smith, B., *The Cost of the National Health Service*, Cambridge University Press, 1956.

Taylor, *Research Perspectives in Education*, Routledge and Kegan Paul, London, 1973.

Tullock, G., *The Politics of Bureaucracy*, Public Affairs Press, Washington DC, 1965.

Vaizey, J., *The Costs of Education*, George Allen & Unwin, London, 1958.

Vaizey, J., *The Political Economy of Education*, Duckworth, London, 1972.

Vickers, C. G., *The Art of Judgment: Policy Making as a Mental Skill*, Chapman and Hall, London, 1965.

Wagner, R. E., *The Public Economy*, Markham, Chicago, 1973.

Ward, A. V., *Resources for Educational Research and Development*, NFER, Slough, 1973.

Weiss, C. H., *Evaluation Research*, Prentic Hall, Englewood Cliffs, 1972.

Wildavsky, A., *The Politics of the Budgetary Process*, Little, Brown, Boston, 1964.

Wildavsky, A., 'Evaluation as an Organisational Problem', *CES University Working Papers* No. 13, London, 1972.

Wildavsky, A., 'The Self Evaluating Organisation', *Public Administration Review*, September-October, 1972.

Wilensky, H. L., *Organisational Intelligence*, Basic Books, New York, 1967.

Wilesnky, H. L. and Lebeaux, C. N., *Industrial Society and Social Welfare*, Free, Press, New York, 1965 ed.

Williams, A., *Output budgeting and the contribution of micro-economics to efficiency in government*, CAS Occasional Papers No 4, HMSO, 1967.

Williams, W., *Social Policy Research and Analysis*, Elsevier, New York, 1971.

Index